FOR THE WORK OF MINISTRY

Northern College and Its Predecessors

ELAINE KAYE

T&T CLARK
EDINBURGH

T&T CLARK LTD
59 GEORGE STREET
EDINBURGH EH2 2LQ
SCOTLAND

First published 1999

ISBN 0 567 08659 3

British Library Cataloguing-in-Publication Data
A catalogue record for this book is available from the British Library

Typeset by Fakenham Photosetting Limited, Fakenham, Norfolk
Printed and bound in Great Britain by MPG Books, Bodmin

FOR THE WORK OF MINISTRY

Contents

List of Illustrations

Acknowledgements

I am greatly indebted to numerous people who have shared their memories, expertise and practical suggestions with me. They include the following: Edmund Banyard, Derrick Barber, Nigel Briggs, Anthony Burnham, Arthur Chadwick, Kenneth Chambers, Elizabeth Charles, Jessie Clare, Margaret Derbyshire, Rosalind Fells, Cyril Grant, Jack Garside, Gerald Gossage, Isobel Grieve, Ann and David Hallas, Kenneth Hibberd, Clifford Hill, David Hudston, Val Huntley, David Jenkins, Paul King, Michael Lay, Gwenith Maddison, Jack McKelvey, Colin Mundy, George Musgrave, Derek Newton, Roy Niblett, Donald Oakley, John Parry, David Phillips, Daphne and Eric Pinder, David Yeo Poulton, Gilbert Preston, Donald Raine, Doreen Rees, David Robinson, Krystyna Rodda, Elizabeth Stewart, Thomas Stiff, John Sutcliffe, Peggy Thomas, Stephen Thornton, Brian Townsend, Kenneth Wadsworth, Eileen White, Wilfred White, John Wilcox, Stanley Wilton, Jean Young and John Young.

David Peel, Principal of Northern College, has been a willing supporter of the enterprise from the beginning. The librarians of the John Rylands University Library at Deansgate, Manchester have been invariably helpful on my numerous visits to consult the Northern College Archive there, as have the librarians of Dr Williams's Library in London. The librarians of Mansfield College have, as always, been cheerful, helpful and hospitable.

Mary and Raymond Shaw in Bradford and Dorothy and Richard Wilkinson in Manchester have provided generous hospitality on several research visits, and transformed work into pleasure.

The following have read through manuscript drafts and offered invaluable comments and criticism, for which I am deeply grateful: Clyde Binfield, Leslie Green, Alan Sell, and Roger Tomes. To Geoffrey Nuttall, I (like so many others) owe more than I could ever repay.

The Congregational Memorial Hall Trust has generously provided a grant towards the cost of publication, and I should like to thank Bernard Reeve, Trust Secretary, for his support.

I am grateful to the Rotherham and Nottingham Local Studies Libraries for permission to reproduce the illustrations of Rotherham Independent Academy and Tollerton Hall.

For the Work of Ministry

I wish to dedicate this work to the memory of my father, Harold Sutcliffe Kaye, former student of the Yorkshire United Independent College, and minister of the Gospel in Whitby and Sutton Coldfield.

Elaine Kaye
Oxford, February 1998

Abbreviations

CQ	*Congregational Quarterly*
CYB	*Congregational Year Books*
CFYB	*Congregational Federation Year Books*
DNB	*Dictionary of National Biography*
DWL	Dr Williams's Library
JRL	John Rylands University Library of Manchester
JURCHS	*Journal of the United Reformed Church History Society*
LIC	Lancashire Independent College
NCA	Northern College Archive
TCHS	*Transactions of the Congregational Historical Society*
URCYB	*United Reformed Church Year Books*

Foreword

Here is an important book. That might seem unlikely even to those who turn to it because of family associations or from denominational loyalty. Institutional histories are always commissioned and usually written *in piam memoriam*, and this history obeys that rule. That does not, however, lessen its significance. This may appear to be the unassuming history of a small, provincial, theological college (so easily diminished by outsiders, and even some well-intentioned insiders, into a 'ministerial training college') serving a cluster of supposedly declining and therefore marginal denominations, but appearances can be deceptive. Here is much more than a celebration of the institutional expression of a sub-set of a sub-culture. It illuminates the development and mentality of an alternative approach to English society. For 'English' the word 'British' should surprisingly often be substituted, and not just because the college is in the Reformed tradition or because its principals have as often as not been Irish, Scottish, or Welsh; and that newly minted word 'spirituality' should here accompany 'mentality'. In sum it is the scope and complexity of this book's terrain, and the clarity with which it has been surveyed, which will strike all serious readers.

Its historical range is almost that of organised Dissent itself, even if the plot thickens in the nineteenth and twentieth centuries. While the dominant denominational accent has been Congregational, the present college incorporates a Presbyterian tradition because it trains men and women for the United Reformed Church, and it reflects the Churches of Christ and Moravian traditions inherited from Overdale College, Birmingham, and Fairfield, near Droylsden, respectively. Consequently the ecclesiological spread is broad, and it is further broadened by the ecumenism implicit in the partnership between all the colleges now based at Luther King House. The geographical spread is broad too, for it is all but nationwide: not indeed London, but Exeter, Plymouth, Bristol, Nottingham, Rotherham, Bradford, Blackburn, Manchester, and beyond. The implications of this are immense, for almost all the varieties of English urban experience are caught by those names. These were the towns whose industry, society, and politics sustained the colleges which have preceded Northern College and explain their physical presence.

Buildings are a perplexity for Christians and a burden for finance committees. College histories prefer to ignore them. Yet most college buildings reflect contemporary standards of relevance and aspiration. They are records which deserve to be read sympathetically: thus Masbro's Academy, in a late Georgian so austere as to be almost workhouse; or Airedale's Undercliffe building, in a Wuthering Classical entirely suited to its windswept eminence; or the up-to-the-mark, more-or-less domesticated shades of Gothic at Emm Lane Bradford, Moorgate Rotherham, Whalley Range Manchester, or Mannamead Plymouth. Each was intended to be an ornament to its townscape, designed by an architect of regional clout, and if Western College Bristol might alone be regarded as architecturally outstanding (though there is a case to be made for Whalley Range), each quite plainly told all who approached them that here was something significant for the quality of contemporary life. They were used, and sometimes lived in (for not all were residential), by transient generations of young men, latterly, of course, joined by women and middle-aged men, whose horizons were bounded only by eternity. More prosaically here was trained an intermediate intelligentsia, for that is what the Nonconformist ministry amounted to in this-worldly terms: young men who would be of consequence in the churches which called them and in the wider community served by those churches. Seen in this light, the colleges were focal points for adult and continuing education, and their principals and staffs provided key members of School Boards and Education Authorities as well as the Athenaeums and Literary and Philosophical Societies which gave Cottonopolis and Worstedopolis their cosmopolitan edge.

They were also focal points for higher education. One of this book's themes is the close relationship between Lancashire Independent College and the emerging University of Manchester; but this was paralleled by similarly fruitful relationships between Western College and the University of Bristol, Paton College and the University of Nottingham, and Yorkshire United Independent College and the University of Edinburgh. When all these local, political, social, and educational links are translated into men and women (for although the colleges were largely male preserves until the 1970s, this intermediate intelligentsia had wives and daughters, and their role in the changing of attitudes cries out for close attention), there begins to emerge a densely textured fabric of connexions and relationships which covers every aspect of British life.

Yet all this is incidental. The colleges' purpose was for the work of ministry. Given their largely Congregational ecclesiology, that purpose presupposed an intelligent, that is to say a liberally interpreted, evangelicalism. It also presupposed a theology which prepared for and thereafter sustained ministry, and which was naturally reflected in both syllabus and discipline. The steady evolution and constant evaluation of what was meant by the word 'college', was implicit in this understanding. Was that purpose ever adequately met?

There are two ways of looking at this. The sensible one is to recognise the inbuilt failure of the whole enterprise. The relationship of a nonconformist institution with established ways, whether clerical or secular, is bound to be problematic. It is fraught with compromise. More practically, it involves a constant financial battle. Then there are the often contradictory expectations of the constituency served by the college and the often wildly variable abilities of candidates called to ministry. By all quantifiable criteria the evangelical Christian is fighting a losing battle.

Yet what strikes the observer is the variety and quality of the work of Northern College and its predecessors. Even in worldly terms it has produced outstanding and successful ministers. The names of Edward Williams, Robert Vaughan, Henry Rogers, D. W. Simon, A. M. Fairbairn, J. B. Paton, R. S. Franks (to select only some who were principals), are enough to demonstrate a sustained intellectual and spiritual engagement with society. Of course there are horror stories, some not to be told here, of opportunities lost and sometimes knowingly ignored. The reader will smile affectionately at the delightful aberration which briefly took Paton, that boldest of collegiate experiments, out to the gothick fantasies of a country estate, but few will smile at the sale of Western College's library by lot at auction, or at the dispersal of Northern College's collection of portraits. Some readers will reflect on the realities of tuition too easily reduced, as one Victorian principal's son put it, to 'lectures which would in almost every case remain the standard for reference and appeal, through a whole pastoral life'.

Even so the abiding message is what Richard Winter Hamilton of Leeds told Yorkshire's Congregationalists in his orotund way in 1831: 'we *will* have the science of theology and the art of preaching'. Given the prior fact of a call, and remembering that the art of preaching is the art of communication, and accepting that from the science of theology should flow our perceptions of pastoral work, indeed of citizenship in all its aspects, then the role of the college remains undiminished and the importance of this book is clear.

Elaine Kaye has shaped faith, doggedness, heroism, enthusiasm, conflict, men, women, buildings, fads, fancies, and dreams into a finely told narrative. The past is illuminated with admirable clarity but, more to the point, it is projected through the present into the future. Of course this is a work *in piam memoriam*. The author is a daughter of the manse. In that sense she is a daughter of what is now Northern College. She also writes as an educationist who is actively involved in the challenges which enliven contemporary theological education. It would be quite unhistorical to say that Northern College is more conscious of such challenges than it and its predecessors have ever been, but it is consciously to the forefront in addressing these challenges. In this it is faithful to its history and confident of its future.

CLYDE BINFIELD
Sheffield

Preface

The role of Nonconformity in English life was of profound significance in the nineteenth and early twentieth centuries. It was a culture as well as a form of belief. No one was more responsible for setting the tone of that way of living, thinking and worshipping than the Nonconformist minister. Though they were despised by some, in an age of outstanding preachers and of ministerial dominance they carried great weight in a wide constituency. Consequently the institutions which educated and formed these ministers had an influence and significance far beyond their size. This work recounts the history of five of them, all Congregational. Their principals were regarded as leaders of the denomination, and most of them were elected as Chairmen of the Congregational Union of England and Wales.

The present Northern College, Manchester, has inherited the traditions and many of the records and books of five such Congregational institutions: Western College, which originated in Ottery St Mary and then moved to several locations in the West Country, finally settling in Bristol; the Yorkshire United Independent College in Bradford, which had begun in Heckmondwike and at one stage provided two colleges, one in Bradford and one in Rotherham; the Lancashire Independent College, which originated in Manchester, but was based for a time in Blackburn; and Paton College, which began in Manchester, but for most of its life was based in Nottingham. Each college attracted deep local loyalty and acted as a focus for Congregationalists for many miles around. Each made its own unique contribution to the texture of Nonconformist life, though their individuality and jealously guarded independence made it difficult to achieve a national policy on ministerial education when one was needed.

Though the colleges were all in England, they had strong links with Wales, whose English-speaking Congregational churches were members of the Congregational Union, and with Scotland, whose denominational life had a different character and history. It is noteworthy how many members of the college staffs, both English and Scottish, were educated in Scotland, whose universities were never closed to English Nonconformists. There were also links with Ireland.

These colleges had to adapt first to a great expansion of Nonconformity in both membership and wealth in the early nineteenth century, and then in the twentieth century to a steep decline. They continually had to battle against lack of financial and moral support from the churches which benefited from the ministry of their students. They educated some who were to achieve distinction as scholars, preachers, administrators and missionaries. But the vast majority were simply faithful pastors and preachers whose cumulative influence cannot be overestimated.

PART ONE

Independent Academies and Colleges in the West and the North of England: 1752–1830s

I

Introduction

OUR story begins in 1752, when John Lavington of Ottery St Mary, Devon, took in some students who were preparing for ministry in Independent churches with the support of the London Congregational Fund Board. Four years later a modest academy opened in Heckmondwike, in the West Riding of Yorkshire, whose students were financed by a group of ministers and prominent laymen in London. From these two small institutions came streams which eventually flowed into the institution known today as Northern College. And before the end of the eighteenth century, another stream had begun its course, this time in Lancashire.

A century earlier, between 1660 and 1662, just over 2,000 clergy and schoolmasters in England and Wales[1] lost their livings because they were unable to accept the terms finally agreed by Parliament in the Act of Uniformity (1662), by which the Church of England was restored under Charles II, and according to which all ministers, lecturers and schoolmasters were required to declare their 'unfeigned Assent and Consent' to everything contained and prescribed in the Book of Common Prayer. Most of them were Presbyterian (1,816), while a relatively small number were Independents (194), and a small minority Baptists (19). Not only did they lose both income and status, but they were subject to severe penalties if they continued to preach, or if they returned to their parishes. Many of them experienced imprisonment. Restrictions and penalties were not confined to clergy and schoolmasters, nor were they applied equally across the country. The Conventicle Act of 1664 was intended to prevent worship which was not conducted according to the rubrics of the Book of Common Prayer and laid down punishments for those caught participating in illegal forms of worship. The Corporation Act of 1661 and the Test Act of 1673 in effect limited all public offices to Anglicans. The Five Mile Act forbade Nonconformist ministers and teachers from residing within five miles of any corporate town, or of the place where they had formerly taught or preached. Henceforward, Nonconformists were recognisable as a distinct section of the community, living under intermittent persecution until the Toleration Act of 1689 gave them the

[1] A. G. Matthews, in *Calamy Revised* (Oxford 1934) estimated that 1,909 were ejected in England. To this number should be added 120 in Wales. See Michael Watts, *The Dissenters: From the Reformation to the French Revolution* (Oxford 1978) 219.

freedom to worship openly as trinitarian Protestant Christians, but remaining subject to many civil restrictions, which made them in effect second class citizens.[2]

Since the time of the Reformation the government had regarded some control of the two universities as necessary in order to achieve sufficient religious conformity and political loyalty for the security of the state. As ordained clergy, college fellows came under the requirements of the Act of Uniformity. Undergraduates too were required to subscribe to the Thirty-nine Articles of the Church of England, in Oxford before matriculation, in Cambridge before receiving a degree. Thus Nonconformists were excluded after 1662 from Oxford (except occasionally as private students) and Cambridge (a few studied there without taking a degree) and from many grammar schools as well. But the Presbyterian and Independent clergy were for the most part learned ministers, themselves educated at one of the two universities. As the 1662 settlement came to be accepted as the status quo, the education of the next generation of Nonconformists (both ministers and laymen) became a matter of concern. The Scottish universities were a solution for some; others went to Utrecht or Leiden in the Netherlands. But for the majority of the able sons of Nonconformist families, the new Dissenting academies became the means of acquiring a sound education.

At first, these academies were informal groups of students in the homes of Presbyterian or Independent ministers; gradually many of them became more formal institutions. Most of them depended on the charisma and ability of one man, and often did not survive his death or retirement. Their most flourishing period was the eighteenth century, when they offered an education which was often broader and more modern than that available in the universities.[3]

It was Richard Frankland's Academy at Rathmell, near Giggleswick, which provided for the education of the second generation of ministers on both the Yorkshire and the Lancashire sides of the Pennines. Richard Frankland (1630–98) was a Presbyterian, educated at Christ's College, Cambridge, and held a living in County Durham before being ejected in 1662. When persecution was at its worst, the Academy had to be peripatetic, but returned to Rathmell after the Toleration Act of 1689.[4]

[2] Roman Catholics, Jews and Unitarians were not accommodated within the Act.

[3] See H. McLachlan, *English Education Under the Test Acts* (Manchester 1931), I. Parker, *Dissenting Academies in England* (Cambridge 1914) and J. W. Ashley Smith, *The Birth of Modern Education* (London 1954). More recent writers have sought to demonstrate that these authors have exaggerated the superiority of these institutions over the universities.

[4] See McLachlan 62–70 and F. Nicholson and E. Axon, *The Older Nonconformity in Kendal: A History of the Unitarian chapel in the Market Place with Transcripts of the Registers and Notices of the Nonconformist Academies of Richard Frankland MA and Caleb Rotheram DD* (Kendal 1915).

Altogether more than 300 students were educated in Frankland's Academy; though only about a third of them became ministers, they included most of the Congregational and Presbyterian ministers in the north of England at the end of the seventeenth century. When Richard Frankland died in 1698, his work was largely taken over by the Independent Timothy Jollie at Attercliffe Hall in Sheffield, though some of his students went to John Chorlton in Manchester. But with the death of Jollie in 1714, ministerial training in the north lapsed, and with it much of the fervour of the early formative period of northern Dissent. By the 1750s, almost all the men trained by Frankland and Jollie had died. The younger ministers now working in the West Riding came from the more liberal academies such as Daventry.

The liberal thinking of the early eighteenth century led to the challenging of traditional trinitarian belief through Arianism[5] and Socinianism.[6] In 1710 William Whiston, Professor of Mathematics at Cambridge, published his widely-read *Essay upon the Apostolical Constitutions*, in which he tried to demonstrate that primitive Christianity accorded with the views of Arius. Two years later he was expelled from the university. Even more widely-read was a work by Samuel Clarke, Rector of St James's, Westminster, *The Scripture Doctrine of the Trinity* (1712), in which he implied that the doctrine of the Trinity was not revealed in Scripture. There is evidence that both these works were discussed in Dissenting academies.

One of the earliest ministers to make known his sympathies with anti-trinitarian thinking was James Peirce, who was called to be the senior Presbyterian minister in Exeter in 1713. He was brought up as an Independent, and after studying at Utrecht and Leiden had served as pastor of a joint Independent/Presbyterian congregation in Cambridge, where he came to know William Whiston before the latter's expulsion from the university. At the time of Peirce's arrival in Exeter, there was already some unease among the Dissenters about the ideas being discussed in Joseph Hallett's Exeter Academy. When Peirce used ambiguous language about the nature of Christ, he was asked by the Committee of Thirteen, the lay trustees of the three Presbyterian meeting houses of Exeter, to preach a sermon in defence of orthodox doctrine; his words failed to satisfy the Committee. There followed a good deal of pamphlet warfare and fevered debate, which finally led to an appeal to

[5] Arius had challenged the orthodox doctrine of the divinity of Christ in the early fourth century. His views were condemned by the Council of Nicaea in 325, but his ideas continued to attract theological explorers.

[6] Fausto Sozzini (Socinus, 1539–1604) was a sixteenth century Italian theologian who denied the essential divinity of Christ. His followers were more radical than Arians.

the Committee of Three Denominations[7] in London to help to resolve the issue by offering advice.[8]

The result was a series of meetings at Salters' Hall in London in February and March 1719, when the Committee brought its proposed 'Advices' before the General Body of London ministers, who resolved (by 57 votes to 53) that 'no human compositions, or interpretations of the doctrine of the Trinity, should be made a part of those articles of the advice.'[9] In March the defeated minority subscribed to a declaration of belief in the doctrine of the Trinity, and were henceforward known as the Subscribers. Their opponents became known as the Non-Subscribers. While the discussion had centred on the scriptural basis of the doctrine of the Trinity, the actual issue at stake was that of subscription rather than doctrine; whether or not ministers should be required to declare their belief in the Trinity and the divinity of Christ. Despite the outcome of the vote, the Exeter trustees decided to exclude both James Peirce and Joseph Hallett, who proceeded to gather a congregation of about 300 in a new meeting house. The effects of this disruption were to be a precipitating factor in the beginnings of the Western Academy a generation later.

From this point forward, most of those congregations which were sympathetic to the discussion of a variety of theological ideas remained as Presbyterians, and eventually became Unitarian. By the middle of the eighteenth century, most of the surviving Dissenting academies were hospitable to the discussion of 'rational theology'. Those for whom subscription to orthodox doctrine was of primary importance remained or became Congregational.

It became all the more important therefore for the orthodox Dissenters to ensure that future ministers were educated in a less heterodox environment. It was also the case that while some of the 'rational Dissenters' were wealthy enough to pay for the education of their sons, those who remained orthodox were usually less wealthy, and therefore relied on outside help towards the cost of ministerial (or other) training and education. The Congregational Fund Board had been founded at a meeting of seven ministers and 14 laymen held in London on 30 December 1695 after the break-up of the 'Happy Union' of Congregational and Presbyterian ministers (founded in 1691) through a failure to resolve contentious issues of theology and church polity. Wealthy members of London churches were persuaded to give generously to a

[7] A committee of four Presbyterians, three Congregationalists and three Baptists set up in 1702 to protect Dissenting interests.

[8] See chapter VI of Allan Brockett, *Nonconformity in Exeter 1650–1875* (Manchester 1962) for a full account of the crisis.

[9] See Michael Watts, *The Dissenters* vol I (Oxford 1978) 375. See also Alan P. F. Sell, *Dissenting Thought and the Life of the Churches* (San Francisco 1990), chapter VI, and Roger Thomas, 'The Salters' Hall Watershed, 1719' in C. G. Bolam et al., *The English Presbyterians* (London 1968).

fund which survives to this day. While a Presbyterian Fund continued to support both Congregational and Presbyterian students and imposed no doctrinal tests, the Congregational Fund Board would support only those of orthodox views. This became even more significant during the eighteenth century. The King's Head Society was formed in 1730 in London specifically to provide for the training of orthodox ministerial students, who had to subscribe to 'A Declaration as to some controverted points of Christian Doctrine'; their supporters were critical of the Congregational Fund Board's requirement that students should have a classical education before beginning ministerial training, though later the two organisations worked together. In 1738 William Coward, a wealthy London merchant, left his estate to make similar provision, and in 1756 a Northern Education Society was formed, also in London, to support such training in the north of England.

Contemporary with this intellectual movement was a religious development of a very different kind – the Evangelical Revival which emerged almost simultaneously in New England, Germany, Wales and England. Zinzendorf, Howel Harris, John and Charles Wesley and George Whitefield were all significant figures in this movement, which affected Anglicans and Dissenters alike. The German Count Nicholas von Zinzendorf (1700–60) was the inspiration behind the Moravian missionary movement, whose strongest English outpost was in the West Riding of Yorkshire through the itinerant ministry of Benjamin Ingham (1712–72), formerly a member of the Methodist 'Holy Club' in Oxford. Howel Harris (1714–73) experienced a conversion experience in 1735 which led him to undertake an itinerant ministry throughout Wales, before founding a religious community at Trevecca in Breconshire. George Whitefield (1714–70) was another member of the Methodist 'Holy Club' at Oxford in the early 1730s, and followed the Wesleys to Georgia. After his return, his firm Calvinism caused a break with the Arminian John Wesley (1703–91); his Welsh followers aligned themselves with the converts of Howel Harris and Daniel Rowland, and others with the Countess of Huntingdon's Connexion in England. He travelled and preached in England as well as Wales, but his English followers usually found a home in Congregationalism. John Wesley's exhaustive itinerant ministry stirred the whole country, but his Arminian views did not find favour with the Congregational churches.

This great movement of itinerant preaching depended on lay support. No lay person was more influential in this respect than Selina, Countess of Huntingdon,[10] whose support was given to George Whitefield, Howel Harris and the Wesleys, as well as numerous other lesser known

[10] Selina, Countess of Huntingdon (1707–91) was converted under Methodist influence in 1739, and after her husband's death in 1746 devoted herself wholly to religious and philanthropic work.

preachers. At first, she worked within the Church of England, taking advantage of her legal right as a widowed peeress to appoint personal chaplains.[11] In 1768 she opened a college to provide an education for evangelical preachers at Trevecca Isaf, near the home of Howel Harris.[12] Her students found it increasingly difficult to obtain episcopal ordination, a situation which was resolved by her 'Plan of Secession', according to which men were ordained directly for her Connexion, the first such ordination taking place in 1783 at Spa Fields, when six Trevecca students were ordained. Many of these men eventually became ministers of Congregational churches.

Her college marked a new departure in theological education, for the students were intended for itinerant as well as settled ministry. 'It was as preachers of the gospel, not as men of learning, that the Trevecca students were sent out to itinerate far and wide and to bring light into the dark corners of the land and of lands across the sea.'[13] Such itinerant preachers were able to respond to the needs of a country undergoing great social and economic upheavals, a country whose population was increasing rapidly, and for whom the ancient parish system was no longer adequate. Evangelism as well as election was understood as central to Christian belief and practice.[14]

The new Dissenting academies/colleges of the late eighteenth century and early nineteenth century laid more stress on evangelism than their predecessors. The orthodox believed 'that the elegant classic, the profound metaphysician, often lost the spirit of the man of God in the task of the man of letters ...'.[15] It is in this tradition, and against this background, that the origins of Northern College are to be discovered.

[11] See Edwin Welch, *Spiritual Pilgrim: A Reassessment of the Life of the Countess of Huntingdon* (Cardiff 1995) 151.

[12] See G. F. Nuttall, *Howel Harris 1714–73: The Last Enthusiast* (Cardiff 1965).

[13] G. F. Nuttall, *The Significance of Trevecca College 1768–91* (London 1969) 7. This published lecture brings out clearly the significance of the college as 'a pioneer in the theological education arising out of the Evangelical Revival'.

[14] See D. Lovegrove, *Established Church, Sectarian People* (Cambridge 1988) 10–13.

[15] D. Bogue and J. Bennett, *History of the Dissenters from 1688 to 1808* vol IV (London 1812) 299.

2

The West Country: The Western Academy

DURING the late seventeenth and early eighteenth centuries, Exeter was one of the most important strongholds of Dissent outside London. In 1672 it was estimated that one-twelfth of the population was Nonconformist, and the severe persecution experienced there in the succeeding seventeen years had the effect of strengthening the cause. By 1715 Nonconformists almost certainly made up at least one quarter of the population,[1] and included many of the wealthy merchant families of the city. Even in 1744, they were at least 16.5 per cent of the population.[2] There were three Presbyterian congregations, James's Meeting, Bow Meeting and Little Meeting. All were flourishing in 1715, and shared four ministers between them – Joseph Hallett, James Peirce, John Lavington and John Withers. The Congregational Meeting in Castle Lane had 400 'hearers' by 1715. A Baptist congregation moved to South Street in 1725, and Quakers met in Wynard's Lane.

In 1691 the Congregational and Presbyterian ministers of Devon and Cornwall had agreed to meet twice a year in general assembly to discuss matters of common interest and hear a sermon, to raise money for the training of ministers, and to arrange for the ordination of qualified candidates. This was one of the very few assemblies which survived into the middle of the next century, despite the severe disruption leading to the Salters' Hall meeting. For all but the first four years of its existence, the Assembly always met in Exeter.

The provision of ministers for succeeding generations was taken seriously. These 'United Brethren' supported students at the Academy founded in Exeter sometime soon after 1690 by the Presbyterian minister of James's Meeting, Joseph Hallett,[3] the son of an ejected minister of the same name who died in 1689. The Academy, open to laymen as well as candidates for ministry, was an institution where liberal enquiry was allowed, if not encouraged; it had the distinction of educating a future

[1] See Allan Brockett, *Nonconformity in Exeter 1650–1875* (Manchester 1962) 71–2 for the evidence for this.

[2] Brockett, 116.

[3] Joseph Hallett II (1656–1722). See *DNB*.

Lord Chancellor, Peter King.[4] In 1710 the theological tutor's son, Joseph Hallett III, began acting as assistant tutor. After reading William Whiston's *Advice for the Study of Divinity* he began a secret correspondence with the author. There was unease among Exeter Nonconformists about the discussions taking place in the Academy[5] which led ultimately to the crisis of 1719. However Joseph Hallett III was ordained alongside John Lavington,[6] a student of more orthodox persuasion, in October 1715.

During the crisis of 1719, brought to a head by the preaching of James Peirce, John Lavington was able to satisfy the Committee of Thirteen of his orthodoxy, as did John Withers; but Joseph Hallett and James Peirce failed to do so. Accordingly, the four Trustees of James's Meeting (of whom two were Lavingtons) expelled them from the Meeting.[7] Henceforward, and until 1753, all candidates for ordination, and new ministers in the area, were required to subscribe to the doctrine of the Trinity. The expulsion of Joseph Hallett II from James's Meeting sounded the death-knell of the Academy, which closed in 1720.

The attempts to hold the Exeter Presbyterians to orthodoxy, and to maintain the Congregationalists and Presbyterians in the Assembly as 'United Brethren', ultimately failed. John Lavington, who had drawn up the formula of trinitarian orthodoxy which the Exeter Committee of Thirteen decided to require of all ministers suspected of unorthodox opinions, continued as minister at Bow Meeting until his death in 1759. For most of that time, from 1729 until 1755, his colleague was John Walrond, who in 1718 as minister at Ottery St Mary had first alerted the London ministers to what was happening in Exeter. Three of John Lavington's sons were candidates for ministry: Andrew Lavington, who died as a student, Samuel Lavington,[8] who attended the Bridgwater Academy until his father grew alarmed at the Arian views of the tutor, John Moore, and sent him to the care of Zephaniah Marryat at Plasterers' Hall, London,[9] and John Lavington II, whose early training

[4] Peter King (1669–1734) was Lord Chancellor 1725–33. In 1713 he defended William Whiston in his trial for heresy.

[5] The youngest Joseph Hallett's later published work, especially *A Free and Impartial Study of the Holy Scriptures Recommended* (London 1729, 1732, 1736, 3 vols), demonstrated his intellectual ability and biblical scholarship, and brought his name to the attention of the German biblical scholar John David Michaelis (1717–91).

[6] John Lavington (d.1759). See *DNB*. The Lavingtons were strong supporters of the Presbyterian congregations.

[7] They were soon appointed ministers of a new Mint Meeting.

[8] In 1753 Samuel Lavington was the last ordination candidate to take the declaration of belief in the Trinity at the Exeter Assembly. He was minister at Great Meeting (later re-named Lavington Chapel), Bideford, 1753–1807.

[9] The Academy of the King's Head Society, which eventually settled at Mile End.

may have been with his father. The removal of Samuel Lavington from the Bridgwater Academy may have reminded the London ministers of the need to provide for the maintenance of orthodox teaching in the West of England, for the matter was now brought to the attention of the Congregational Fund Board.

In the 1740s the Board supported 48 such students, and the number rose to 63 in the 1760s. Until 1752 most of these were being educated either at Mile End Academy (which became Homerton Academy in 1770) or at the Welsh Academy which moved from Haverfordwest to Abergavenny, thence to Oswestry and elsewhere in the Welsh Borders until it finally settled in Brecon as Brecon Memorial College in the middle of the nineteenth century.[10]

It was therefore the Congregational Fund Board which agreed to support the initiative of a group of Congregational ministers (including John Lavington senior) which met privately in Exeter in 1752 and decided to invite the younger John Lavington, ordained in 1739 and now minister at Ottery St Mary, to take in four students who had already been examined by members of the Board and found qualified. The Board would provide each one with £12 per annum. Lavington agreed, and the Academy was based at his house in Broad Street, where one or two students were admitted each year. The course lasted four years, admission being dependent on a reasonable prior classical education. By the time John Lavington died in 1764,[11] eighteen students had received all or part of their training under him. He was much respected by orthodox and liberal alike, though his own orthodoxy can be verified from three surviving manuscript notebooks of student notes on his lectures, which include a section on 'Corruptions of the Socinians to be guarded against'.[12] On the Sunday after his death, Micaijah Towgood of Exeter said of him from the pulpit, 'He was more pious, more learned, and more useful than us all.'

Micaijah Towgood[13] meanwhile had joined his cousin Stephen Towgood as a joint pastor of James's Meeting in Exeter in 1750. He was a former student of the Taunton Academy[14] and 'believed in the Trinity

[10] Later it moved to Swansea, and thence to Aberystwyth.

[11] His exact year of birth is not known, but is likely to have been c.1720. He therefore died comparatively young.

[12] These books, transcribed by Thomas Reader and further copied by S. Rooker, have been preserved in the New College Archive, WES 5–7, at DWL.

[13] Micaijah Towgood (1700–92). See *DNB*. His *Dissenting Gentleman's Letters* (1746–8) was a classic defence of Nonconformity, and was re-published in the early nineteenth century.

[14] Taunton Academy was established c.1670, and continued under three theological tutors until 1759. Micaijah Towgood would have been taught by Henry Grove (1683–1738), who managed to avoid any public speculation on the doctrine of the Trinity, but corresponded with Samuel Clarke. For Henry Grove, see *DNB*.

after the Arian fashion'.[15] In 1753 he was responsible with others for proposing a motion which in effect abolished the customary practice of requiring that candidates for ordination should make a trinitarian declaration. He relaxed the communion discipline of his congregation, in not asking for a profession of articles of faith, but rather requiring primarily that communicants should live a godly life and understand the meaning of the service. When a second Exeter Academy was opened under Samuel Merivale in either 1760 or 1761, Micaijah Towgood was appointed one of the tutors (of biblical exegesis) alongside his pastoral duties. For the next few years there were thus rival academies in the West Country for orthodox and liberal.[16]

The initially modest orthodox Academy was run on the old style, in that the location was determined by the choice of tutor. After John Lavington's death in 1764, James Rooker[17] was chosen as tutor and the Academy moved to Bridport, Dorset, where James Rooker had since 1742 been minister of a church founded by seceders from a Presbyterian meeting.[18] A native of Walsall, he had been educated at the Bedworth Academy under John Kirkpatrick. But there was continuity from Ottery in that one of John Lavington's pupils who succeeded him as minister at Ottery, Samuel Buncombe,[19] ran a preparatory classical course, supported by the London King's Head Society, for students who then went on to Bridport. Rooker had preached at Buncombe's ordination in 1760. Eight students transferred from Ottery to Bridport in 1764, and by 1769 they were occupying new premises by Bridport's East Bridge; a further eleven entered before James Rooker's resignation in 1779.

One of James Rooker's students, Joseph Chadwick,[20] wrote an account of his student days in response to an enquiry from Joshua Wilson, on 4 February 1820. Chadwick was reaching the end of his ministerial life but his memory was clear. James Rooker he remembered as 'a very pious character, rigidly attached to all the sentiments commonly called Calvinistic, but at the same time very humane & compassionate & peculiarly attentive to the comfort of the students, when under any

[15] See Alan P. F. Sell, 'A Little Friendly Light: The Candour of Bourn, Taylor and Towgood' in *JURCHS* V (1987–92) 517–40 and 580–613, reprinted in Sell, *Dissenting Thought* (1990)

[16] The Exeter Academy closed in 1771. A third Exeter Academy opened in 1799, but lasted for only six years.

[17] James Rooker (1728/9–1780). See Alan P. F. Sell, 'The Walsall Riots, the Rooker Family and Eighteenth-Century Dissent' in Sell, *Dissenting Thought* (1990).

[18] John Lavington Senior had delivered the sermon at his ordination on 16 October 1751.

[19] Samuel Buncombe (1734–94). See *Evangelical Magazine* 1794, 309–17 and 337–9.

[20] Joseph Chadwick (1751–1841) was the great-grandson of another Joseph Chadwick, ejected from the living of Winsford, Somerset in 1662.

mental or corporal indisposition'. The students had acquired some classical education before entering the Academy, and therefore it was not felt necessary to give much attention to Greek and Latin, 'a few verses only being translated by us out of the Greek Testament every morning, a portion of Turretini's System of Scholastic theology[21] in Latin translated likewise once a week'. He then gives further insight into both the teaching methods and the books studied:

> We had also to learn the Hebrew Grammar & once a week to translate a few verses out of the Hebrew Bible, with the usual points, & to attend to other weekly Lectures read to us by our Tutor from Dr Watts' Logic (an invaluable book),[22] especially his excellent chapter on the doctrine or subject of *Prejudice*), Dr Watts' Geography & Astronomy,[23] Dr Gibbons' Rhetoric,[24] Rowning's Natural Philosophy,[25] & Mr Lavington's Divinity Lectures, in manuscript, one of wch we were to transcribe for future use every week. We had also to compose in the first years short essays on given subjects, 3 of which I remember were on the 4th commandment, the Redemption of Time, & Pride; & in the last year, when (& *not before*) we were sent forth to preach, we composed sermons, partly from texts given us by the Tutor & partly from our own choice.[26]

After James Rooker's resignation because of a stroke in 1779, the Academy moved to Taunton, where Thomas Reader[27] had been minister at Paul's Meeting since 1771. He acted also as tutor until 1794. Like James Rooker, he had spent time at the Bedworth Academy, but had also attended Doddridge's Academy in Northampton, before moving to Wareham as minister. He spent the whole of the rest of his ministerial life in the West of England. Nineteen students entered the Academy at Taunton.

[21] This was probably the *Institutio Theologiae Elenchticae* (3 vols, Geneva 1679–85) by François Turretin (1623–87). It was a work of strict Calvinist theology, the most important systematic theological work written in Geneva in the seventeenth century. It was studied in Scotland and in New England into the middle of the nineteenth century. Turretin's son, Jean-Alphonse (1671–1737) was a more moderate Calvinist.

[22] Isaac Watts, *Logic: or, the Right Use of Reason in the Enquiry after Truth* (London 1724) was used as a textbook in the universities of Oxford, Cambridge and New England.

[23] Isaac Watts, *The Knowledge of the Heavens and the Earth Made Easy: Or, The First Principles of Astronomy and Geography Explain'd by the Use of Globes and Maps* (London 1726).

[24] Thomas Gibbons, *Rhetoric* (London 1767). Thomas Gibbons (1720–85) was a tutor at Mile End Academy.

[25] John Rowning (1701?–71) published *A Compendious System of Natural Philosophy* between 1735 and 1744. This was used in the University of Oxford in the 1750s.

[26] New College MS L54/4/71, DWL.

[27] Thomas Reader (1725–94). See *Evangelical Magazine* 1794, 485–94, 441–8.

One of his students was James Small,[28] a native of Taunton, who married James Rooker's daughter. He was minister at Axminster when invited to succeed Thomas Reader, so the Academy moved yet again. Within two years the Congregational Fund Board announced its decision to discontinue the Academy, a decision which was modified only after a strong appeal from the secretary of the Western Calvinistic Association. The Board agreed to maintain some financial support, but on a lesser scale. The formation of a local Society to raise supplementary funds enabled the Academy to continue. For the next 32 years, James Small undertook all the teaching, of classics and mathematics (of which he was particularly fond) as well as theology, resisting the pleading of his friends to take on an assistant 'with a pertinacity which his best friends sincerely lamented'. Fifty-three students entered his Academy, though the numbers at any one time were few.[29]

In 1827 the Congregational Fund Board experienced severe financial problems and had to withdraw all support for many years. The Academy's Report for 1827 therefore addressed the local churches: 'It now remains for one hundred independent churches of the four western counties to determine, whether an Institution, which has been a *blessing*, and which, with the contemplated advantages, may become a still *greater blessing*, shall utterly fail, or rise with an accession of strength and efficiency.'[30] There was a good response, and a meeting was held in Exeter on 19 November 1828, after the retirement of James Small, to determine the Academy's future.

It was agreed to put it on a more formal basis, with a fixed location, a stronger committee and a wider curriculum. Exeter was deemed the most suitable place, and two houses in Alphington Terrace were rented. George Payne,[31] the theological tutor at the Blackburn Independent Academy since 1823, was persuaded to move to Exeter (with two of his students), and soon established his reputation in Devon. He was already known through his contributions to the *Evangelical Magazine* and *Eclectic Review* and before long was in great demand as a preacher. The Academy now achieved wider public notice.

Payne was the son of an Oxfordshire cooper who in adult life became a Baptist minister at Walgrave, Northamptonshire and was one of the

[28] James Small (1759–1834). See *Evangelical Magazine* 1834, 265–9.

[29] The early students at the Academy are all listed in J. C. Johnstone, 'The Story of Western College', *TCHS* VII (1916–18) 98–109. A more comprehensive list of students up to 1912, with fuller information, appears in the *Western College Annual Report* for 1912, 10–29.

[30] Quoted in the *Evangelical Magazine* 1829 158–9

[31] George Payne (1781–1848). See George Payne, *Lectures on Christian Theology* 2 vols (London 1850) with a memoir by J. Pyer and reminiscences by R. Wardlaw, and *DNB*. For a discussion of his ethics see Alan P. F. Sell, 'A renewed plea for "impractical" divinity', *Studies in Christian Ethics*, VII/2, 1995, 68–91.

founders of the Baptist Missionary Society. The younger Payne was baptised by John Clayton at the King's Weigh House when he was a student at Hoxton and after further study at Glasgow University served as assistant to Edward Parsons in York for a year, and then as coadjutor to George Lambert in Hull. He returned to Scotland in 1812 to become minister of a new chapel in Albany Street, Edinburgh, formed by a group who seceded from James Haldane's church over the issue of baptism. He was one of the leaders in the formation of the Congregational Union of Scotland in 1812 and of the Edinburgh Itinerant Society, and his gifts as a preacher were widely appreciated. After 12 years in Edinburgh he had moved south to Blackburn, and combined the ministry at Mount Street Chapel with teaching at the Academy.

He published several theological works while he was in Exeter. His *Lectures on Divine Sovereignty, Election, the Atonement, Justification, and Regeneration* (1836) was often used as a textbook. His moderate Calvinism owed much to the influence of Edward Williams of the Rotherham Academy (with whom he had corresponded in some depth while in Hull[32]), to Jonathan Edwards, the American Calvinist theologian, and to Ralph Wardlaw, the Scottish Congregational minister and theologian whom he had known in Glasgow when a student. His biographer referred to his learning as 'varied and respectable, though not what scholars would call extensive and profound', pointing out that he was never able to read German works in the original, but had to rely on English translations.[33] However, he achieved widespread recognition: he was elected Chairman of the Congregational Union of England and Wales in 1836, and eight years later was invited to give the recently established Congregational Lectures in London, for which he chose the subject of 'Original Sin'.[34] In 1841 he attended the Manchester conference on the Corn Laws, and was the one minister present to give evidence of having read works on political economy.[35] He was tireless in travelling round the West Country and to London in search of funds.

Within three years the Academy moved into new and larger premises north of the city centre at Marlfield House, Pennsylvania,[36] which was purchased for £2,450. Five years later, the Congregational Fund Board renewed its support and promised an annual grant of £120. The number of students now fluctuated between about six and twelve.

A series of assistant tutors helped George Payne with the teaching. Daniel Currie (1829–31), a former student at Axminster Academy, died in office, still only 30. Jonathan Glyde (1831–5) was related to the

[32] Payne, xxxi–xlvi.
[33] J. Pyer, ibid, cxi.
[34] Published in 1845 as *The Doctrine of Original Sin.*
[35] I am indebted to Roger Tomes for this information.
[36] An area first developed in the 1820s by a Quaker businessman, Joseph Sparkes.

Lavington family on both sides. He was educated at Highbury, and came to the Western Academy as tutor when he was only 23. Within four years, George Hadfield, who heard him preach in Exeter, had persuaded him to go north to Bradford, where he had a distinguished ministry for almost twenty years and did much to raise standards of public worship.[37] John White Pope (1836–9) stayed on as tutor for three years after taking the Academy course. Later in life he was a private tutor at University College, London. Orlando Thomas Dobbin (1840–5), a former student of Hoxton Academy, was an Irishman of some scholarly attainment who eventually joined the Church of England.

Of the 100 students who passed through the Academy between 1752 and 1832 the majority (62) remained in ministry in the West Country until retirement. Twelve moved to another denomination (eight became Anglican, two Unitarian and two Baptist). Almost all the rest remained in the Congregational ministry but a few spent some years in other parts of the country. One, Richard Knill, was a missionary with the London Missionary Society in Nagercoil for three years. The 31 students who studied under George Payne, however, included no fewer than eight who served with the London Missionary Society, and those whose ministry was confined to the West Country were in the minority (seven). One student, Samuel Martin, was later elected to the Chair of the Congregational Union, in 1862.[38]

The Western Academy was never prominent in itinerant ministry – the Baptists were more active in Devon in this respect – but it served as a focus for Congregationalists in the West Country.[39] Itinerant ministry was however to the forefront of the work of the Academies in the north of England which we are now to consider.

[37] Jonathan Glyde (1808–54). See *CYB 1856* 214, *Evangelical Magazine* 1855 121–7, and G. W. Conder (ed), *Memoir and Remains of Jonathan Glyde* (London 1858).

[38] See *Western College Annual Report* for 1912.

[39] The Academy remained in Exeter until 1845. Its later history in the West Country is recounted in Chapter 9.

3

Yorkshire[1]

Heckmondwike and Northowram

Dissent had always been relatively strong in the West Riding of Yorkshire, and especially in the villages on the hills near Halifax and Huddersfield, where most of the people were involved in some way or another with the cloth industry. But after the deaths of those who had lived through the years of persecution, religious life within all the denominations reached a low point, and churches ceased to command respect from those outside. Among the Dissenters, the spread of Arian ideas, especially among the clergy, coincided with, and, according to some, led to, falling congregations. Anglicans suffered both from the practice of plural livings and religious indifference, and from impossibly large parishes affected by industrialisation. When John Wesley visited Huddersfield on 9 May 1757 he wrote, 'A wilder people I never saw in England.' According to the Countess of Huntingdon's biographer, Henry Venn, who became vicar of Huddersfield in 1759, 'found his parish in worse than Egyptian darkness'.[2] Joseph Cockin, one of James Scott's early students and later a celebrated preacher in the West Riding, recalled the hostility of his father and friends to his growing interest in religion when a boy in Honley, which led to his being thrown out of the family home for a long period.[3] His experience was not unique.

There were, however, already promises of revival. William Grimshaw (1708–63),[4] the eccentric but highly esteemed clergyman who became vicar of Haworth in 1742, made a profound impact on the surrounding area. He welcomed John Wesley, George Whitefield, and William Romaine to his pulpit; the number of communicants in his church rose from 12 to 1200. Benjamin Ingham gathered support for the Moravians in the 1730s and 1740s and was instrumental in the foundation of the Moravian Settlement at Fulneck. However, for Heckmondwike, where the Yorkshire Academy began, the most significant influence was to be

[1] The accounts of the colleges of Yorkshire are much indebted to K. W. Wadsworth's excellent *Yorkshire United Independent College* (London 1954).

[2] *The Life and Times of Selina, Countess of Huntingdon* vol I (London 1844) 276. The author was described on the title page as 'a Member of the Houses of Shirley and Hastings', but was subsequently identified as A. C. H. Seymour.

[3] See John Cockin (ed), *Memoirs of the Rev Joseph Cockin* (London 1841).

[4] See Frank Baker, *William Grimshaw 1708–63* (London 1963) and *DNB*.

that of Henry Venn (1725–97),[5] who arrived in Huddersfield as Vicar in 1759.

Dissent had always been strong in the Spen Valley and surrounding area, and Heckmondwike had no parish church until 1830. The Independent church at Heckmondwike had its origin in the years of persecution after 1662. A small gathered congregation formed a church on 29 July 1674, and on the following 5 November Josiah Holdsworth was ordained pastor there. Born in Wakefield, Holdsworth was a graduate of St John's College, Cambridge. He served for a short time as chaplain to the Presbyterian Sir Richard Hoghton of Hoghton, very close to Tockholes and Blackburn. He was ejected from the living of Sutton upon Derwent in 1662, and probably preached clandestinely until the Declaration of Indulgence of 1672 allowed him to acquire a licence (at Heckmondwike). After his ordination, and for the last eleven years of his life, he and his congregation ran the constant risk of being apprehended for breaking the law. For a time, they met at night.[6] Holdsworth died, aged 46, only months after Charles II, and so did not survive long enough to experience the happier atmosphere that resulted from the Toleration Act of 1689. Two more ministers served the church before James Scott arrived: David Noble (1686–1709) and John Kirkby (1710–53).

Later generations looked back on those early years of Independency in West Yorkshire as 'the heroic years', the years when the ecumenically-minded Presbyterian Oliver Heywood toured the county preaching, often in danger. To the people of West Yorkshire Oliver Heywood meant as much as Richard Baxter and John Bunyan did to others.

By 1751 John Kirkby, minister at Heckmondwike, was elderly and wished to retire; but according to the custom of the time, he was prepared to wait until a successor could be found. Nobody realised at this time that the church was at the centre of a crucial division in the development of dissenting religious thought, through the lives of two men who were cousins, both called Joseph Priestley. The Priestley family lived a few miles away at Birstall. The younger Joseph Priestley (1733–1804) had lost his parents when young, and was brought up by his aunt, Mrs Keighley, at Old Hall, Heckmondwike. Mrs Keighley was a member of the Independent Chapel, but had wide sympathies; her home was 'the resort of all the Dissenting ministers in neighbourhood without distinction, and those who were the most obnoxious on account of their heresy were almost as welcome to her, if she thought them honest and good men (which she was not unwilling to do), as any others'.[7] Here the

[5] See H. Venn, *The Life and a Selection from the Letters of Henry Venn* (London 1834), and *DNB*.

[6] See Oliver Heywood, *His Autobiography, Diaries, Anecdote and Event Books* vol III (edited J. H. Turner, Bingley 1883) 214.

[7] *Memoirs of Dr Joseph Priestley* (Centenary edition, London 1904) 4.

young Joseph Priestley took a keen interest in everything under discussion, and enjoyed private lessons from a number of local clergymen, including John Kirkby. It seems that he was particularly influenced by his discussions with John Walker, one of the candidates considered (but rejected) as successor to John Kirkby in 1751. When he applied for church membership a year later, the elders rejected him because, in his own words, 'when they interrogated me on the subject of *the sin of Adam*, I appeared not to be quite orthodox, not thinking that all the human race (supposing them not to have any sin of their own) were liable to the wrath of God and the pains of hell for ever, on account of that sin only.'[8] A year later Joseph Priestley entered Daventry Academy, and embarked on the course which was eventually to lead him to be one of the celebrated intellectuals of his age, scientist, philosopher, unitarian minister.[9]

The older Joseph Priestley was one of the elders or deacons of the Heckmondwike Independent church; these elders held to orthodox belief, and were determined to avoid a minister with even a faint hint of Arianism in his preaching. Many of them were involved in the cloth trade, which, alongside the production of carpets and blankets, was so firmly established here. When they consulted the Revd Alvery Jackson, the Baptist minister of Barnoldswick, who occasionally preached in Heckmondwike, concerning a possible successor to John Kirkby, they were told of James Scott, an outstanding orthodox preacher from Scotland, then minister at Tockholes, a village on the southwest border of Blackburn. The elders went across the Pennines to hear him preach, and promptly invited him to move to Heckmondwike. He was loath to leave a place at which he had only recently arrived, and had reservations about the 'gifted brethren' he was told had become accustomed to speaking during John Kirkby's years of infirmity;[10] but it was not until two years later, after much pleading, that he finally agreed to move to the Spen Valley.

James Scott (1710–83) came from the border country near Lauder and had studied at Melrose Grammar School and at Edinburgh University (though there is no record of his having taken a degree) before working as a private tutor to the sons of George Peter, laird of Chappell. Writing later of his move to England, he recorded that he was 'educated a Presbyterian, in opposition to episcopacy, but not in opposition to the Congregational order. I was in some measure persuaded that Congregational churches were the institutions of Christ before I left Scotland –

[8] Ibid 7.

[9] Joseph Priestley (1733–1804). See *DNB*.

[10] Despite assurances to the contrary, these 'gifted brethren', who rejected any form of contact with other Christian churches, caused Scott a great deal of trouble until they were asked to leave in 1760.

which was one reason of my complying with an invitation to this country.'[11] Having turned down an invitation to minister in the next parish to his birthplace, in 1739 he moved to the north of England to serve as minister first at Stainton and then at Horton-in-Craven. His reputation as a preacher in the orthodox tradition grew, and he received several invitations to other churches. In 1751 he accepted a call to Tockholes, one of the six Lancashire Congregational or Presbyterian churches which had not been influenced by the prevailing Arian and Socinian ideas. He found the members receptive to his requirement that they should learn the Catechism of the Westminster Assembly by heart.

By the time James Scott was called to Heckmondwike, most other local Nonconformist ministers were sympathetic to Arianism.[12] This was a matter of concern beyond the limits of the West Riding. The sister of the orthodox Joseph Priestley was married to Edward Hitchin (c.1726–74), minister of the largest Independent meeting house in London at White Row. Hitchin regularly visited his wife's family in the Spen Valley, and often spoke of 'the gloomy condition' of the local Nonconformity. When James Scott arrived, the two men often met and talked and evidently shared and lamented the same depressing view of the surrounding religious life.

How was the orthodox reformed faith to be handed on unless future ministers had the opportunity of an appropriate education? The son of Heckmondwike's first minister was educated at Richard Frankland's Academy at Rathmell, but since 1714 Nonconformist ministerial training in the north had lapsed, and with it much of the fervour of that early formative period of northern Dissent.

From the conversation between Hitchin and Scott, and that of others, arose the idea of reviving an academy for training pastors and itinerant preachers in the north of England; unlike the earlier academies which had not confined admission to ministerial candidates, this was to admit intending ministers only. 'The awful want of gospel ministers, and the cloud of socinian darkness spreading over the northern counties of England, occasioned a few ministers and gentlemen in London to deliberate on some happy method, by which congregations might be blessed with godly preachers; sound in the faith, and exemplary in their lives.'[13] A meeting on 24 May 1756 in London formally set up the Northern Education Society, with Dr John Guyse, an active member of the King's Head Society, as chairman and Hitchin as secretary. They

[11] Quoted in Frank Peel, *Nonconformity in the Spen Valley* (Heckmondwike 1891) 139.

[12] Frank Peel, *Spen Valley: Past and Present* (Heckmondwike 1893) 412.

[13] *An Account of the Rise, Nature and Progress of a Society for Educating Young Men for the Work of the Ministry, in the West Riding of the County of York* (n. d. but c.1765). Congregational Library, DWL.

appointed James Scott as tutor to the academy. At a further meeting on 14 June, it was agreed that no young man should be proposed until 'he hath produced an account in writing of the reason of his hope, and of what he apprehends to be the principal doctrines of Christianity'. Such candidates were to be examined by local committees of ministers and laymen, and a report made to the subscribers. The Society would then provide £15 per annum for the support of each accepted student. The course was to last for four years, during which time the students would live in the tutor's household.

Before agreeing to the suggestion of appointing Scott as tutor, William Fuller, a London banker who was soon to become the treasurer of the Northern Education Society, wrote to the Heckmondwike minister asking him for his views on doctrine and discipline. Fuller was a staunch Calvinist and an active member of the King's Head Society. Scott's reply, dated 27 March 1756, was as follows:

> I have considered the Savoy Confession on the subject [of church order], and do heartily approve of it with some small exceptions. I believe visible saints are the only fit matter of the visible church; that Jesus Christ hath given power to a particular congregation or church to manage all the concerns of the church according to the scripture rule with respect to the choice of officers, the admission, censuring and exclusion of members of it, to be admitted on a profession of faith and obedience. I have read, and do approve of Dr Owen's view of the gospel church, except his opinion with respect to ruling elders, which I am not clear about, but do rather incline to the Rev. Mr. Bragge's sentiment as I understand it upon reading his book on church discipline, viz. that Jesus Christ hath not appointed the office of the ruling elder as distinct from the teaching elder, but that the power, rule and government is in the whole church; that the elder brethren ought especially to be helpers to the elders by this office.[14]

This seems to have satisfied Mr Fuller, who became a generous supporter of the Heckmondwike Academy. Scott for his part wanted guidance on the curriculum expected at an English college, and sought advice, particularly from the Mile End Academy,[15] which provided tuition for students supported by the Congregational Fund Board and the King's Head Society. Joseph Priestley had decided against entering Mile End when he learned that its students were expected to subscribe to ten articles of Calvinist faith.

The Academy opened in August 1756.[16] Each applicant had to give

[14] Quoted in Frank Peel, *Nonconformity in the Spen Valley* (1891) 138.

[15] John Conder was theological tutor at Mile End; the tutors responsible for preparatory work in classics and logic were John Walker and Thomas Gibbons.

[16] One year after this academy opened, another opened across the Pennines at Warrington for 'rational Dissenters', with the younger Joseph Priestley as one of the lecturers.

Figure 1: Heckmondwike Academy at Southfield
Source: W. Scruton, Pen and Pencil Pictures of Old Bradford *(Bradford 1889)*

evidence of personal piety and faith. The first three students to be admitted were Richard Plumbe,[17] Timothy Priestley (brother of the younger Joseph Priestley)[18] and Thomas Waldegrave.[19] They lived with James Scott and his wife in their home in Millbridge, on the site of the original meeting house by the river Spen.[20] Apart from Henry Venn, in whose house he met most of the local Evangelical leaders, Scott's nearest sympathetic ministerial neighbour was John Pye[21] of Nether Chapel, Sheffield, who rode across the moors to Heckmondwike regularly to discuss the state of the churches and the affairs of the Academy with its tutor. His greatest good fortune was the arrival of Henry Venn as Vicar of Huddersfield in 1759, for Venn was a keen and effective Evangelical, who had accompanied George Whitefield on a preaching tour, and who was one of the Countess of Huntingdon's chaplains.[22] In Huddersfield, he 'prophesied over the dry bones, and a wonderful rising followed'.[23] He was sympathetic to Calvinism and catholic in his attitude to other denominations. Thus under his influence thirteen men became ministers, most of them in Independent churches, trained in Scott's Academy.

Little is known specifically about the syllabus followed at the Academy, but we can assume from that fact that one or two of the students had done preparatory studies before entering, that they were expected to begin their course with some knowledge of classical studies, that biblical studies in Greek and Hebrew would have formed a large part of the curriculum, and that the doctrine taught would have been strictly Calvinist. Everything was taught by Scott himself, alongside his pastoral duties. Of the 57 students who completed their course with James Scott, only two seem to have adopted Arian or Socinian views in later years.

Gradually the Academy became known over a wide area, and the number of visitors increased. This led in 1761 to a custom which continued until well into the second half of the twentieth century, whereby visitors were invited and made welcome for the whole of one day in the year (but were not expected at other times). This was the

[17] Richard Plumbe (d.1791) had two pastorates, at Charlesworth, Derbyshire 1760–71 and Castlegate, Nottingham 1772–91.

[18] Timothy Priestley (1734–1814) had four pastorates, at Kipping, Thornton; Cannon Street, Manchester; Lock Chapel, Dublin; and Jewin Street, London.

[19] Thomas Waldegrave (1732–1812) had been brought up by a Roman Catholic uncle. His two pastorates were first at Scott's former church in Tockholes, and then at Bury St Edmunds. See B. Nightingale, *History of the Old Independent Chapel, Tockholes, near Blackburn, Lancashire* (London and Manchester 1886).

[20] This building has not survived.

[21] John Pye (c.1718–1773) was the grandfather of John Pye Smith, President of Homerton College 1806–50.

[22] See H. Venn (1834), and *DNB*.

[23] *Life and Letters of the Countess of Huntingdon* vol I 276.

occasion which became known as the Heckmondwike Lecture: an evening lecture was given at Lower Chapel, followed by two morning lectures at Upper Chapel and 'a good plain dinner'. It gradually evolved into the great gathering of the year for West Riding Congregationalists, and continued late into the twentieth century.[24]

As the number of students slowly increased, it became impossible to accommodate them all in the tutor's own house. Scott's wife Esther, to whom he was devoted, predeceased him in 1763. In 1768 he bought a small estate up the hill at Southfield, Norristhorpe, for the Academy,[25] and did all his teaching there until the walk up from Heckmondwike proved too taxing. In his final months the Academy returned to the centre of the town.

One of his former students wrote of Scott:

> ... his appearance was commanding, his manner grave and solid, his doctrine sound and uncorrupt; savouring much of the old Puritans. His voice was strong, and though not very sonorous, by no means disagreeable; his style indeed was not the most correct; – often mixed with Scotticisms; and his compositions were allied to those of the old Divines, who, after raising the doctrine, divided and subdivided into an host of particulars. ... He was a Divine of the old stamp of the Scottish school.[26]

Another spoke of his being 'mighty in the Scriptures. ... He was almost a living concordance.'[27] He could be forbidding, especially to strangers, but once the 'thick rind' was broken through, he was friendly and agreeable. He was no 'trimmer' but 'a staunch and uniform Dissenter, i.e. he did not look one way and row another.'[28] His exhortation was not limited to students or members of his own church. More than a century later Frank Peel recalled hearing old people say that 'when idlers who were gossiping in the street on Sunday mornings saw him coming towards his chapel

[24] In the nineteenth century a fair was held in the town as part of the celebrations, and the railway company laid on special day excursions. Even after the closure of the Yorkshire United Independent College in 1958, the students of the Northern College had to attend the Lecture, regardless of the fact that it fell during the middle of examinations.

[25] The building in which Scott taught was later used as a weaver's shed and eventually pulled down in the 1920s, though the surrounding cottages remain. Stones from the building now form part of the pedestal of the pulpit (dated 1929) of Norristhorpe United Reformed Church, and also part of a sundial which stood in the grounds of the Yorkshire United Independent College in Emm Lane until that building was sold. It is now returned to Heckmondwike, where it stands in the grounds of Upper Chapel, alongside the gravestones of James and Esther Scott.

[26] Quoted in the *Evangelical Magazine* 1814, 501–2.

[27] Jonathan Toothill, *Funeral Sermon for the Rev James Scott* (Huddersfield 1783) 30.

[28] Ibid 31.

from Millbridge, they were in the habit of going into their houses to avoid the inevitable remonstrance or exhortation.'[29]

Sixty-seven students were admitted to the Academy when Scott was tutor, ten of whom had not completed the course before Scott died.[30] These men helped to create a new climate in the northern counties. The majority remained in the ministry in the north of England for their entire working life, some of them in recently-formed churches which owed their origins to student preaching. The Northern Education Society was fulsome in its circular of c.1765: 'The streams of this fountain have been signally blessed for refreshing, and making fruitful many congregations, which were like dry and barren wildernesses.' One of the most distinguished former students, Joseph Cockin, who founded the West Riding Itinerant Society, wrote in the *Evangelical Magazine* in November 1795 of the Academy's students that 'by their instrumentality decayed congregations have been revived, and many new ones raised up.' Though the students were not supposed to preach in local churches until the final year of their course, Scott found it hard to refuse requests from struggling congregations without ministers.

After Scott's death in 1783, the London Committee had to find another minister who could assume responsibility for the ten students still in training. They chose a former student, Samuel Walker, minister at Northowram, a few miles away near Halifax. Northowram, like Heckmondwike, had a long and honourable Nonconformist tradition, for it was there that Oliver Heywood had gathered a church in 1672 after gaining a licence to preach. The chapel building was erected in 1687.[31] Samuel Walker became the church's fourth minister in 1774 and appears to have been very popular at first. In 1783 the students, together with the Academy's books and apparatus (science was on the curriculum), moved to the Manse at Northowram, a short distance from the chapel. Next door to the Manse was a smaller building in which the previous minister, Robert Hesketh, had kept a school, which was now used for the Academy.[32]

For reasons not entirely clear, Samuel Walker's relations with his congregation and students did not prosper, and he resigned the pastorate in 1793.[33] By this time the number of students had fallen, and many of the subscribers, including William Fuller, the treasurer, had withdrawn their support. The Academy therefore was closed in 1794, and the four

[29] Frank Peel, *Nonconformity in the Spen Valley* (1891) 171.

[30] *Rotherham Independent College Annual Report 1888* lists all the students educated at Heckmondwike. The Surman Index at Dr Williams's Library provides biographical information about them.

[31] A new chapel building was opened in 1837, which now forms Heywood Memorial Church, a congregation of the United Reformed Church.

[32] These two houses still stand in the main street of Northowram.

[33] Very little further is known of Samuel Walker.

remaining students were placed under the personal tuition of William Vint of Idle, near Bradford.

From this point and for almost a century Yorkshire ministerial education developed through two separate branches, one on the outskirts of Bradford, the other in Rotherham. Both claimed to be the heir of Scott's Academy at Heckmondwike.

ROTHERHAM

On 27 June 1794 William Fuller wrote from London to Joshua Walker, a wealthy furnace owner of Rotherham, whose father Samuel (no relation of Samuel Walker of Northowram) had helped to found and finance the building of Masbro' Independent Chapel.[34] The letter explained the decision to withdraw support from Samuel Walker at Northowram, and asked Joshua Walker to bring the whole matter to the attention of the leading laymen and ministers of the West Riding. A general meeting was then convened in Leeds in July by William Moorhouse at which 20 ministers and 12 laymen were present.[35] A committee of ten was appointed to make plans for a new academy for ministerial students, which it was at first assumed would be in the Halifax area. At a meeting held in Halifax on 11 September, it was decided to seek two tutors, who were to be 'Calvinist Independent Dissenters'. Board and lodging would be provided free of charge for students. Meanwhile the committee had acquired the Academy's library at Northowram. On 8 October it was agreed that the Academy would be situated in a large town, and Joshua Walker of Rotherham was appointed treasurer. This appointment was to be crucial, because Joshua Walker knew that Masbro' Independent Chapel, in a village on the west side of Rotherham, was looking for a new minister, and he also knew that one of the possible candidates had a reputation as a sound tutor of ministerial candidates. In addition, Walker was a very wealthy man.

The committee approached Edward Williams, then at Carrs Lane, Birmingham, as possible tutor. Edward Williams had already been approached by the Masbro' Chapel, and the committee was ready to establish the new academy there if Williams were prepared to accept both positions. The fatal illness of his wife postponed a decision, but finally in August 1795, a month after her death, he agreed to accept both invitations.

[34] See C. J. Chislett (ed), *Masbro' Independent Chapel* (Rotherham 1960). Samuel Walker's firm built Southwark Bridge and Wear Bridge, Sunderland. The Walkers were one of the chief families of Rotherham.

[35] See *An Account of the Rotherham Independent Academy* (1797), DWL and NCA. J. Gilbert attributed its authorship to Edward Williams.

The choice of Edward Williams[36] gave the new Academy an excellent foundation, for he was one of Congregationalism's outstanding theologians at the time. Like many of his generation, he had moved from his family background in the Church of England to Independency through the influence of evangelical preachers, in his case Calvinistic Methodists in his native north Wales (Welsh was his native tongue). He had joined the Independent church at Denbigh, and through the influence of Daniel Lloyd, its minister, enrolled as a student in the Dissenting Academy at Abergavenny, where Lloyd himself was educated. From here he was called to be minister first at Ross-on-Wye, then in 1777 at Oswestry. It was in Oswestry that he began teaching students at the request and expense of Lady Glenorchy,[37] and then from 1782 to take charge of his own old Academy, which moved to Oswestry. When his health eventually broke down under the strain he moved to Birmingham to be minister at Carrs Lane. But he missed his students, and when he was first approached unofficially about the possibility of taking on an academy in Yorkshire, he wrote to an unknown correspondent:

> My soul often has longed for the company of pious young men for the Ministry, and pined in secret for the loss, like that of a mother for her children; insomuch, that I have had serious thoughts of announcing my design of taking two or three under my care, if such as are truly promising could be procured; and have been treating for a house with that view. You will not wonder, therefore, if I compare your letter to the sounding horn of the huntsman . . .[38]

On the other hand, he did not want to teach to the exclusion of pastoral ministry. He felt that he had both talents, and 'could not satisfy my conscience, nor think of my future account with comfort, were I, without pressing necessity, to hide one of them'.[39]

Williams held a good balance between learning and evangelical conviction. In a letter to the Yorkshire committee dated 20 August 1795, he told them that one of the factors which persuaded him to accept their invitation was the fact that they 'are peculiarly intent on the *religious* qualifications of the young men whom they mean to recommend as students. . . . I am fully assured that an *unconverted ministry* is the bane of the Christian cause, and the dead weight of the churches.'[40] But this

[36] Edward Williams (1750–1813). See J. Gilbert, *Memoir of the Life and Writings of Edward Williams* (London 1825), W. T. Owen, *Edward Williams DD 1750–1813: His Life, Thought and Influence* (Cardiff 1963) and *DNB*.

[37] Willielma Campbell, Viscountess Glenorchy (1741–86) was a patron of evangelical preachers in both Scotland and England. See *DNB*.

[38] Quoted in J. Gilbert (1825) 373.

[39] Quoted ibid 374.

[40] Quoted in *An Account of the Rotherham Independent Academy* 35.

was not for him an argument 'against literature and the study of improvement, since God produces effects in grace as well as nature, by the use of means.'[41]

A work which he edited in 1800, *The Christian Preacher* (which included extracts from works by both English and French writers of the previous two centuries), was evidence 'that the best elements in the Older Dissent and in the Methodist Revival met in him'.[42] The work was dedicated to his present and past students, and reveals something of the ideals of preaching he put before them, including the necessity for both 'the glowing heart' and the disciplined mind. In his own contribution to the book, on 'The Preacher's Library', he recommended that the furniture and books of the minister's study should make up at least half of the whole furniture of the house.

The Academy opened on 5 November 1795, with ten probationer students, in a new building financed by Joshua Walker[43] which stood 'on a gentle eminence' not far from the Independent chapel.[44] It is difficult for the visitor today to imagine the building being 'surrounded by garden and pasture grounds', as Edward Williams described it in 1797.[45] It was 'finished in a neat but plain manner'. There were three floors: the ground floor included a hall 25 feet by 18, and a library 25 feet square, while the bedrooms and studies filled the two upper floors. The extant engraving and early photograph of the building (see Figure 2) show the college as extended in 1812[46] but one can see that in its original form it was an impressive if plain classical building, surrounded by trees.

The committee of the Academy, which represented the subscribers, almost all of whom came from the West Riding, was drawn from the local area, and so was able to take a much closer interest in its affairs than did the London committee of the Heckmondwike and Northowram Academies.[47]An appeal for new equipment was issued, and the committee was encouraged 'by the cheerful contribution of some ladies in the neighbourhood for a large, new pair of globes, on the best construction,

[41] *Account* 4.

[42] Owen 73.

[43] At first Walker received interest on the £500 he provided, but before his death in 1815 he conveyed the ownership of the building to the Committee by deed of gift.

[44] This chapel building still stands, and is now a carpet warehouse. The memorial tablets, many of them to former members of Rotherham's staff, remain on the walls; at the side of the building is the graveyard and the small mausoleum built for the Walker family.

[45] *Account* 45. College Road, in which both college and chapel stood, is now intersected by a large roundabout and dual carriageway.

[46] Copies are in Rotherham Local Studies Library, and one is reproduced in Tony Munford, *Victorian Rotherham* (Huddersfield 1989). This building was eventually pulled down. Falding Street now marks the site.

[47] London representatives continued to collect subscriptions however: William Fuller, Ebenezer Maitland, Benjamin Mills and James Neale.

Figure 2: Rotherham Independent Academy, Masbro'
Source: Rotherham Public Library

with recent improvements by Dr Herschel'.[48] Not only was it responsible for appointing the staff and raising the funds, but it was able to take an interest beyond that of simply receiving reports on the admission and progress of students. It actually examined the students before admission and prior to each annual general meeting, when orations in Latin and Greek were delivered by selected students. There is an early example of this superintendence in the admission of the Academy's most distinguished alumnus, John Pye Smith.[49] The minute for 4 January 1797 records his admission, but goes on to record that 'on account of some imprudent conduct ... he be suspended from the further benefits of this Institution until the next Vacation'. His offence was to have been associated with a newspaper, *The Sheffield Iris*, which had been critical of the militia's breaking up a crowd during public demonstrations in the previous year. He was warned that the Academy committee 'disapproved of too much openness and decision in political sentiments'.[50]

The course of instruction was normally to be four years, but could be extended to five. Since there were so few opportunities for Dissenters to acquire a good education, the curriculum of necessity had to include basic education in arts and science as well as more advanced study of theology, philosophy and biblical studies. As at the Western Academy under James Rooker, text-books included Rowning's *Natural Philosophy* and Isaac Watts' *Logic* and works by François and Jean-Alphonse Turretin. There was a strong emphasis on languages, especially Latin, Greek and Hebrew. Mathematics, divinity, church history, astronomy and geography also found a place. Though James Scott at Heckmondwike and Samuel Walker at Northowram each had to teach all subjects, the new academy aspired to a higher standard, and within two months of the opening appointed a second member of staff to act as classical tutor. Maurice Phillips, a former student of Edward Williams at Oswestry, combined teaching with ministry at Zion Chapel, Attercliffe, Sheffield from 1802 until 1810.[51]

By 1803 Williams had been made responsible not only for the teaching, but for the boarding of the students, for which he was given an allowance of £25 per annum.[52] In a time of rising prices this soon proved insufficient. But an accompanying decline in subscriptions led the

[48] *Account.*

[49] John Pye Smith (1774–1851). See John Medway, *Memoirs of the Life and Writings of John Pye Smith* (London 1853). He was for many years principal of Homerton Academy.

[50] Quoted in Wadsworth, *Yorkshire United Independent College* (1954) 63.

[51] Maurice Phillips (1767–1822). His first ministry, from 1790 until 1796, was at Brigstock, Northants. His later career was as a schoolmaster.

[52] He had married Jane Yeomans of Worcester in 1796, and so again lived in a family household.

Committee to instruct him 'to discontinue the allowance of Butter to the Bread and Milk given to the students to Breakfast and to make such other reasonable retrenchments in the expenditure as he may think necessary', adding 'and that a Letter be addressed to the Students to admonish them cheerfully to submit to such necessary regulations'.[53] The response of the students is not recorded. He had supplemented his salary by taking in three boys under the age of 15 for general education, with the agreement of the committee. Three years later Maurice Phillips resigned on account of the low salary and moved to Mill Hill School as headmaster. His successor as tutor from 1810 to 1817 was Joseph Gilbert, a student at the Academy 1806–10, the future biographer of Edward Williams.[54]

During his years at Rotherham, Williams published two important theological treatises: *An Essay on the Equity of Divine Government, and the Sovereignty of Divine Grace* (London 1809) and *A Defence of Moderate Calvinism* (London 1812), expressing a moderate Calvinism tempered by the evangelical spirit;[55] his ideal would have been to reconcile Calvinist and Arminian ideas.[56] Both books were the fruit of many years of thought and reflection, and had an influence beyond his own lifetime. Williams's theology was less dogmatic than orthodox Calvinism about human destiny, was reserved about the idea that God predestines some to election and others to damnation, and stressed human responsibility for the preaching of the gospel. He was steeped in the Puritanism of his forebears, and, together with Edward Parsons of Leeds, edited the works of John Owen, Jonathan Edwards (a particularly strong influence on him), Isaac Watts and Philip Doddridge. His own works were later edited by Evan Davies in four volumes and published in 1862. His lecture notes survive in two large handwritten volumes in Dr Williams's Library.[57] The elegant handwriting suggests a person of clear, logical thinking.

Not only was he an outstanding scholar, but he played a leading role in the affairs of English Congregationalism, and in the country's religious life as a whole. He was involved in the foundation and editing of the *Evangelical Magazine*. He was one of those instrumental in the formation of the London Missionary Society. And he was a firm supporter of the movement to form a Congregational Union which was

[53] Rotherham Independent Academy Committee Minute Book, entry for 30 June 1808.

[54] For Joseph Gilbert (1779–1852) see *DNB*. He later had a long ministry at Friar Lane, Nottingham.

[55] See D. Bebbington, *Evangelicalism in Modern Britain: A History from the 1730s to the 1980s* (London 1989), 63–5 for a discussion of Moderate Calvinism in historical context.

[56] See Owen, 94–113, and R. T. Jones, *Congregationalism in England 1662–1962* (London 1962), 170–1, for a discussion of Williams's theological system.

[57] MS L23, DWL.

under discussion in the first decade of the nineteenth century. When the Congregational Union of England and Wales was finally created in 1832, most of Williams's proposals for such a union were adopted.[58] In addition he and Maurice Phillips were active members of the West Riding Itinerant Society.

When Williams died on 9 March 1813 aged 62, 49 students had been educated in his academy. His contemporaries and successors were in no doubt that he was one of the great theologians of his age. His thinking was mediated to the next generation primarily through the teaching and writing of his pupil, John Pye Smith, at Homerton Academy.

The committee was eager to find a successor who would further enhance the reputation of the Academy, and were gratified when James Bennett agreed to move from Romsey to become theological tutor at Rotherham.[59] James Bennett was a Londoner whose Anglican parents had attended one of the Countess of Huntingdon's chapels. After a period in business in London and Bath (where he heard the great evangelical preacher William Jay) he had experienced an evangelical conversion, which led him to seek admission to David Bogue's Academy at Gosport in 1793. From here he became minister of the Congregational church in Romsey, Hampshire, where, during a ministry of 17 years, his congregation increased sevenfold. He not only undertook evangelistic tours, but continued his linguistic and theological studies in the early hours of each day. He came to Rotherham with a great reputation as a preacher, known to a wide circle through his regular contributions to the *Evangelical Magazine* and the *Eclectic Review*, and his active support for the London Missionary Society. Collaboration with his former tutor, David Bogue, had resulted in the publication of the authoritative *History of the Dissenters* in four volumes during the years 1808 to 1812.

During the first eight months of his ministry at Masbro' Chapel 50 new members joined the church. He worked immensely hard in both Academy and local church life and twice his health broke down. He had a particular enthusiasm for oriental languages – Hebrew, Syriac, Arabic and Aramaic – as well as Latin, Greek, French and German. The number of students applying to the Academy (it was renamed as a College after 1814) began to increase, and within two years of his arrival the building had to be extended to enable eight more students to be accommodated (making a total of 21). In 1841 he gave the Congregational Lecture on 'The Theology of the Early Church'.[60]

When the classical tutor, Joseph Gilbert, left in 1817 he was succeeded

[58] See Owen, 92–3.

[59] James Bennett (1774–1862). See *Memorials of the Rev James Bennett* (London 1863), *CYB 1863* 206–8 and *DNB*.

[60] Published as *The Theology of the Early Christian Church, Exhibited in Quotations from the Writers of the First Three Centuries* (London 1841).

by Thomas Smith,[61] a graduate of Edinburgh University who had been employed as a private tutor to the family of Robert Spear, the benefactor of William Roby's Academy in Manchester. He was to remain at the Rotherham Academy for 32 years.

In 1827 there was some discussion in the Academy's committee concerning 'insubordination among the students', which may well have been related to Bennett's second breakdown. He decided that the time had come to move, and in 1828 he accepted an invitation to minister at Silver Street, London, where again the membership rose dramatically.[62] His last attendance at an Annual Meeting of subscribers in Rotherham happily coincided with a celebration of the repeal of the Test and Corporation Acts in 1828. Seventy students passed through the College during his tenure, including John Hoppus, later of University College, London, and Samuel McAll, president of Hackney College from 1860 until 1881.

The committee now made a list of men to be approached with a view to becoming theological tutor.[63] The fifth on the list was Clement Perrot, a minister in Guernsey, and it was his name which was eventually brought to the committee meeting and approved on 5 February 1829. It was not a good choice. Within two years the committee was again discussing insubordination among the students, and the numbers declined. It was a wise decision for both tutor and college when Perrot handed in his resignation in June 1833. The College now entered upon a difficult period during which local feelings of loyalty to the College were not matched by financial support.

IDLE

The Academy at Idle began in a more modest way than did the one in Rotherham, but very gradually established a firm base of support in the local community and slowly built up its academic reputation.

Idle, belying its name, was a hard-working industrial village on the edge of Bradford. Like Heckmondwike and Rotherham, it had a long and honourable Nonconformist tradition. Upper Chapel dated back to 1715 when John Buck became minister, and the first building to 1717.[64] The last minister before the arrival of William Vint was Joseph Dawson

[61] Thomas Smith (1786–1853). See *CYB 1854* 250–3.

[62] He carried on preaching until he was 86. During that London ministry he was elected chairman of the Congregational Union in 1840. When he died the anonymous obituarist in the *CYB 1863* wrote of him as 'almost the last of the generation of worthies of the Independent Nonconformists who have done so much to uplift the sacred cause from the degradation to which in previous days it had been subjected.'

[63] The list was as follows: Dr Wardlaw, W. Orme, H. J. Burder, Greville Ewing, Clement Perrot, Andrew Reed, John Ely, A. C. Simpson, Joseph Gilbert, Walter Scott, Thomas Binney.

[64] J. G. Miall, *Congregationalism in Yorkshire* (London 1868) 294.

(1740–1813), a friend of the younger Joseph Priestley, who combined ministry with teaching, medicine, and managing an iron works; according to Idle's historian, ministry was the lowest priority among his many interests.[65] He was 'a man of great liberality and kindness, though an Arian in sentiment'.[66] The membership sank to no more than half a dozen. Under the influence of the preaching of Joseph Cockin, who was then minister at Kipping, a few miles away, and an old Heckmondwike student, the congregation favoured a minister of more orthodox persuasion when Joseph Dawson left, and called William Vint, one of Samuel Walker's former students at Northowram. Vint began his ministry in 1790, and soon filled the chapel, which was then rebuilt to house a growing congregation.

William Vint (1768–1834) was a Northumbrian who acquired a love of walking through roaming over his native hills. Under the influence of his minister, James Somerville, he enrolled as a student at Northowram in 1785, and by choice walked the 100 miles from and to his home each term. He must have made a great impression as a student preacher, for he received calls from several churches in the north of England before deciding to accept the invitation to Idle.

As a former Northowram student he was well known locally, so it was natural for the Northern Education Society to ask Vint to act as tutor to the remaining students when Walker's Academy closed in 1794. This he did for a year, until two students received calls and the remaining two moved to the new Academy at Rotherham. This left the Bradford area without an academy or source of student preachers. One of the London supporters of the Northern Education Society, Edward Hanson, who came from Yorkshire and retained an interest in the prosperity of orthodox Dissent there, invited Vint to take two students into his home for ministerial training at Hanson's expense. The arrangement began in 1800, when four students began their training.

It was agreed that the students, who according to the Trust Deed would all subscribe to the doctrines of the Westminster Assembly's Shorter Catechism, would undertake a four-year course in the following subjects: Latin, Greek, Hebrew, English, logic rhetoric, geography, church history, theology (all taught by one tutor). Subscriptions were invited, and arrangements made for a meeting of subscribers to receive reports and elect a committee. When Edward Hanson died in 1806, his will (dated 1802) provided for an income of £150 per annum in support of the Academy. This, together with rising subscriptions, allowed not only for the support of four students, but also for the provision of new dormitories and studies adjoining the parsonage in 1809. Gradually a library was built

[65] J. H. Turner, *Nonconformity in Idle, with a History of Airedale College* (Bradford 1876) 47.

[66] Ibid 294.

up, through both donations and purchases. Among the reference books acquired, according to the *Annual Reports*, were the *Encyclopaedia Britannica*, Walter Wilson's *History of Dissenting Churches*, Horne's *Introduction to the Critical Study and Knowledge of the Holy Scriptures*, Jackson's *Antiquities*, and the works of Philip Doddridge.

One could not, however, call the accommodation spacious. In 1827, the 18 students shared two dormitories, and though each had a study, it was only five feet ten inches square.[67] The setting was bracing, at the top of the village. Although Thomas Rawson Taylor, who was a student from 1826 until 1830, called Idle a 'dirty, grovelling, manufacturing village', he told his sister that 'a walk of five minutes brings us to a point whence we have a view of some of the finest scenery of Airedale, which, lying west, presents every evening an enchanting sunset scene.'[68]

The original agreement was that students should preach during their first two years only at the discretion of the tutor. Judging by the support which local congregations received from the students throughout Vint's years as tutor, this discretion must have been liberal. And it seems that Vint expected his students not to flinch at walking long distances over the moors to village churches, any more than he did. In 1818 Amos Blackburn, a student, wrote: 'It is now three months since I commenced preaching the Gospel (as a student) in which time I have preached between 40 and 50 times, which is more than three times a week, and I have walked 560 miles for that purpose.'[69] The Report of 1819–20 recorded that 'like apostolic men, [the students] have travelled on foot, and in the course of the last twelve months, the miles which each has travelled in this manner, when added together, make a total exceeding 17,400 miles.'

Vint himself was tireless in itinerant ministry. He preached for the Itinerant Society (formed in 1811 at the instigation of Joseph Cockin) and for the West Riding Home Missionary Society, formed in 1819 to complement the work being done to support missions overseas. Much of the work of these societies was done by Idle students, and many Congregational churches were either newly formed or revived during these early years of the nineteenth century.[70] Each year's Report referred

[67] See W. S. Matthews, *Memoirs and Select Remains of T. R. Taylor* (London 1836).

[68] Thomas Rawson Taylor to his sister 11 September 1827, quoted in Matthews, *Memoirs* 50–1. The cotton and worsted trade had spread to Idle by 1800.

[69] Quoted in J. H. Turner, *Nonconformity in Idle, with the History of Airedale College* (Bradford 1876) 136.

[70] After referring to 63 places of worship within 30 miles of Idle, the *Annual Report* for 1826–7 listed as revived congregations: Pudsey, Bingley, Kipping, Mixenden, Eastwood, Ossett, Hopton; and as newly gathered ones: Pateley Bridge, Ripon, Wortley, Stainland, Elland, Otley and Tadcaster. The following year's report claimed that the number of regular attenders at Independent churches in Yorkshire and Lancashire had doubled in recent years.

to congregations revived as a result of the Academy's work. 'The Academy at Idle must ... be considered the life blood of our Itinerant Society.'[71] It proved increasingly difficult to respond to all the requests for preaching which poured in. Despite the emphasis on preaching and pastoral work, the details of the examinations in the annual reports reveal that a great deal of linguistic work was done; as well as studies in Latin, Greek and Hebrew, some of the Gospels were studied in Syriac, some chapters in Daniel and Ezra were read in Aramaic, and works in French were often included.

In 1825 the Annual Report referred to the fact that the number of requests for preachers each week regularly exceeded the number of students, and expressed the view that 'the increase and prosperity of the Independent denomination, in a very important division of the Kingdom, will, in a great measure, depend on the enlargement of the Academy at Idle,' and added, 'Our Institution has had its day of small things.' A year later, this ambition was reflected in a change of name from Academy to College, and an extension of the course to five years. The Annual General Meeting on 21 June in that year resolved 'that as the ordinary schools of the country have of late years been generally styled Academies, this institution for the sake of distinction shall be hereafter denominated Airedale Independent College.' At the same time, William Vint ceased to be Idle's minister, and gave all his time to teaching. There were now thoughts of moving to a new and larger site and of finding a second tutor. A special appeal was launched, which resulted in one outstanding donation.

The Balme family was well known among Bradford Nonconformists. John Balme, who had taken a leading part in the building of Horton Lane Congregational Church, was survived by three daughters, two of them married. Before the unmarried daughter Sarah, 'long distinguished for her liberal, yet unostentatious charities',[72] died, she had expressed to her sister, Mary Bacon, a wish to leave money for the purchase of a site for the removal of Idle College to Bradford. Mrs Bacon accordingly made contact with members of the College's committee, and offered to purchase a site for building in addition to donating a local estate to yield income towards its support, in the names of herself and her deceased sister.

Events then moved fast. A specially convened building committee met in Horton Lane Church on 15 March and agreed to accept Mrs Bacon's offer and to seek plans for a new building.[73] By July an architect (Mr Clark of Leeds) had been chosen. A site on the edge of Bradford at Undercliffe was selected, high up, facing both the Aire valley and the

[71] *Annual Report 1813–14*, NCA.
[72] See *CYB 1855* 288–9.
[73] Airedale College Building Committee Minute Book, NCA.

moors, on what was then open ground, where the air was quite as bracing as at Idle. There seems to have been some disagreement between William Vint and the building committee about both site and style of building, for the minute for 22 April 1831 recorded that he was willing to move to Undercliffe, 'but at the same time enters his protest against both the site and the plan of the projected college'. The committee nevertheless decided to proceed, expressing the hope that 'time will heal those painful feelings which have been so unfortunately excited'.

The laying of the foundation stone on 20 June 1831 was the occasion of a great gathering of a thousand Nonconformist ministers and lay people from the West Riding, and received widespread publicity. The Revd Richard Hamilton,[74] the well-known minister of Albion Independent chapel in Leeds, gave an impassioned speech, vindicating the separation of Dissenters from the Church of England 'on the ground of its departure from the purity and simplicity of church government which characterized primitive Christianity'.[75] He maintained the superiority of Dissenters in both preaching and theology:

> We are convinced that the British Universities are quite unfitted to conduct the education of our ministry. Their pre-eminence of many advantages we at once concede. We have nothing approaching them as to kind or degree in our Institutions. But we *will* have the science of theology and the art of preaching. It would be to mock our clerical brethren to speak of their divinity or their preaching otherwise than as most undigested and superficial. Indeed mind and information seem little wanted in the routine of duties whose ritual prescribes each word and whose rubric ordains each posture; in which all that is to be said and to be sung, the very method of an announcement, the spreading forth of a hand, – is literally provided and must be slavishly pursued. This is the fault of their system. They are as much behind us as ministers as we are behind them as scholars.[76]

He caused considerable controversy by also taking the opportunity to attack what he saw as the Unitarian appropriation of Presbyterian trusts. He was speaking with the confidence generated by the recent repeal of the Test and Corporations Acts, and in a town which was to develop one of the strongest bases of Nonconformist support in the country.

About two weeks after this event, the secretary of the building committee, John Peele Clapham, wrote to the Revd John Blackburn, editor of the *Congregational Magazine*, enclosing a lithographic sketch of the proposed new building, in Grecian style, which he hoped Blackburn would publish. It would, he believed, help others to realise that 'the Congregational Dissenters of the North have not neglected that

[74] Richard Winter Hamilton (1794–1848) was Chairman of the Congregational Union in 1847. See *DNB*.

[75] *Annual Report 1830–1* 41.

[76] Ibid 29–30.

attention to Architectural propriety which is not less due to the growing importance of our Denomination, than it is required by the Educational Advance in good taste which Society at large is so rapidly making.'[77]

Before the building was completed, William Vint fell ill and had to resign. He died, aged 66, on 13 March 1834, just ten days after the students and two new tutors had moved into the new college premises, to begin a new and confident stage in the College's history.

[77] J. P. Clapham to J. Blackburn 8 July 1831. DWL.

4

Lancashire

Early Co-operation

Nonconformity had never been as strong in Lancashire as in the West Riding of Yorkshire, and there were few Lancashire Independent churches at the end of the eighteenth century which could trace their origins back to the seventeenth century. Robert Halley, writing in 1869, listed six Congregational churches, all of them originally Presbyterian, who had adopted Congregational principles in response to the increasing Arianism among the Presbyterian churches: St Helen's, Greenacres, Darwen, Whitworth, Elswick and Tockholes.[1] Late eighteenth century Lancashire Nonconformity was rural rather than urban, settled, unimaginative, apt to be self-satisfied. Yet this was the period which saw the great expansion of the cotton trade, the rapid growth of towns and a spectacular increase in population.

Although the renewal of Congregationalism cannot be attributed solely to any one person or place, the village of Tockholes, three and a half miles south-west of Blackburn, can be identified in retrospect as having played a significant role. Its Nonconformist chapel, initially Presbyterian, could trace its origins back to the years before 1662.[2] Like many others, the gathered congregation continued to meet, despite the Act of Uniformity and the 'Clarendon Code', in St Michael's Chapel of Ease until they were able to build their own meeting house in the valley below the main road. It was licensed in 1710. The presence nearby of the most influential Presbyterian family in Lancashire, the Hoghtons of Hoghton Tower, was a great support to the congregation during the years of persecution before 1689.[3] They had two large square pews in the centre of the chapel, with the family shield and monogram on the door panels. Two of the earliest ministers, Robert Waddington (minister 1700–15) and James Towers (minister 1722–49), were former students

[1] R. Halley, *Lancashire: Its Puritanism and Nonconformity* vol II (Manchester 1869) 420.

[2] For the history of the Tockholes congregation, see B. Nightingale, *History of the Old Independent Chapel, Tockholes, near Blackburn, Lancashire* (Manchester and London 1886).

[3] A century later the orthodox Presbyterian Sir Henry Hoghton was MP for Preston 1768–95. Like many other orthodox Presbyterians he was prepared to fulfil the legal requirement of receiving the Anglican sacrament on occasion.

of Richard Frankland's Academy. When Scottish weavers and traders began to move into the Blackburn area in the mid-eighteenth century, many of them found the form of service at Tockholes more congenial and familiar than any in Blackburn, and would walk out there on Sundays.

This was the congregation which called James Scott from the Scottish Borders to be its minister in 1751. During his short ministry there, before being persuaded to cross the border into Yorkshire, Scott made a deep impression by his earnest visiting and forceful preaching, which contrasted sharply with the rational preaching of so many others. It was not only Arian ideas, but a lack of religious fervour, 'a sort of creeping paralysis', what appeared to be 'a tradition rather than a faith',[4] which differentiated the ministry of so many Presbyterian ministers from that of someone like James Scott at Tockholes. 'That may be said of this little church which can be said of few others in the county of a like age, that it has never once faltered in its attachment to great Evangelical principles.'[5] Within a year of the opening of his Academy at Heckmondwike, Scott had sent one of his students, Thomas Waldegrave, to succeed him at Tockholes. And in the succeeding years, it was his former students who renewed the life of the churches in St Helen's (Isaac Sharp), Elswick (Robert Simpson), Forton (James Grimshaw), and elsewhere.

Many of the Lancashire Presbyterian ministers, especially those trained in Northampton and Daventry, wished to see a successor to Caleb Rotheram's Academy at Kendal, which closed in 1752. John Seddon, the Presbyterian minister at Warrington, who was a former student of the Kendal Academy, and held Socinian views, was able to raise funds, especially in Manchester, Liverpool, Bolton and Warrington, for the new Academy which opened in Warrington in 1757. John Taylor[6] was appointed as theological tutor, and Joseph Priestley joined the staff four years later. Three hundred and ninety three students passed through the Warrington Academy before its closure in 1786, but of these, only 55 were actually preparing for ministry. It was an Academy in the earlier tradition, educating the sons of wealthy Dissenters for a variety of professions. Without doubt, the Warrington Academy promoted exciting intellectual exploration, especially in science, which was not matched in the contemporary universities, and it has an honourable place in educational history.[7] But its liberal theology provoked a vigorous reaction among the more orthodox Dissenters of Lancashire.

[4] R. Halley, vol II (1869) 398.

[5] B. Nightingale, *Lancashire Nonconformity* vol II (London and Manchester 1891) 46.

[6] John Taylor (1694–1761), a native of Lancaster, an Arminian and Arian who nevertheless had a great veneration for Puritan tradition. See *DNB*.

[7] Its work was continued in Manchester New College, the forerunner of the present Harris Manchester College, Oxford. See H. McLachlan, *Warrington Academy: Its*

The influence of James Scott has to be attributed chiefly to his Scottish upbringing and education. But simultaneously, the English Evangelical Revival was reaching Lancashire through the preaching of the Wesleys, George Whitefield and Jonathan Scott.[8] Scott, an army officer, was converted through the preaching of the evangelical William Romaine at Oathall, Sussex, a house belonging to the Countess of Huntingdon. In 1769 he left the army and began life as an itinerant preacher in the north west. Many Congregational churches in Shropshire, Cheshire, Staffordshire and Lancashire owe their original foundation to him. He began visiting Lancashire in 1773. He refused an invitation to become permanent minister there, but was ordained as a 'presbyter or teacher at large' by a group of Congregational ministers at Lancaster on 18 September 1776.[9] He continued to work tirelessly as an itinerant preacher in Lancashire and neighbouring counties for many more years, finally settling in Matlock in a house left to him by his patron, Lady Glenorchy.

However, the greatest of the Lancashire itinerant preachers, following in the tradition of men like Jonathan Scott, was William Roby, who first preached under the patronage of the Countess of Huntingdon. He has a greater claim than anyone else to be regarded as the initiator of ministerial education in Lancashire during and after the Evangelical Revival.

William Roby[10] was born into a nominally Anglican family in Wigan. His father, a schoolmaster, hoped to see him continue from Wigan Grammar School to university and ordination to the priesthood in the traditional manner. The young Roby however began to take religion particularly seriously, and at first this drew him away from, rather than towards, his father's ambitions. Listening in St Paul's Church, Wigan,[11] to the preaching of John Johnson, one of the first six students to be ordained from Trevecca College in 1783[12], he became conscious of his unfitness for the 'awful responsibility' of ministry and accepted a post as a schoolmaster. Two years later, the call to ministry prevailed. John

History and Influence (Manchester 1943), and P. O'Brien, *Warrington Academy 1757–86: Its Predecessors and Successors* (Wigan 1989).

[8] Jonathan Scott (1735–1807). See Dugald Macfadyen, 'The Apostolic Labours of Captain Jonathan Scott' in *TCHS* 3 (1907–8) 48–66.

[9] Two of the ministers taking part, Abraham Allat of Forton and Timothy Priestley of Manchester, were former Heckmondwike students. See *Evangelical Magazine* 1807, 539.

[10] For William Roby (1766–1830), see W. G. Robinson, *William Roby and the Revival of Independency in the North* (London 1954), and *DNB*.

[11] St Paul's was opened in 1785 as a Countess of Huntingdon's Chapel. See Nightingale, vol IV, 75–84.

[12] This was at the 'primary ordination' of the Countess of Huntingdon's Connexion after her secession from the Church of England.

Johnson commended him to the Countess of Huntingdon, who agreed to support him at her college at Trevecca. Though he found the experience unhappy and unprofitable, and left after only six weeks, the Countess did not withdraw her support, but sent him to Malvern as a private chaplain, and then to several other places for short periods, as was her practice. After this, it was with much relief (especially as he was now engaged to be married) that he accepted an invitation from John Johnson to be his colleague in Wigan in 1788. Almost immediately John Johnson moved to Tyldesley to establish a new church, and left Roby in sole charge in Wigan. He was ordained as minister of the Countess of Huntingdon's Connexion on 20 September 1789 at Ebenezer Chapel, London. Five months later he married Sarah Roper in Worcester Parish Church. Her support was vital to him throughout the forty years of their marriage.

Though he now had a settled pastorate, he used it as a base for a lifetime of sacrificial itinerant ministry, often discouraging and unappreciated:

> The connexion of itinerant with stated labours is arduous, requiring a healthy and vigorous constitution; and the toil is often increased by the thoughtless inattention of the individuals to whose benefit itinerant labours are devoted. Often I have walked in dark, wintry, stormy nights three, four, or five miles, preached and returned home, without tasting any refreshment. The toil is often attended with discouragement.[13]

Yet there was a more positive side, for by this form of ministry 'many individuals are brought to serious concern, drawn to a stated attendance, congregations collected, churches formed, places of worship erected, and permanent interests established.'[14] Without living to see it, Roby laid the foundation for the flourishing Congregationalism of nineteenth-century Lancashire.

The service at St Paul's, Wigan, was liturgical and the minister wore surplice and gown in the Anglican manner. As minister there, Roby preached on the Articles of the Church of England, to which he was still loyal. At the same time he defended Calvinism against Socinianism. Through his friendship with men such as Robert Simpson, then at Bolton, and Isaac Sharp of St Helen's, both ex-students of the Heckmondwike Academy, he was now drawn to the principles of the gathered church, and decided to seek service as a Dissenting minister.

It was at this stage (1795) that he received and accepted a call to Cannon Street Meeting House in Manchester, a congregation which had seceded from the Presbyterian Cross Street Chapel, Manchester's first Dissenting place of worship, in 1761. It had attracted Scottish immigrants as well as others who as Anglicans had been influenced by

[13] W. Roby, MS Memoir, quoted in Robinson, 36.
[14] Ibid.

evangelical preachers. In the years since its licence had first been granted, it had had three ministers: Caleb Warhurst (who died in 1765), Timothy Priestley (who though a very good preacher was dismissed in 1784 after becoming entangled in financial difficulties)[15] and David Bradberry, a follower of George Whitefield. The last-named had to preside over a disagreement in the church concerning 'ruling elders', which led to a further secession in 1788 to the new Mosley Street Meeting House. Roby was therefore faced with the challenge of building up a congregation weakened by dissension and division.

From the beginning, and until his death in 1830, Roby was untiring in pastoral work, preaching, and building up the fellowship among his fellow clergy and congregations. One of the students whom he trained while at Manchester wrote of him: 'It was one of the first and most anxious objects of Mr Roby ... to imbue the more regular Dissenters to whom he united himself with somewhat more of the fervent zeal and itinerant exertion and character of the connexion which he had left.'[16] The congregation increased from 150 to 1200 (500 of whom were members), necessitating the building of a new and larger church in Grosvenor Street (now re-named Roby Street) in 1807 – though a small group remained behind and formed themselves into a separate church.

There was hardly any aspect of the Protestant religious life of Manchester or the surrounding district in which Roby was not involved, whether it was the Sunday School movement, the British and Foreign Bible Society, or the Royal Lancastrian Free School. At the national level, he was one of the founders of the London Missionary Society in 1795 and a supporter for the rest of his life. His itinerant preaching inspired the foundation of many new Congregational churches in the area. It was his efforts to support and later to train others to follow him in this itinerant evangelism which led ultimately to the formation of the Lancashire Independent College.

The Independent theologians of the seventeenth century had assumed fellowship and mutual oversight among the gathered congregations. The Savoy Declaration of 1658 had laid down that Churches of Christ 'ought to hold communion amongst themselves for their peace, increase of love, and mutual edification'.[17] In the years of persecution it was impossible to organise any formal associations, but after the Toleration Act of 1689 attempts had been made to form societies for mutual support, and a few, such as the Exeter Assembly and the Congregational Fund Board, had survived. In Lancashire, representatives of four divisions of the county met regularly, and General Meetings were held twice a year, at least until

[15] See J. Waddington, *Congregational History 1800–1850* (London 1878) 52.

[16] James Turner, quoted in Robinson, 57.

[17] *The Savoy Declaration of the Institution of Churches, and the Order Appointed in Them by Jesus Christ* XIV (1658).

1700. But the complacency which characterised many congregations in the middle of the eighteenth century, and the predominance of Arian Presbyterians in those which survived, had allowed this aspect of church polity to lapse, until the revival of evangelism gave a new impetus to the formation of local associations for both home and foreign missionary effort (some of which were inter-denominational).[18] One of the first was the Hampshire Union in 1781; many others followed, and by 1806, when the Lancashire Congregational Union was formed, thirteen county associations already existed. One of the differences between these associations and those of a century earlier was that they often included lay members.

It was the Lancashire County Union which sponsored the ministerial education which grew into the Lancashire Independent College, though not before Roby had anticipated their support by training ministers himself. The first attempt at an association of Lancashire churches and ministers was made in 1786 at a meeting in Bolton. This seems to have lapsed, until in August 1798 twelve ministers (of whom Roby was one) from Lancashire, Cheshire, Derbyshire and Yorkshire formed an association at a meeting at Tintwistle. One of its purposes was 'the wider extension of the Gospel', which led to the formation of an Itinerant Society in 1801.[19] The need for support for the itinerant preachers convinced them that a stronger association was needed. It was in 1806, therefore, that a Lancashire Congregational Union was founded at a meeting in Mosley Street Chapel, Manchester, with 24 Lancashire ministers and a few from over the border in neighbouring counties. Needless to say, Roby was a member of its committee. From this Union there developed a network of itinerant preaching and a great expansion and renewal of Congregational churches.

Roby's Academy 1803–8

'It is desirable that [itinerant preachers] commence with as complete a stock of ministerial furniture as they can previously acquire, and that they guard against [itinerancy's] dissipating tendency.' So wrote Roby in his Memoir.[20] While discussions concerning the formation of a county union were continuing, Roby had challenged his fellow ministers to sponsor an 'itinerant seminary' to train suitable young men as itinerant

[18] G. F. Nuttall, 'Assembly and Association in Dissent 1689–1831' in G. Cuming and D. Baker (eds), *Councils and Assemblies*, Studies in Church History VII (Oxford 1971), provides a detailed account of these movements. Baptist local associations usually preceded the formation of Congregational ones.

[19] See B. Nightingale, *The Story of the Lancashire Congregational Union 1806–1906* (1906) for an account of the foundation of the Union.

[20] Quoted in Robinson, 36n.

preachers within a space of 12–15 months, without demanding knowledge of biblical languages. The challenge was not taken up. But Roby entered into correspondence with the Scottish evangelists James and Robert Haldane,[21] which resulted in their trying to persuade him to leave Manchester in order to conduct seminaries in Scotland financed by Robert Haldane. Roby, however, felt his work was still in Manchester. This was confirmed when a Manchester benefactor of such a seminary declared himself – Robert Spear, a member of Mosley Street Meeting, where his father had been a deacon.

Robert Spear[22] was a cotton merchant who made sufficient money to be able to retire when he was 46 and move to the Cheshire countryside, and eventually to Edinburgh. For over a decade he was a very generous benefactor to ministerial training, not only in Manchester but also at Rotherham. He was the first treasurer of the Lancashire Congregational Union and supported several evangelistic enterprises, including the London Missionary Society. He now offered to pay for the board and lodging of students for a two-year course and to provide books for a library. As William Roby would give his services free, and as no expense was to be involved in using the Mosley Street vestry for teaching, an academy on a modest scale was now possible.

The Academy, which opened in 1803, lasted for five years, until Robert Spear's retirement and removal from Manchester and consequent withdrawal of financial support led to its dissolution. During the five years of its existence at least fourteen men were trained.[23] Despite Roby's earlier suggestion that no languages other than English need be taught to potential itinerant preachers, he included Latin, Greek and Hebrew, and sometimes required students to translate the Greek Testament into Latin at sight. W. G. Robinson recounts a story which illustrates both the standard of education achieved and the attitude of some Anglican clergy to Dissenting ministers. A new curate at Wharton, near Bolton, fresh from Oxford, wrote a note in Latin to Thomas Jackson, Roby's former pupil, asking if he might borrow a copy of Cicero's *Orations*, expecting to confound the Independent minister. He was taken aback not only to receive the book, but also a greeting in Greek.[24]

The course was an intensive one of two years, with no holiday breaks. According to a former student, 'The timid and diffident were sure to meet with kindness and encouragement; while the self-sufficient and vain were

[21] Robert Haldane (1779–1853) and James Haldane (1768–1851) had founded a Congregational church in Edinburgh in 1799. In 1808 both adopted Baptist views.

[22] Robert Spear (1762–1817). See William Jay, *Autobiography* (ed G. Radford and J. A. James) second edition (London 1855) 432–7.

[23] See C. E. Surman, 'Roby's Academy, Manchester, 1803–8', *TCHS* 13 (1937–9) 41–53 for a discussion of the students and their careers.

[24] Robinson, 116.

as sure to be repressed.'[25] The students worked on their own in the mornings while their tutor was busy with his own ministerial duties, then met at 2 p.m. for lectures and class work in English grammar and composition, logic, biblical languages, history, geography, astronomy, 'use of the globes' and philosophy. They studied Isaac Watts's *Logic*, Hugh Blair's works on rhetoric and Greek, John Hutchinson's works on philosophy, and the systematic theology which Roby himself had prepared and presented in 80 lectures. Although the method of teaching involved a great deal of memorising, Roby 'appeared rather like a Father instructing his sons than with the stiffness of the Professor', and he interspersed some of the lectures with anecdotes.

Every week the students were required to present their tutor with a sermon for criticism. Early in the week, they prepared an outline for comment, at which stage Roby would 'carefully point out the want of logical arrangement where it was obvious: paucity of ideas, and suggested several that should be added; errors in theology; deficiency in spirit and application, etc.'.[26] It was then presented at the end of the week 'written in a fair hand', while the student waited anxiously for comment. Roby taught his students that itinerancy was integral to complete ministry; at least six spent part of their later careers in full-time itinerancy.[27]

Roby continued to train individuals after the formal closure of the Academy (Surman lists nine such men). The most famous was the missionary, Robert Moffat,[28] but he was only one of many whom Roby inspired for missionary work overseas.[29]

LEAF SQUARE ACADEMY 1811–13

Roby's Academy was the joint enterprise of a single tutor (who was also minister of a large church) and one benefactor. Such limited resources were not worthy of a county growing rapidly in wealth and population. When it was known that Robert Spear could no longer provide financial support on the same scale as previously, Roby ensured that the issue of ministerial education was brought to the fore in the meetings of the new Lancashire Congregational Union. At its third meeting in April 1809, it

[25] MS Memoir (NCA) quoted in full, Robinson, 116–19. The Northern College Archive also includes a handwritten copy of Roby's theological lectures, forming a 'System of Divinity', running to nearly 1,000 quarto pages.

[26] Robinson, 119.

[27] Surman, 46–52.

[28] For Robert Moffat (1795–1883) see *DNB*. Moffat's 460 pages of notes on Roby's lectures on theology are in the London Missionary Society Archive at the London University School of Oriental and African Studies.

[29] See W. G. Robinson, 'William Roby's Missionary Candidates' in *TCHS* 16 (1949–51) 82–90.

was resolved: 'That it appears highly expedient that an Academical Institution for the education of young men for the Ministry be established for the benefit of the Independent churches in the Counties of Lancaster, Chester and Derby.'[30] Two months later Roby, Joseph Fletcher of Blackburn, Noah Blackburn of Delph (a former Heckmondwike student) and Robert Spear (who was still active in the Association) were asked to 'mature' a plan for an Academy to be put to the next meeting.

On 13 July the Union agreed to establish a joint Academy and Grammar School, and funds were solicited. There was a growing demand for good education for the sons of Nonconformist laymen and ministers at a time when most of the endowed public schools were closed to non-Anglicans. There was also concern that future deacons and members of Independent churches as well as their ministers should keep pace with improving educational standards, that all of them should 'be able to meet the foe in armour of equal strength and with weapons of equal temper so that if their enemies wore swords they might wear them too,' and be able to 'repel and render innoxious the impotent darts of sophistry and scepticism.'[31] Mill Hill Grammar School had just been founded (1807) with the same end in view, and two years later a Protestant Dissenters' Grammar School was founded in Yorkshire (the forerunner of Silcoates School).

The combination of School and Academy did not prove advantageous to the Academy, although it was hoped at first that the School would generate sufficient funds to support the Academy. The School opened first, in January 1811, with George Phillips[32] appointed as President of both School and Academy. Sadly, ill health soon forced him to resign and he died before the year ended.

His successor as head of the School was John Reynolds.[33] Reynolds was an unusual person in such a context, for he was the son of a physician-in-ordinary to George III, educated at Westminster School and Oriel College, Oxford, and served for a time as a royal page. Subsequently he was attracted by the preaching of Dissenting ministers, and was recommended to Leaf Square by John Pye Smith of Homerton. He was a successful schoolmaster, and 'few perhaps ever maintained a stricter system of discipline with less severity.'[34] The School, which was advertised in the

[30] Minute book, Leaf Square Academy and School, NCA.

[31] John Clunie in the report of Leaf Square School for 1814, quoted in C. E. Surman, 'Leaf Square Academy, Pendleton, 1811–13' in *TCHS* 13 (1937–9) 114.

[32] George Phillips (1784–1811) was a Welshman who had been educated at Wymondley Academy and Glasgow University.

[33] John Reynolds (1782–1862) was later (1843) Chairman of the Congregational Union of England and Wales, and father of H. R. Reynolds, President of Cheshunt College 1860–95.

[34] Raffles MS, quoted by C. E. Surman, *TCHS* 13 111.

Evangelical Magazine and the Manchester newspapers, attracted a number of pupils, including the sons of several prominent Congregational ministers. Three assistant staff were appointed, one of them being John Dalton,[35] who taught mathematics for two and a half days a week.

Meanwhile, George Phillips's successor as President of the Academy was another Welshman, Jenkin Lewis, an older man who had served as assistant to Edward Williams at Abergavenny and later took over that Academy when it moved to Wrexham.[36] Ministerial students were slow in applying, and the total number of students educated between June 1811, when the first three were admitted, and December 1813, when the Academy closed, was only four; of these, three continued their training elsewhere after the closure. Although the School did well, it did not provide sufficient finance for the support of the ministerial candidates, and money ran out. It proved much easier to pass resolutions about ministerial training than to raise funds for it, despite appeals to all the churches in the district.

When it was decided to dissolve the Academy, the School continued for many years as a private venture under the direction of John Clunie,[37] who succeeded John Reynolds in September 1813.

Blackburn Independent Academy 1816–43

Roby and his supporters were undaunted by this failure, and kept the issue at the forefront of the deliberations of the Lancashire Congregational Union. Although Roby was finally to lose all support from Robert Spear when the latter left the district for Edinburgh in 1816, he now benefited from the guiding hands of two men whose skill and reputation were crucial in establishing the next enterprise on a permanent footing – George Hadfield and Thomas Raffles.

George Hadfield[38] was born in Sheffield but practised as a lawyer in Fountain Street, Manchester, for 40 years. He was an active member of Mosley Street Chapel, took a prominent role in both the political and the religious life of the north of England, and was a generous benefactor of

[35] John Dalton (1766–1844), chemist, mathematician and natural philosopher. See *DNB*.

[36] Jenkin Lewis (1760–1831) later minister at Newport, Monmouthshire. See *Dictionary of Welsh Biography Down to 1940* (London 1959).

[37] John Clunie (1784–1858) was educated at Hoxton Academy and Glasgow University. In later years he was a great supporter of Blackburn Independent Academy, the Lancashire Independent College, and the Lancashire Congregational Union.

[38] George Hadfield (1787–1879). See James Griffin, *Memories of the Past* (Manchester 1883) 264–310, F. Wrigley, 'George Hadfield, Joseph Parker and other correspondents' in *CQ* 17 (1939) 455–8, and *DNB*. See also 'The Personal Narrative of George Hadfield' (1882) MS in Manchester Central Library.

Congregational institutions. He was one of the original sponsors of the Congregational Library in London. An eager controversialist, he has been described as 'perhaps the bitterest disestablisher the Congregationalists ever produced'.[39] The rates controversy, the Anti-Corn Law League, the controversy over Lady Hewley's Charity,[40] the Dissenters' Chapels Bill, disestablishment, all attracted his forensic skills. But he was also a supporter of the Peace Society, and could act as pacifier as well as controversialist. 'Some would have said that the critical and aggressive side of Nonconformity was unduly developed in him, and the criticism would have been just, provided it was not taken as giving a complete view of his character.'[41] When he was 65 he was finally elected as a Member of Parliament for Sheffield, and sat until he was 87.[42] When Edward Miall rose to speak in the House of Commons in favour of the disestablishment of the Church of England, Hadfield said to him, 'Miall, fear God, and you need not fear any man.'[43] He was a meticulous committee person (though it was 'an old and settled rule' with him never to take the chair[44]), a pertinacious debater, and an effective advocate. The extant Leaf Square Minute Book is in his hand, carefully documented, and the box of correspondence preserved in the Northern College Archive reveals how closely involved he was in all the affairs of the Blackburn Academy. It was fortunate to have him as secretary, and although the extent of his commitment varied according to his other legal responsibilities, his contacts and influence were crucial in securing the necessary support for the continuation of the enterprise.

In 1816 Thomas Raffles,[45] like George Hadfield, was still a young man, though already marked out as a future leader; he was to become one of the 'weighty' ministers of Congregationalism. He came to Liverpool to be minister of the newly-built Great George Street Church in 1812, after study at Homerton and five years of ministry at Hammersmith. It was not long before he was drawn into the affairs of the County Union. His diary entry for 5 August 1815 included the following:

> On Friday, the 4th, I attended a meeting in Bethesda vestry, for the purpose of considering the propriety of an academy, or academies, for this county.

[39] W. R. Ward, *Religion and Society in England 1740–1850* (London 1972) 125.

[40] Lady Hewley's Trust Deed of 1704 had conveyed property to Presbyterian trustees for the benefit of Dissenting ministers. When the trustees became Unitarian, the orthodox Dissenters challenged their right to act as trustees of the Trust, and after a long and bitter struggle, eventually won their case.

[41] J. Guinness Rogers, *Autobiography* (London 1903) 68.

[42] According to Francis Wrigley, he twice refused a baronetcy. See 'George Hadfield, Joseph Parker and Other Correspondents', *CQ* 17 (1939) 455.

[43] A. Miall, *Life of Edward Miall* (London 1884) 320.

[44] George Hadfield to Gilbert Wardlaw, 11 April 1830, NCA.

[45] Thomas Raffles (1788–1863). See T. S. Raffles, *Memoirs of the Life and Ministry of the Rev Thomas Raffles* (London 1864) and *DNB*.

> A long discussion – great division of sentiment – a committee appointed to consider the subject and report, of which, contrary to my wish, I am one.[46]

Over the next 45 years, Raffles proved to be one of the greatest friends and wisest advisers of the Lancashire college, and his support enhanced its reputation.

The debate continued over the next two months. Some of the protagonists wanted individual ministers present to take two or three students each rather than establish another Academy, but their view did not prevail against the arguments of George Hadfield and other laymen. On 28 October 1815 a committee was appointed to supervise the arrangements for the new institution, and to decide on a theological tutor.

Their choice fell on Joseph Fletcher,[47] minister of Blackburn Congregational Church since 1807, and with the choice of tutor was determined the location of the new Academy. Fletcher, at 32 still a comparatively young man, was the son of a Chester goldsmith, educated at Hoxton Academy, during which time he benefited from John Clayton's[48] ministry at the King's Weigh House, until he and a fellow student, George Payne, set a new tradition by winning Dr Williams's scholarships for three years' study at Glasgow University, at the instigation of Thomas Wilson, Hoxton's treasurer. Thomas Wilson hoped that further study at a Scottish university would make them 'more fitted to defend the truth against the attacks of learned infidels and sceptics'.[49] Their frequent discussions while enjoying the hospitality of Ralph and Gilbert Wardlaw were as beneficial educationally as was their attendance at lectures. At the age of 22 Fletcher was invited, on the recommendation of Dr Robert Simpson, the former Heckmondwike student who was now principal of Hoxton, to succeed James McQuhae at the Blackburn chapel, and began his regular ministry in April 1807. William Roby was one of the ministers who took part in his ordination. The group of Tockholes members who lived in Blackburn had decided to form their own meeting in the town in 1777, and had persuaded the minister, James McQuhae (a native of Scotland) to move from Tockholes to the new church in Blackburn with them. He had built up the church in Chapel Street to a membership of 69 in a ministry of over 25 years, and soon after Joseph Fletcher arrived, the building had to be enlarged.

Fletcher's reputation was such that soon after settling in Blackburn he was invited, though without success, to return to Hoxton as classical

[46] Quoted in T. S. Raffles, 135.

[47] Joseph Fletcher (1784–1843). See Joseph Fletcher Jun., *Memoirs of the Life and Correspondence of the Late Rev. Joseph Fletcher DD* (London 1846) and *DNB*.

[48] John Clayton (1754–1843) was a former student at Trevecca. See *DNB*.

[49] J. Waddington, *Congregational History 1800 to 1850* (London 1878) 149.

tutor. Within four years he had received, but again refused, an invitation to Newington Chapel in Liverpool. Already he was contributing regularly to the *Eclectic Review*, and after the publication of *Principles and Institutions of the Roman Catholic Religion* (1816), a series of lectures given in response to claims made by the priest of the nearby Roman Catholic Church,[50] he received, but yet again refused, an invitation to a church in London.

As he wished to continue in pastoral charge of Chapel Street, he had made it a condition of his acceptance of the post of theological tutor at the new academy that he should be assisted by a classical tutor. The committee therefore appointed William Hope, a native of Blackburn who had been brought up and educated in Scotland.[51]

The Academy was to be administered by a committee of eight ministers and thirteen laymen. Each candidate for the four-year course was to provide 'a testimony to the suitableness of his character and qualifications' from his own church, a written account of 'his views of Divine truth', his religious experience, and his motives in seeking to enter Christian ministry. In addition he was to deliver a short address to the committee, who soon found that they had to begin their meetings at 7 am in order to fulfil this as well as the rest of the required business. A house in Ainsworth St (number 43), next door to Joseph Fletcher's own house, was procured as Academy House. In the first few years the students did not live there, but were lodged in 'the Houses of serious persons'.[52]

The first meeting of the newly-constituted committee of the Blackburn Independent Academy, with William Roby in the chair, was held on the day after Christmas Day, 1816, when four candidates were interviewed and accepted as probationers. They included W. H. Stowell, a future principal of Rotherham Independent College, and they were the first of 49 students who completed the course at Blackburn during the next 27 years; a further ten moved from Blackburn to complete their course in Manchester.

The committee cannot have been completely surprised in 1822 to learn that Joseph Fletcher had been invited to a large church in Stepney, London, and that he had now decided that the time had come to move. He had a distinguished ministry in London for the next 20 years, and played a leading part in denominational affairs.[53]

[50] Lancashire had remained a stronghold of Roman Catholicism after the Reformation.

[51] William Johnstone Hope (1788–1853) was tutor 1816–19, after which he spent thirty years as headmaster of the Congregational School, Lewisham (later Caterham School). See *CYB 1855* 218.

[52] These arrangements were recorded by George Hadfield in the Leaf Square Minute Book.

[53] Thus he was chairman of the Congregational Union of England and Wales in 1837.

The committee first pleaded with William Roby to accept the post of theological tutor, offering to move to Manchester if he would accept. But he replied that teaching combined with pastoral work was too much to contemplate at 'the advanced period of my life'.[54] They therefore turned to George Payne, with whom Joseph Fletcher had studied at Hoxton and in Glasgow.[55] In November 1822 the Academy committee heard that Payne was likely to be invited to become minister at Mount Street Chapel (formed by a group of Scots who had had a disagreement with Joseph Fletcher over church government) in Blackburn.[56] They agreed to appoint him as theological tutor with a salary of £150 per annum. He began work in the Academy in 1823 and remained for six years. The fact that some of his students moved with him when he took up the position of theological tutor to the Western Academy in 1829 suggests that he was an inspiring teacher. His first substantial work, *The Elements of Mental and Moral Science* (1828, reissued 1842, 1845) was written in Blackburn, and earned him the degree of LL D from Glasgow University. Like Fletcher, whom he immediately preceded as Chairman of the Congregational Union in 1836, he was a regular contributor to the *Eclectic Review* and the *Evangelical Magazine*.

Not long after George Payne arrived, a severe depression in Lancashire caused a falling-off in subscriptions. There was talk of reducing the staff to one, a move which Payne strenuously resisted, with 'a painful feeling'. He asked the committee to consider moving from Blackburn, a request supported by the students, who noted that the 'ministerial, scientific and literary resources' of Liverpool and Manchester were almost wholly lacking in Blackburn.[57] The restraining factor, which weighed heavily with many members of the Committee, was a substantial endowment from Roger Cunliffe, the Academy's first treasurer, which could only be used for so long as the Academy remained in Blackburn. Payne was disappointed and left in 1829, while the Academy remained, for the time being, in its existing home.

Payne's successor was Gilbert Wardlaw,[58] who had already worked at the Academy as classical tutor at Blackburn for two years from 1821 until 1823, when still a very young man. Now 31, he was a former student of the Glasgow Theological Academy, where he was taught by his more famous uncle, Ralph Wardlaw.[59] He had followed George

[54] William Roby to John Clunie 19 August 1822, NCA.

[55] See pp 16–17 for George Payne.

[56] See Nightingale vol II, 69.

[57] Memorandum from Blackburn students to the Committee 3 April 1827 NCA Box 19.

[58] Gilbert Wardlaw (1798–1873). See *CYB 1874* 559–61.

[59] Ralph Wardlaw (1779–1853) three times refused invitations to teach at or preside over English Congregational colleges between 1828 and 1842. See *DNB*.

Payne as minister at Albany Street in Edinburgh, and now followed him again to Blackburn.

Six men served as classical tutor during the life of the Academy at Blackburn. William Hope was succeeded by William Howle 1819–21. Following Gilbert Wardlaw's brief period as tutor 1821–3, Ebenezer Miller from the Glasgow Theological Academy acted as tutor from 1824 until 1827, when he went on to have a varied career including eight years as headmaster of Silcoates. He was followed by the most distinguished of Blackburn's classical tutors, William Lindsay Alexander,[60] a graduate of St Andrews University who joined the Academy as tutor when he was just nineteen, before further study in Edinburgh and a distinguished career as minister of North College Street Church; finally he was principal of the Theological Hall in Edinburgh. He published a number of memoirs, commentaries and works of theology in later life. The last tutor, who stayed for ten years, was a former student of the Academy, Daniel Burgess Hayward,[61] who had come to Blackburn through the influence of Thomas Raffles in Liverpool.

Although the Blackburn area had a strong Nonconformist tradition, it was not the most suitable location for a Lancashire college in the early nineteenth century. The population, prosperity and influence of Manchester were increasing so rapidly that it is not surprising to find frequent discussions about moving the Academy there. The Blackburn premises were very unsatisfactory, for many of the studies had no heating, there was no garden or open space round the building, and the ground floor rooms looked straight onto the street. Although the map showed Blackburn situated in the middle of Lancashire, it did not have easy access to most of the flourishing Congregational churches of the county, which were now mostly in Manchester and the surrounding area. These factors finally outweighed the advantages of the Cunliffe bequest, and on 20 December 1838 it was finally resolved, with one dissentient, to move to Manchester. Within a month of the committee's definite decision the whole constituency of the proposed college had met and prepared for the move. While plans for the new college were made energetically in Manchester, the work at Blackburn continued under Gilbert Wardlaw and Daniel Hayward until April 1843. The number of students applying and being accepted began to show a modest increase. The Lancashire college was now about to move from the periphery into the centre of the intellectual life of Victorian Dissent.

[60] See J. Ross, *W. Lindsay Alexander* (London 1887) and *CYB 1886* 146–9.
[61] Daniel Burgess Hayward (1798–1874). See *CYB 1875* 330–2.

PART TWO

The Move to the City: 1830s–1914

5

The Expansion of Nonconformity

By the year 1833, Congregationalists had a new mood of self-confidence. The repeal in 1828 of the Test and Corporation Acts of the late seventeenth century, after a strenuous campaign inside and outside parliament, marked a new stage in the position of Nonconformists within English society. Catholic Emancipation a year later gave a similar status to Roman Catholics. No longer were members of town councils or holders of office under the Crown required to make some form of subscription to the beliefs of the Church of England. The repeal of the Five Mile and Conventicle Acts eleven years earlier had removed other irksome, if usually disregarded, restrictions. In practical terms the result of this legislation was not dramatic, and there was no immediate great increase in the number of Dissenting (or Roman Catholic) town councillors or Members of Parliament. But the psychological effect was profound. Although many real or perceived grievances remained – above all the very existence of the Established Church[1] – Dissenters were no longer entirely second class citizens. A new confidence prevailed, which was now expressed politically as well as socially, architecturally as well as intellectually. Dissenters became Nonconformists. Thomas Binney's statement, published as an appendix to his speech at the laying of the foundation stone of the new King's Weigh House in 1833 that 'the Established Church is a great national evil', was widely reported, quoted out of context, discussed, denigrated and applauded. When the Reform Act of 1832 extended parliamentary representation to areas where Dissent was comparatively strong, a process began, slowly at first, through which Nonconformity became a recognisable political force in the middle and late nineteenth century. Some contemporaries saw this rather depressingly as the transfer of power 'from one class of society, the gentlemen of England, professing the faith of the Church of England, to another class of society, the shopkeepers, being Dissenters from the Church, many of them Socinians,

[1] The Anti-State Church Society was founded in 1844, evolving into the Society for the Liberation of Religion from State Patronage and Control (known as the Liberation Society) in 1853. For the best short account of this movement (which did not succeed) see D. Thompson, 'The Liberation Society 1844–68' in P. Hollis (ed), *Pressure from Without in Early Victorian England* (London 1974).

others atheists'.[2] Others heralded it as the beginning of a new era of equality.

The newly self-confident Congregationalists were increasing in numbers, particularly in the rapidly developing industrial towns and cities of England.[3] 'Our age is pre-eminently the age of great cities', wrote the Lancashire Independent College's first president, Robert Vaughan, in his influential work, published as the College opened, *The Age of Great Cities* (1843); '... the strength of Protestantism is a strength on the side of industry, of human improvement, and of the civilization which leads to the formation of great cities.'[4] Although Manchester did not officially become a city until 1853, it was already a very prosperous and populous industrial centre when the Lancashire Independent College opened there in 1843. Bradford, to which Airedale moved in 1833, did not become a city until 1897, but it too was a rapidly developing centre of population and industry. Cotton and wool were the foundations of this prosperity. Exeter, home of the Western Academy until 1845, was already a city; Plymouth, to which it moved, was not officially a city, but together with Devonport and Stonehouse was the centre of a large conurbation. Rotherham was an industrial town, but did not expand in the same way as Bradford and Manchester, and its college eventually had to submit to Bradford's dominance when it could no longer sustain its independent existence. Colleges were now in the centres of industrial England, ready to play their part in the development of Victorian civic life.[5]

No subject excited more controversy in this period, both locally and nationally, than education – not so much the process of education, but rather its control. The provision of a national school system was greatly hampered by the rivalry between Anglicans and Dissenters for influence over religious education, and no Nonconformist college principal could hope to remain neutral in this political battle. In a lower key, but still significant, was the campaign to abolish religious tests at Oxford and Cambridge.[6] After the repeal of the Test and Corporation Acts, the argument that universities should admit all sections of society gathered strength, though the idea of admitting Roman Catholics as well as

[2] The Duke of Wellington, Prime Minister 1828–30, to John Wilson Croker, former Secretary to the Admiralty, 6 March 1833, quoted in J. C. D. Clark, *English Society 1688–1832: Social Structure and Political Practice During the Ancien Regime* (Cambridge 1985) 413.

[3] This was confirmed by the Religious Census of 1851.

[4] R. Vaughan, *The Age of Great Cities: Or, Modern Society in its Relation to Intelligence, Morals and Religion* (London 1843) 77.

[5] Spring Hill College opened in Birmingham in 1838.

[6] See David Bebbington, 'The Dissenting Idea of a University: Oxford and Cambridge in Nonconformist Thought in the Nineteenth Century', Hulsean Prize Essay, University of Cambridge 1973, for a detailed account of Dissenting attitudes to higher education.

Dissenters alarmed some Nonconformist leaders. The campaign to abolish these university tests, in which Robert Vaughan, through the pages of the *British Quarterly Review*, played a significant role, continued from the early 1830s until the passing of the University Tests Act of 1871.

An alternative to liberalising the two ancient universities (and Durham, founded in 1832) was the creation of new ones free from religious tests and more experimental in curriculum. Writing in 1812, David Bogue and James Bennett considered that a university 'upon a liberal plan, open to all denominations', in a central part of England, would find support from Dissenters.[7] Eight years later, the idea of a university in London first took shape in the mind of the poet Thomas Campbell[8] while visiting Germany to collect material for a general survey of European literature. He was so impressed by the new University of Bonn, founded in 1818, and by the prevailing mutual tolerance there between Catholics and Protestant, that on returning to England he discussed the idea with friends in London and aroused a good deal of interest. After eight years of earnest discussion and planning between Dissenters and liberal thinkers of many different religious persuasions or none, University College opened its doors in Gower Street to students regardless of religious affiliation. One of its most active promoters was Francis Cox,[9] a Baptist minister who was the first librarian of the college; amongst the public supporters of the enterprise were Joseph Fletcher of Stepney, late of the Blackburn Independent Academy, and Thomas Wilson,[10] a prominent Congregational layman and treasurer of Hoxton/Highbury Academy, who was elected a member of the founding Council.

Dissenters and Anglicans were unable to agree about the conditions for establishing chairs in theology, hence the subject's exclusion from the curriculum, which led Thomas Arnold to denounce it as 'that godless institution in Gower Street'. King's College, Strand, was opened in 1831 under the patronage of George IV as a specifically Anglican foundation in response. Neither college granted degrees, but pressure to do so led eight years later to the foundation of the University of London as a degree-giving body for both University College and the newer King's College. The new university proved a great asset to the Congregational theological colleges, and provided the means for raising their standard of

[7] See D. Bogue and J. Bennett, *History of Dissenters from 1688 to 1808* vol IV (London 1812) 309–10.

[8] Thomas Campbell (1777–1844), poet and writer. See *DNB*.

[9] Francis Augustus Cox (1783–1853, Baptist minister in Hackney, Secretary of the General Body of Dissenting Ministers in London, and later campaigner for the disestablishment of the Church of England. See *DNB*.

[10] Thomas Wilson (1764–1843). See *DNB*.

education, for they were given the opportunity of affiliation, enabling their students to take external arts degrees of the university.[11] All the northern colleges and the Western College had taken this opportunity before 1850.

University College also offered teaching opportunities to men excluded from Oxford and Cambridge. The first two principals of the Lancashire Independent College, Robert Vaughan and Henry Rogers, were both professors at University College in the 1830s, and the first professor of philosophy, John Hoppus,[12] was a former student of the Rotherham Independent Academy. Through their connection with the College they were able to meet a wide circle of writers and thinkers.

The Congregationalists[13] now greatly outnumbered Presbyterians, who by the early nineteenth century were mostly avowed Unitarians.[14] Since 1800 the idea of forming a Congregational Union had been discussed, but it was not until 1831, after fierce arguments, that a formal plan was drawn up at a meeting in London, and sent round for approval to county unions; it was finally agreed in May 1832.[15] The new Congregational Union of England and Wales had to struggle with the tension between the strong tradition of independence among local churches and the need to provide mutual support and a more coherent common theology and policy.[16] By no means all county unions were favourable, and it was a long time before the Congregational Union could be said to represent almost all Congregational churches.

The Union's activities provided a forum for discussion of common problems, for exhortation in response to the challenges of the age, and for the mobilisation of opinion against social and religious discrimination. Assemblies, open to lay members and theological students as well as ministers, were held twice yearly, in London in May and in different provincial centres in the autumn. The day before the planning meeting for the new Union, a Congregational Library had been opened in Blomfield Street at the instigation of Thomas Wilson, and it was here that

[11] It was not until 1901 that London University established a degree in Theology.

[12] John Hoppus (1789–1875). See *CYB 1876* 341–3 and *DNB*.

[13] This term was now used more frequently than 'Independents'.

[14] The Unitarian Relief Act of 1812 had effectively given Unitarians the same rights as other Nonconformists.

[15] See Albert Peel, *These Hundred Years: A History of the Congregational Union of England and Wales 1831–1931* (London 1931) for an account of the formation of the Union.

[16] In 1833 the new Union agreed a 'Declaration of the Faith, Church Order, and Discipline of the Congregational, or Independent Dissenters'. In his history of the Union, Albert Peel described this Declaration as 'popular rather than scholastic, the product of preachers rather than of theologians. There is a want of theological precision that would have shocked the seventeenth century divines, but this accurately represented the mind of the churches at this period' (75).

the meetings of the Congregational Union Council were held. The Library promoted an annual series of Congregational Lectures, delivered each year from 1833, many of them by the principals of the theological colleges.

By the end of the 1830s, there were eleven theological colleges educating future Congregational ministers. These colleges faced many common problems, and it was through the new Union that the first conference of Congregational college representatives met at Blomfield Street in 1845.[17] In January 1865 and June 1872 similar conferences were held, leading to the formation of an Examination Board, the Senatus Academicus, which was to offer diplomas, at the level of 'Associate' and 'Fellow', in theology (ATS and FTS) to students in Nonconformist colleges, at a time when such degrees were not available outside Oxford and Cambridge. The work of the Senatus, whose examiners were members of staff of the English and Welsh theological colleges and Scottish theologians, extended from 1880 until 1902, by which time London University was offering a BD degree.[18] Other attempts to co-ordinate the work of theological colleges, their qualifications for entry, syllabuses, and staffing, always encountered the strong local loyalties of the Independent tradition, and made it very difficult for the denomination to respond to contemporary needs in ministerial education.

There was however a growing sense of identity among Congregationalists, as among Nonconformists as a whole, encouraged by the campaigns for political and social equality. The bond between orthodox Evangelicals, both Dissenting and Anglican, had weakened, though there was one challenge which faced them both: the growth of Roman Catholicism, spurred by the influx of Irish immigrants, and, linked with this in many Protestant minds, the (Anglo-Catholic) Oxford Movement, which owed its origin to the Assize Sermon preached in Oxford by John Keble in 1833.

It was against this background that the colleges planned their strategy in the years after 1832. As the century progressed, there were many intellectual challenges to the Christian faith which demanded a church and ministry equipped to respond, not least the advanced biblical and theological thinking which emanated from the German Protestant universities. Among the teachers in the theological colleges discussed in these pages were some who took their place in the national intellectual

[17] See *Minutes of the Proceedings of a Conference of Delegates from the Committees of Various Theological Colleges Connected with the Independent Churches of England and Wales held in the Congregational Library 7–8 January 1845* (1845).

[18] The Minute Book of the Senatus Academicus is in DWL, New College MS 491/1.

life of their generation – men such as A. M. Fairbairn, J. B. Paton, A. S. Peake, Henry Rogers and Robert Vaughan. Holding the balance between evangelical faith and intellectual exploration was a perpetual challenge to every theological college.

6

Lancashire

Manchester in 1843

When Roby's Academy opened in 1803, the population of Manchester was 70,000, almost double what it had been 20 years earlier. But by the time the building of the new Lancashire Independent College was in progress in 1841, it had increased to 243,000.[1] During the intervening years, Manchester had attracted attention not only from the whole country, but from America and Europe too, as a city[2] of both great wealth and great agitation. In 1819 a fundamentally peaceable political demonstration on St Peter's Fields, Manchester, was forcibly broken up by the militia, causing the death of 11 people and the wounding of about 400. Manchester was henceforward irrevocably linked with the 'Peterloo Massacre'. When the Manchester Exchange was extended in 1838, it became the largest Exchange room in Europe.[3] The Manchester–Liverpool railway, opened in 1830, and the addition of six more lines before 1846, spurred the growth of both trade and population, so that the city was generally regarded as the foremost British commercial centre outside London. Yet these developments were uncontrolled by any local authority, as Manchester was officially not even an incorporated town until 1838, though it had become a parliamentary constituency in 1832. The diocese of Manchester was created in 1847.

During the years when the new college was being built, two important national political movements had strong links with Manchester. The Anti-Corn Law League had begun in Manchester in 1838 as the Manchester Anti-Corn Law Association, and it was from Manchester that 100 tons of propaganda, using the new cheap rates of postage, flooded across the whole country,[4] urging the repeal of the laws which regulated the price of corn in the interests of the landed classes, to the detriment of the middle and working classes (especially after a series of bad harvests). It was in Manchester that almost 700 ministers, mostly

[1] By the end of the century, it had reached half a million.

[2] It was not officially a city until 1853, but in size, wealth and prestige it was more than the equal of any other city.

[3] Asa Briggs, *Victorian Cities* (London 1963) 107. Chapter 3 of this work provides a comprehensive discussion of nineteenth-century Manchester.

[4] Ibid 119.

Nonconformist, met together in August 1841 and condemned the system of protection represented by the Corn Laws. The Free Trade Hall in Manchester was opened three months before the formal opening of the Lancashire Independent College. The two leaders of the national Anti-Corn Law League, Richard Cobden and John Bright, were both Lancashire MPs, and among others actively involved was the ubiquitous George Hadfield. The working classes, on the other hand, fearing middle-class domination as much as that of the landed classes, gave no support to the League, but sought radical parliamentary reform through the Chartist movement. It was in Manchester that the National Charter Association was founded in 1840, and the city continued to be a centre of Chartist agitation until the failure of the movement in 1848.

The social aspects of life in the city were already the subject of close scrutiny and interest. The Manchester Statistical Society (the first of many such societies), whose reports were often quoted in Parliament, was founded in 1833. One of its most active members was the medical officer of the Ancoats and Ardwick Dispensary, Dr James Kay (later Sir James Kay-Shuttleworth),[5] whose *The Physical and Moral Condition of the Working Classes Employed in the Cotton Manufacture in Manchester* (1832), produced in the wake of a terrible cholera epidemic in the city, was a pioneering study of the new ways of life developing in industrial centres of population. The city attracted attention well beyond Britain; the most significant foreign observer was Friedrich Engels from Germany, whose *Condition of the Working-Class in England in 1844* (1845, English translation, New York 1886, London 1892) was based largely on evidence collected from the experience of visiting his father's factory, Ermen and Engels, during a stay of 21 months in Manchester, and provided much of the evidence for Marx's critique of capitalism.

Writers too were drawn to make Manchester the setting for their novels. Disraeli set his trilogy of novels, *Coningsby*, *Sybil*, and *Tancred*, in the Manchester of the mid-1840s. A vivid and sensitive novel, *Mary Barton: A Tale of Manchester Life*, depicting both the dignity and the horror of working-class life, appeared anonymously in 1848, attracting wide attention, and not a little controversy. Its author was soon identified as Elizabeth Gaskell, wife of the leading Unitarian minister at Cross Street in Manchester.

The intellectual life of the city centred round the Manchester Literary and Philosophical Society (founded 1781), the Portico Library in Mosley Street, the Royal Manchester Institution for the Pursuit of Science (1821) and the Manchester Athenaeum, completed in 1839, providing reading rooms, lectures, concerts and a library. The *Manchester Guardian*, which appeared in 1821 as a response to the Peterloo Massacre, was read far

[5] Sir James Kay-Shuttleworth (1804–77). See *DNB*.

beyond the confines of the city. For those most deeply concerned about the need for social reform, Cross Street Unitarian Chapel, 'where the bourgeoisie of Manchester worshipped God,'[6] was the most attractive meeting place. Many of its members, and both of its ministers, William Gaskell and John Robberds, were former students of the Warrington Academy. James Kay was a regular attender, as was Richard Cobden, who received his early training in public speaking there.

The leading Congregational church in central Manchester was Mosley Street (later Cavendish Street), where R. S. M'all had attracted many former members of Grosvenor Street Chapel after the death of William Roby in 1830. Robert Halley,[7] a man of wide sympathy and profound learning, was called as minister in 1839; his wisdom was to prove a great strength on the Council of the new Lancashire College. Many leading Manchester citizens, including, for a time, both John Owens[8] and John Rylands,[9] were members. Altogether, the Nonconformists outnumbered Anglicans in mid-nineteenth century Manchester.

Manchester was about to become a significant centre of higher education. The Manchester Unitarian College returned from York to Manchester (where it had been 1786–1803) in 1840. A Wesleyan College opened in Didsbury, South Manchester, in 1842. And already there was developing in the mind of John Owens and his business partner, George Faulkner, the idea of founding a college in Manchester free from religious tests, an idea put into effect as Owens College in 1851.[10] This college was to play an important role in the education of the men admitted to the Lancashire Independent College.

LANCASHIRE INDEPENDENT COLLEGE: PREPARATION AND OPENING

As soon as the decision to move the Blackburn Independent Academy was taken in 1838, circular letters were prepared and sent round, subcommittees appointed, enquiries about possible sites made, and appeals for money circulated. George Hadfield undertook to be treasurer

[6] Valentine Cunningham, *Everywhere Spoken Against: Dissent in the Victorian Novel* (Oxford 1975) 131.

[7] Robert Halley (1796–1876) was educated at Homerton college under John Pye Smith. In 1854 he was elected to the chair of the Congregational Union. From 1857–72 he was principal of New College, London. His history of Lancashire Nonconformity (2 vols 1869) revealed him to be a historian of more than denominational sympathy. See *DNB*.

[8] John Owens (1790–1846), manufacturer. See *DNB*.

[9] John Rylands (1801–88), cotton manufacturer. His widow established the John Rylands Library, opened in 1899, in his memory. See *DNB*.

[10] Owens College was eventually transformed into the Victoria University of Manchester. See J. Thompson, *The Owens College* (Manchester 1886).

of the Appeal, and pursued the task with great vigour; the depression in Lancashire trade made his task harder, and gave him many a sleepless night. He immediately immersed himself in the planning of every aspect of the College. He wrote to James Bennett at Rotherham, Thomas Binney in London and Robert Halley at Highbury, seeking advice on the relative merits of residential and non-residential colleges.[11] Their advice was equivocal, but the committee eventually decided in favour of a residential college.

The first circular from Hadfield went out on 1 January 1839. It referred to the inconvenient location of Blackburn, 'which is so difficult of access from various parts of the country'; the 'baneful effect' of the Unitarian College in Manchester, and of the Unitarian 'usurpation' of Nonconformist chapels and endowments, which required an alternative influence; and the regrettable influence of the Roman Catholic College at Stonyhurst in 'disseminating Popish tenets in the county'. As a rallying call it had considerable success, for £12,500 was raised within a short time.

The first task was to find a suitable site. Manchester was growing rapidly, and several new estates were being offered for sale. Two suitable ones were identified: the estate of Samuel Brooks in Withington, and another in Prestwich. On a vote, that of Samuel Brooks, a prosperous banker with both Quaker and Congregational connections, was preferred. The estate, named Whalley Range after Samuel Brooks's birthplace of Whalley, near Blackburn, was about two and a half miles from the city centre. A plot of seven acres, set on the edge of prosperous middle-class Manchester, was selected and purchased for £3,558.6s.8d.

The next stage, before the formal purchase, was to set up a Trust Deed for the management of the College. Ever mindful of the way in which, in his view, a small group of Unitarian trustees had 'usurped' the endowment left by the orthodox Lady Hewley, George Hadfield was determined to provide safeguards against any similar appropriation for the new institution. Therefore a significant role in the administration was given, not only to the trustees, but also to the subscribers. An Annual General Meeting of subscribers was to have power to fill vacancies among the trustees as well as to appoint an executive committee to conduct regular business during the year. An attached schedule, listing eleven 'doctrinal sentiments' to be accepted by all potential students, was so constructed 'as not to render it impossible for the committee to admit to the benefits of the Institution, any individual of Evangelical sentiments and decided piety'.[12] The Deed was executed on 19 June 1840. The 30

[11] This correspondence is in the Northern College Archive.

[12] Reports of the Several Committees of the Lancashire Independent College presented to the Subscribers and Friends at the General Meeting, 7 April 1841 (1841) 5.

trustees were headed by Thomas Raffles, John Pye Smith, Ralph Wardlaw, Joseph Fletcher and Robert Halley.

The Building Committee agreed at its first meeting (22 July 1839) that the new college should be capable of accommodating 50 students, each to have a study and a bed in a dormitory, with two commodious houses (that is, with five or six bedrooms) for resident professors. A dining room was to be provided, sufficiently large to seat the residents, and a library at least equal in size; three lecture rooms, as well as kitchens and servants' quarters, would also be provided. Architectural designs were then invited in the usual manner, with prizes of 100 and 50 guineas to be offered for the two best designs.

It was the design of J. G. Irwin[13] which was chosen at the end of 1839 from 36 plans submitted by 27 architects. Building tenders were then invited, and that of Hogg, Bedford and Farquharson, for £13,682, was accepted. Immediately plans were made for the laying of a foundation stone on 23 September 1840 by George Hadfield, with Thomas Raffles presiding. It was decided that various objects should be buried in a cavity in the foundation stone, including a bible, a history of the Lancashire County Union (probably an account written by R. Slate), reports of the Blackburn Academy, a list of subscribers, various other reports, and silver coins of the House of Hanover.

This occasion was widely reported and vividly remembered for reasons quite unplanned and unforeseen. Several thousand people had assembled for the event in mid-morning when it began to rain. A covered platform which had been provided for the female members of the families with tickets was soon occupied by 'one hundred ladies, including many of the young and beautiful, attired in the light and elegant costumes of the season just passing from us, their countenances beaming with animation and an expression of interest in what was taking place.'[14] But the opening hymn was suddenly accompanied by a loud crash and piercing screams. One of the supports had given way, and propelled the platform's occupants violently to the ground. Fortunately no one was killed, but many (including George Hadfield's daughter) were badly hurt. The foundation stone was hurriedly laid and the selected objects buried,[15] while the party resorted to Rusholme Road Congregational Chapel, two miles away, for recovery and relief.

George Hadfield had prepared a lengthy speech for the occasion, which it was decided to defer; it was actually delivered three months later on 17 December in Rusholme Road Chapel. It was a eulogy of the great

[13] J. G. Irwin went bankrupt before the building was completed, and the work was taken over by his principal assistant, Mr Chester.

[14] Transactions of the Congregational Churches, November 1840, quoted in Joseph Thompson, *Lancashire Independent College 1843–93* (Manchester 1893) 44.

[15] To the best of our knowledge, they have never been removed.

Figure 3: Lancashire Independent College
Source: centenary booklet of the College (photo by R. W. Berry)

men of the Puritan tradition, an expression of admiration for the high standards of education among the descendants of the Puritans in the United States, and a forthright condemnation of the growth of Unitarian influence – a rallying call to his hearers to support and build up a college worthy of their tradition, 'assuredly, the most important undertaking for the spread of evangelical truth, that was ever begun by Dissenters of our denomination, in this or any other part of the United Kingdom'. However, the speech did end on an eirenic note: 'Attached as we are to the principles of religious liberty, which so strongly characterize the Congregational denomination, we trust the day will come when the sectarian interests of the different classes of Christians will either be lost sight of, or placed in their true and very subordinate position . . .'[16]

The central point of the building now beginning to rise in Whalley Range was a tall Gothic tower 92 feet high, above a grand entrance which was flanked on each side by long wings of three storeys, the ground floor prefaced by arcades – the whole width being 261 feet. The front of the building housed the communal rooms – dining room, library, lecture rooms, together with the professors' houses while two receding wings 149 feet deep provided the students' studies and bedrooms. The kitchens were in the basement. There was no chapel, as according to Congregational practice every student was required to become the member of a local church and to attend Sunday morning service there.[17] The building material was brick, faced at the front with Yorkshire stone.

The success of the new enterprise ultimately depended on the quality of the staff, and it was to this matter that the Education Committee gave its main attention. No longer was one tutor to combine pastoral ministry with sole responsibility for the senior years of ministerial education. It was agreed that there should be three departments, with a 'professor'[18] in charge of each: theological, biblical and literary. The professor in theology was to lecture on philosophy, church polity, doctrine (on which the students were to write a weekly paper), and to conduct a weekly sermon class. The biblical studies professor was to teach Hebrew and Greek and lecture on both Old and New Testaments; in addition he was to give lectures on the Reformation. The professor of 'literature' had a wide remit, to teach Latin and Greek texts, logic, mathematics, ancient history and English grammar.

[16] *An Address Intended to have been Delivered on the Occasion of the Laying of the Foundation Stone of Lancashire Independent College by George Hadfield* (Manchester 1842) 76.

[17] After the opening of the college, a service was held on Sunday evenings in the library for people in the neighbourhood as well as staff and students who were not preaching elsewhere.

[18] This was a courtesy term used in Nonconformist colleges for most members of staff.

Anticipating a potentially embarrassing situation, in April 1842 Gilbert Wardlaw had announced his resignation from the Blackburn Academy, and planned to return to Scotland. His deteriorating eyesight (eventually leading to blindness) made him reluctant to contemplate the greater demands to be made of the theological tutor of the new institution. Daniel Hayward, Blackburn's arts tutor, refused the chair of general literature at Manchester, and 'retired' at the age of 45 to Hadleigh in Suffolk.

The committee was therefore free to search for a completely new staff. The first two invitations were issued in February 1842, to Dr Ralph Wardlaw of Glasgow (Gilbert Wardlaw's uncle, who was already 63) as theological professor, and to Dr Samuel Davidson of Ulster as biblical professor. Ralph Wardlaw refused, as he had refused other invitations to teach in English theological colleges, but Samuel Davidson[19] accepted readily. In December an invitation to Charles Peter Mason, of London University, to be professor of literature was issued and accepted. He was to prepare students for the London University degree of Bachelor of Arts.[20]

In the following month Robert Vaughan[21] of London was invited to be president and theological tutor, with a salary of £400 and a house. His acceptance of this post, after much heart-searching and consultation, immediately set the intellectual tone of the new college at a level which would gain respect not only from Dissenters but from wider religious and academic circles. A man with 'an air of authority', blended with 'great kindness and urbanity', his striking presence immediately made an impact on Manchester Nonconformity. He was at his most impressive on a large public platform. One of his later students commented that 'he had the appearance of a well-to-do archdeacon or deacon in the Establishment.'[22] He was a model of the middle class urbanity to which many Nonconformists now aspired. Aged 48, he had been minister for the preceding eighteen years of Hornton Street Congregational Church, Kensington, combining it since 1834 with the Chair of Ancient and

[19] Samuel Davidson (1806–98). See A. J. Davidson (ed), *The Autobiography and Diary of Samuel Davidson* (Edinburgh 1899) and *DNB*.

[20] C. P. Mason was later known as the author of a series of books on English grammar.

[21] Robert Vaughan (1795–1868). See *Robert Vaughan: A Memorial* (London 1869) and *DNB*. See also Clyde Binfield, 'Hebrews Hellenized: English Evangelical Nonconformity and Culture 1840–1940' in S. Gilley and W. J. Sheils, *A History of Religion in Britain: Practice and Belief from Pre-Roman Times to the Present* (Oxford 1994).

[22] H. G. Parrish, *From the World to the Pulpit* (London 1863) 160. This book was published anonymously, but the author, a student at the College between 1856 and 1861, was easily identified. A few years later he was ordained priest in the Church of England.

Modern History at University College, London. By 1843 he had not only been awarded the degree of DD from Glasgow University (in 1836) but had numerous publications to his credit. He achieved all this without the advantage of any college or university education.

Vaughan was born to Anglican parents of Welsh descent in the west of England in 1795. He early showed an enthusiasm for scholarly work by spending the guinea he received when he was twelve on Raleigh's *History of the World*. In his inaugural lecture at University College, delivered when he was 39, he spoke of history as 'a theme which has furnished some of the most heart-felt delights of my earliest boyhood, and one which in later life has never ceased to develop new and deeper sources of attraction'.[23] He came under the influence of William Thorp, Independent minister at Castle Green, Bristol, and was trained by him for the ministry; it is not known why he did not seek admission to a college. In 1819 he was called to be minister at Angel Street, Worcester, where William Jay of Bath and John Angell James of Carrs Lane, Birmingham, both took part in his ordination. After six years he succeeded John Leifchild in Kensington.

During his early years in Kensington he published several works. The earliest was a collection of manuscript sources in two volumes on the life and ideas of John Wycliffe, *The Life and Opinions of John de Wycliffe* (London 1828); this was followed by similar manuscript collections on *The Protectorate of Oliver Cromwell* (two volumes, London 1838) and *The History of England under the House of Stuart Including the Commonwealth* (two volumes, London 1840).

His inaugural lecture at University College, London, as Professor of Ancient and Modern History, at a time when the study of history at Oxford and Cambridge was limited to ancient history within the departments of classics, was a thoughtful and ground-breaking examination of the study of history.[24] For Vaughan, '... if any one place would be more appropriate than another, as originating that intellectual reform which should assign to history its due prominence in the class of liberal studies, that place is the University of London.'[25] History, he believed, must be presented as a means of improving the human mind, 'the pole-star of the enlightened'; it was far more than the dull recording of facts: 'There is hardly a fault less endurable than dullness.'[26] The method he proposed to use in his lectures involved a brief outline of the period to be studied, followed by a more detailed examination in respect of five

[23] R. Vaughan, *On the Study of History* (London 1834).

[24] Published as *On the Study of History* (1834).

[25] Ibid 43.

[26] Ibid 41, 11.

themes: legislation and government; commerce, science and art; literature; religion; and national character. Thus he proposed to give more time to analysis than to narrative.

It was perhaps appropriate that the year he moved to Manchester saw the publication of his *The Age of Great Cities*.[27] Mary Hora[28] has pointed out that there is a close connection between the themes of this work and an earlier book of his on Congregationalism,[29] revealing that for him there was a close correlation between Congregationalism and prosperous city life. To those who saw cities as 'the great evil of the age,' Vaughan argued that the city represented 'whatever is most valuable in our social and religious state as a people'. The strength of Protestantism 'is a strength on the side of industry, of human improvement, and of the civilization which leads to the formation of great cities'.[30] Living in Manchester did not appear to change his mind on this issue. When Elizabeth Gaskell's *Mary Barton: A Tale of Manchester Life* was published in 1848, revealing some of the terrible living and working conditions of Manchester workers, his review was critical, complaining that it did a 'very great injustice to the employers'.[31]

One theme appeared constantly in Vaughan's work: Dissent must aspire to a higher educational standard. He had already argued, in his book on *Religious Parties in England* that Dissenters, both lay and ministerial, should raise their literary ambitions, for 'a party without literature must be a party without power.'[32] Dissenters should also recover the literature which was already theirs; '... while we do not mean to impeach the ancestry of other religious bodies, we mean to claim an ancestry of our own, and one second, as we think, in its honourable qualities to no other. ... The gold was not without alloy, but it was there.'[33]

Much consideration had been given to the question of charging students. It had been the practice at Blackburn to provide not only free tuition but also free residence. 'Is there not reason to fear that the small scale, and exclusively gratuitous character, of Dissenting Collegiate

[27] R. Vaughan, *The Age of Great Cities: or, Modern Society Viewed in its Relation to Intelligence, Morals and Religion* (London 1843). In *Cities Perceived: Urban Society in European and American Thought 1820–1940* (Manchester 1985) Andrew Lees calls Vaughan's book 'the most sweeping and impassioned statement of the urban ethos to appear anytime in England or anywhere in the century.' (45)

[28] In a forthcoming article in *JURCHS*.

[29] R. Vaughan, *Congregationalism: Or, the Polity of Independent churches, Viewed in Relation to the State and Tendencies of Modern Society* (London 1842).

[30] *Age of Great Cities* 77.

[31] *British Quarterly Review* IX (February 1849) 117–36.

[32] R. Vaughan, *Religious Parties in England: Their Principles, History and Present Duty* (London 1839) 134.

[33] 'Protestant Nonconformity in its Relation to Learning and Piety'. An inaugural lecture at the opening of the Lancashire Independent College, April 1843 (1843) 9.

Establishments, have operated unfavourably, to some extent on our ministry?' asked Thomas Raffles in his report to the Provisional Committee in December 1842. 'Have they never repelled pious young men of a respectable standing in society, by the aspect of inferiority they have presented, and thus suppressed in such persons the rising desire for the work?' After discussion, the Education Committee proposed, and the main committee agreed, that the college should not automatically provide free board, but that those whose family means were sufficient should pay for themselves. Those who were not in this position, but who were recommended by affluent churches, might be supported by some of the church's wealthier members, which would have the advantage of providing a close personal link between church and college. Others could be funded through the founding of an Educational Society, similar to those on the American model, or by the endowment of a few scholarships. If all this led to greater care in the selection of students, that could not but be beneficial.

The work at Blackburn ended on 20 April 1843, and the opening of the new college took place a few days later. A large gathering met in Grosvenor Street Chapel on the evening of 25 April to hear Dr John Harris, president of Cheshunt College, speak on 'The Importance of an Educated Ministry'. The following morning, after a prayer meeting in Zion Chapel, the subscribers, friends and invited guests[34] met in the new library to hear Dr Raffles give an account of the steps by which the idea of a worthy Lancashire Independent College had come to fruition, and to hear Dr Vaughan elaborate, with passing references to Gibbon, Milton and Bacon, on 'Protestant Nonconformity in its Relation to Learning and Piety'. Lunch and speeches followed. A final meeting on the same evening in the Corn Exchange stimulated many additional subscriptions, almost eradicating the debt, though still leaving some furnishing and the laying out of the grounds to be paid for.

The work of the College actually began on the following 30 August. In the intervening period the various subcommittees worked hard to assemble appropriate books, portraits and furnishings. The 2,000 books moved from Blackburn were in many cases dilapidated, and the collection as a whole was considered quite inadequate for the work to be done in Manchester. Fortunately, many gifts were forthcoming, the largest being a collection of 770 valuable books from Dr John Clunie, secretary to the Committee. When almost 4000 volumes had been assembled and placed in the new oak bookcases, the library provided an atmosphere conducive to study.

[34] The guests included Thomas Binney of the King's Weigh House and John Angell James of Carrs Lane, Birmingham. It was a happy coincidence that the Mayor of Manchester at the time was James Kershaw, one of the college's trustees.

The portraits hanging on the walls placed the College firmly within its tradition. Richard Baxter, Henry Newcome and John Owen represented the seventeenth century, while William Roby, Robert Spear, Joseph Fletcher and Thomas Raffles represented contemporary Congregationalism. The portrait of John Owen, Congregationalism's greatest seventeenth century theologian, was the gift of George Hadfield, who had been alerted not only to its existence, but to its impending sale, by James Sherman of the Surrey Chapel.[35]

When academic work began at the end of August, thirteen students moved from Blackburn, and another seven were admitted to begin their course. Amongst the new students were two who were to achieve some public distinction, one in a comparatively short life, the other in a very long one. Robert Alfred Vaughan,[36] who was the son of the president, was already a graduate of London University before entering the Lancashire College. His ministry at Ebenezer Chapel, Birmingham, from 1850 until his resignation because of ill-health in 1855, and his *Hours with the Mystics* (1856) promised an outstanding ministry which was cut short by his death at the age of 34.

James Guinness Rogers was a graduate of Trinity College, Dublin, and left the college to enjoy a long and noted ministry in London, where he was regarded as 'the representative of sober yet convinced Nonconformity'.[37] Enoch Mellor, admitted in 1846 as a graduate (of Edinburgh University), became a noted preacher in the north of England.[38]

The committee laid down a timetable for the daily routine of the College, beginning with morning worship at 7 a.m., ending with supper at 9.30 p.m., after which (at 10 p.m.) the doors were to be locked. Punctuality and good order were to be kept with the assistance of a system of fines. Forty years later, Guinness Rogers doubted that this was a wise system: 'It was certainly strange that students who were Christian professors, and were dedicated by their own intelligent and voluntary act to the work of the ministry, should be placed under a discipline more exacting, more severe, and more calculated to repress the growth of self-

[35] The portrait, painted by Bayley, a pupil of van Dyke, was identified c.1830, and bought by J. Winter from the estate of G. Polhill, Chipsted, Kent. Only two other portraits of John Owen were known, one in Bristol Baptist College, the other in the possession of Henry Owen Hall of Hackney. See *Manchester Times* 14 May 1842.

[36] Robert Alfred Vaughan (1823–57). See R. A. Vaughan, *Essays and Remains*, with a memoir by R. Vaughan (London 1858), and *DNB*.

[37] Alexander Gordon in *DNB*. James Guinness Rogers (1822–1911) was Chairman of the Congregational Union in 1874. For many years he was a friend of Gladstone. See J. Guinness Rogers, *An Autobiography* (London 1903).

[38] Enoch Mellor (1823–81) was subsequently minister of Square Chapel, Halifax, and Great George Street, Liverpool, and was elected to the Chair of the Congregational Union in 1863. See *CYB 1882* 315–8.

reliance than that applied to youths fresh from school and without any special qualification for self-government.'[39]

By the time the Annual General Meeting for 1844 was held on 23 December of that year, there were 24 students in the College, a bequest from Moses Hadfield had provided what was to prove the first of many scholarships to help needy students, a large list of subscribers (mostly from Lancashire, but also a good number from London) had been created, and the building was completed and furnished. The Committee was justifiably proud:

> It is a satisfaction to [the Committee] to think, that the Congregational body have now a convenient and capacious pile of college buildings, with suitable grounds laid out, all in a completed state, situated in the midst of this wealthy and populous district, and adapted, if its interior economy correspond, to exert a mighty moral influence upon all the neighbourhood around.

CONTROVERSY 1843–59

Within eighteen months of the opening of the College, the difference of approach between the forthright 'Puritan' solicitor (George Hadfield) and the more conciliatory former Kensington preacher (Robert Vaughan), used to mixing with more aristocratically connected Nonconformists, led to a clash which lost the College one of its strongest supporters. According to Guinness Rogers, Vaughan had not been Hadfield's choice as President,[40] and the two men did not find co-operation easy.

It was after considerable correspondence with Thomas Raffles in the preceding months that George Hadfield proposed to the meeting of the Committee on 11 November 1844 that Raffles, the Committee's chairman, should inform the President 'that his undertaking the Editorship of the *British Quarterly Review* as proposed in a printed circular published by himself, for the discussion of politics, and literary, scientific and other subjects, would be incompatible with the momentous duties of his office and calling as President and Theological Professor in this College'. The acceptance of this arrangement by the Committee would, he believed, be a breach of the Trust Deed.[41] The Committee's refusal to support him, and their view that the matter was 'completely beyond their province', led to his withdrawal from any further close

[39] J. G. Rogers in *The Congregationalist* March 1882, 198, quoted J. Thompson, *Lancashire Independent College 1843–93* 99.

[40] J. Guinness Rogers, 69.

[41] LIC Book of Proceedings of Subscribers and Committee 1842–50, NCA.

involvement with the College's affairs. He had discovered that his political principles and those of the new president were a long way apart on several important issues, including state education and church disestablishment, and that they differed too on political strategy; where Hadfield was forthright, Vaughan was conciliatory. Hadfield therefore parted company with the College, and found other outlets for his campaigning energy. Some years later, he welcomed the opportunity to pursue his interests in the House of Commons, where he was a frequent speaker after his election as MP for Sheffield in 1852.

It was Vaughan's literary interests and ambitions, and his wish to be a moderating influence, which led to his proposal to edit a journal. In 1844, the favourable response of the *Eclectic Review* (edited by the Baptist Thomas Price and widely read in Congregational circles) to the Anti-State Church conference held in London in April, provided Vaughan with the kind of opening he desired. He deplored what he viewed as the unbalanced liberalism of the *Eclectic Review*, not only on the subject of disestablishment, but also on education, for he rejected the policy of 'voluntaryism' – the idea that it was not the business of the state but rather that of the different denominations of Christians to provide education – a policy which had been officially adopted at the annual meeting of the Congregational Union in Leeds in 1843. Vaughan did not share the fear of an Anglican monopoly and refused to accept the implication that a religious education provided by the state along Anglican principles was worse than no education. In this stand, he was supported by two prominent members of the denomination, Thomas Binney of the King's Weigh House and Henry Rogers, the man who was to succeed him as president of the Lancashire College.

He was not deterred by Hadfield's opposition, and his new journal, the *British Quarterly Review*, which first appeared in May 1845, found many sponsors in Lancashire. It soon gained a high reputation as a thoughtful and moderate journal with a wide range of interest. Political issues, current literature, religious questions, all found a place. The second number, in autumn 1845, for example, carried articles on the Church of Scotland (this was not long after the Great Disruption), university tests, the Corn Laws, Ireland, and the Tractarians. Vaughan's characteristic moderation was expressed in his discussion of the ways in which Nonconformists had contributed towards generating the 'faults' of the Tractarians:

> It is in an undue disparagement of the mode and symbol in worship; in a neglect of the aids which religion desires from its own natural and hallowed association; in a too common want of sympathy with general literature, and even with their own literature; and, above all, in the excess to which they have often pushed the principles of ecclesiastical democracy – in all these respects nonconformists have done much to give prominence

> to that tangent point from which so many have gone off in a widely different direction.[42]

Guinness Rogers, a student at the time of the dispute between Vaughan and Hadfield, later observed that the President, 'under the influence of London Dissent', '... felt it to be part of his great mission to strengthen all the conservative forces there might be in our churches' and noted that, while the students were sympathetic to radicalism, their support was on the side of Vaughan rather than Hadfield.[43]

If Vaughan was able to rally general support for his 'conservative' stance at this stage of his presidency, the crisis which erupted twelve years later was too powerful for any peaceful resolution, and led indirectly to his own resignation. In the intervening years, the College's work developed steadily, though it did not entirely escape the temptation to bolster numbers by accepting students whose academic attainment or potential were not of an appropriate standard. This was partly dealt with by establishing a preparatory class. There was a gradual increase in the number of students, aided by the endowment of three Shorrock scholarships by Eccles Shorrock, a trustee from Darwen. Whereas the College opened with 20 students, there were 30 in 1853, and 42 in 1862. The attendance of some students at the classics classes at the newly-founded Owens College after 1851 helped to raise the general standards.

When C. P. Mason resigned in 1849 to take up a teaching post in a school in London, he was replaced by Robert Halley, son of the Mosley Street minister, who remained for six years until he went out to India as principal of Doveton Institution and Protestant College, Madras, in 1856.[44] At this point there was considerable discussion as to whether students might not take most of their arts course at Owens College, freeing Lancashire Independent College to be a purely theological college. The students presented a memorandum to the Committee (dated 22 February 1855), pressing the case for continuing and increasing their attendance at the Owens College classes: 'Meeting on common ground with students not of our college our prejudices have been lessened and our best sympathies cultivated, while we have felt urged on to the utmost exertion ...'; competing for the College's scholarships and prizes had produced 'a more manly spirit of industry' during the arts course. They were highly appreciative of the 'generous attention' they had always

[42] *British Quarterly Review* vol I (1845) 456–7.

[43] J. Guinness Rogers, *An Autobiography* (London 1903) 69.

[44] Robert Halley (1827–85). He had attended classes at Manchester New College before studying at Coward College and University College, London, and spending a year in Bonn. After returning from India he was principal of Tettenhall College, Wolverhampton, for seven years, and finally minister at Arundel, Sussex.

received from the Owens College tutors.[45] In particular, the students were deeply impressed by the Open Lectures on 'The Relation of Religion to the Life of the Scholar' given each year by A. J. Scott,[46] first principal of Owens College.[47] These lectures contrasted favourably with the rather dull system of lecturing and note-taking which was the custom at most theological colleges, including Lancashire.

But the Committee timorously decided otherwise; fearing that the College would have no control over either the behaviour of the students or the lectures of the staff at Owens, they felt the risks were too great, and shrank from involvement in Manchester's great educational enterprise. Two new professors were therefore appointed to replace Robert Halley at the College, Theophilus Dwight Hall[48] to teach classics, and Alfred Newth[49] to teach mathematics, philosophy and Hebrew. For the time being, the students received all their tuition within the College.

Work proceeded steadily until a sudden irruption in 1857 led to the resignation of two of the four members of staff. The crisis which shook the College in 1857 was of wider significance in the intellectual life of the time, being the first public manifestation of unease about the kind of biblical criticism which was already common in Germany.[50] From the opening of the College, biblical studies had been in the hands of Samuel Davidson,[51] a former Presbyterian scholar from Belfast whose

[45] Memorandum, quoted in J. Thompson, *Lancashire Independent College 1843–93* 120.

[46] Alexander James Scott (1805–66) was a Church of Scotland minister who was principal of Owens College 1851–7. See J. P. Newell, 'A Nestor of Nonconformist Heretics: A. J. Scott (1805–66)' in *JURCHS* 3/1 (1983) and *DNB*.

[47] See F. J. Powicke, *David Worthington Simon* (London 1912) 19, 34.

[48] Theophilus Dwight Hall was the son of a Congregational minister, George Hall of Henfield, Sussex. He was a graduate and gold medallist of University College, London, and had been a tutor at Mill Hill School. He was the author of several manuals for teaching Latin, Greek and English, published when he was principal of the Collegiate School, Bowdon, after leaving the Lancashire College. He co-operated with Sir William Smith on the latter's Latin dictionary.

[49] Alfred Newth (1811–75) was a former student of John Pye Smith. A modest and scholarly man, he came to the College after pastoral ministry in Christchurch and Oundle, and was to remain until his death 21 years later. His brother, Samuel Newth, had recently become a professor at, and was later to be principal of, New College, London. See *CYB 1876* 355–8.

[50] For recent detailed studies of the Davidson controversy, see John Lea, 'The Davidson Controversy' in *Durham University Journal* 68 (new series 37) 1975, 15–32, and F. Roger Tomes, '"We are hardly prepared for this style of teaching yet": Samuel Davidson and Lancashire Independent College' *JURCHS* 5/7 (1995) 398–414. See also John Rogerson, 'Samuel Davidson and his Dismissal in 1857', chapter XIV of his *Old Testament Criticism in the Nineteenth Century* (London 1984), and Willis B. Glover, *Evangelical Nonconformists and Higher Criticism in the Nineteenth Century* (London 1954).

[51] For Samuel Davidson (1806–98) see A. J. Davidson (ed), *The Autobiography and Diary of Samuel Davidson* (Edinburgh 1899) and *DNB*.

sympathies towards Congregationalism caused him to welcome the invitation to the Lancashire College in 1843. When he arrived, he already had two published works to his credit, *Lectures on Biblical Criticism* (Edinburgh 1839) and *Sacred Hermeneutics Developed and Applied* (Edinburgh 1843); the latter, a book of 700 pages which revealed an extensive knowledge of German scholarship, has been described by a twentieth-century Old Testament scholar as 'one of the most informative and fair-minded accounts of German criticism to be published in the first half of the nineteenth century in Britain'.[52] A year after settling in Manchester he paid his first visit to Germany and met many of the leading biblical scholars, including August Tholuck in Halle and Johann Neander in Berlin. His work was evidently appreciated there, for he was only the second English scholar[53] to have the degree of D Theol conferred on him by the University of Halle. German scholars visited him in Manchester, where works continued to flow from his pen while he was teaching, including a three-volume *Introduction to the New Testament*, published 1848–51. He was described by a critical member of the Committee as being 'of a very crotchety turn of mind,' and seems to have fallen into the habit of taking the opposite view from that of the President in most matters.[54] However, there is no hint in examiners' reports of any criticism of or dissatisfaction with his teaching. He inspired at least one student, David Worthington Simon (who was to become principal of three theological colleges in later life), to serious study of German theology. 'Indeed, Simon's whole life-work may be said to have been determined in those days when he was admitted to Dr Davidson's study and family circle as a privileged friend.'[55] It is uncertain whether Davidson knew of the work on the Old Testament of Francis Newman,[56] who was teaching nearby at Manchester New College when the Lancashire College opened, and whose *A History of the Hebrew Monarchy* (London 1847, published anonymously at first) was one of a number of critical biblical works being published by Unitarian scholars.

In 1854, Davidson was invited by Longmans to share in the revision of a work in four volumes by Thomas Hartwell Horne, *Introduction to the Critical Study and Knowledge of the Sacred Scriptures* (first published in

[52] John Rogerson, *Old Testament Criticism in the Nineteenth Century* (London 1984).

[53] The first was Dr Samuel Lee (1783–1852) of Cambridge.

[54] See 'The Autobiography of David Everard Ford', ed Albert Peel, in *TCHS* 11 1930–2.

[55] Thus wrote Simon's fellow-student, John Brown, in Powicke, 33. Simon was a student at the College 1849–54.

[56] Francis William Newman (1805–97), Fellow of Balliol College, Oxford 1826–30, Classical Professor at Manchester New College 1840–6, Professor of Latin, University College, London 1846–69, brother of John Henry Newman. See *Who was Who 1897–1915* and *DNB*.

1818) for a tenth edition. He agreed to work on the second volume, on the Old Testament, in partnership with S. Prideaux Tregelles,[57] on condition that he was allowed to rewrite the work rather than simply revise the section allotted to him; 'he considered that he would be doing a service to religion in Great Britain by helping to acquaint English people with the sounder views already prevalent in Germany,' wrote one of his former students.[58] His volume, a work of 1,100 pages published in October 1856, provided the most detailed information yet available in English about critical studies in Germany.

The following month, when the College Committee met on 24 November, the Revd David Everard Ford, minister of Richmond Chapel, Broughton, felt it his duty to speak, though with 'deep reluctance': 'Our biblical professor had been suspected of holding such parley with our enemies in the gate, as involved an attainder of treachery; and it was only right, as an act of justice to him, to ourselves, and to the cause of revealed religion, that the matter should undergo a thorough investigation.'[59] He claimed to have received many letters expressing alarm at the opinions expressed in the book, implying that Davidson had not upheld the plenary inspiration of the Bible – more likely to have been prompted by a letter from S. P. Tregelles in *The Record*,[60] and ensuing references in other papers, than by reading the whole volume. Another ministerial member of the Committee, John Kelly,[61] of Crescent Chapel, Liverpool, suggested the convening of a subcommittee to consider the matter; this was agreed, and he, Robert Halley, P. Thomson, W. R. Thorburn, R. M. Davies and James Gwyther, all well-respected local Congregational ministers, were appointed.

Their report, drawn up after several long meetings and much private study, took two hours to read at the meeting of the Committee on the following 16 February (1857). The main recommendation, which was

[57] Samuel Prideaux Tregelles (1813–75), biblical scholar. See *DNB*.

[58] James Allanson Picton, chapter VI, 'The College Crisis' in Davidson, op cit 41.

[59] 'Autobiography' 278. He added, '... if during a long life I had rendered no further service to the cause of truth and righteousness than on that occasion, I should feel, on a dying bed, that I had not altogether lived in vain' (279). David Everard Ford was a lifelong friend of Thomas Binney. At his funeral, Alexander Thomson spoke of him as 'a conspicuous example, of what I might call the rich, full-bodied theology of the fervent, unhesitating faith of a former generation.' See *CYB 1876* 335, and *DNB*.

[60] *The Record* 3 November 1856. Tregelles wrote of the sorrow he had experienced in observing 'that Dr Davidson has used this work as the occasion for avowing and bringing into notice many sentiments and theories with regard to scripture which his former works would not have intimated that he held, and his adoption of which was *wholly unknown* to Mr Horne and myself.'

[61] John Kelly (1801–76) was a former student of Idle Independent Academy who exercised the whole of his ministry in Liverpool. He had been chairman of the Congregational Union in 1851. See *CYB 1877* 384–7 and *DNB*.

accepted, was that Davidson should be asked to prepare 'such an explanation of parts of his book which are deemed objectionable, as may remove misunderstanding, which his own language may have occasioned, conciliate opposition, which his own haste may have provoked, make concession where concession may be justly due, and thus take the most effectual means of vindicating himself from unjust and malevolent aspersions.'[62]

Davidson had in fact examined the theories about the authorship and sources of the Pentateuch very carefully, and did not rush to support every new German hypothesis. But for those who had acquired a dread of German biblical scholarship and who clung to a theory of plenary inspiration, rumours about the book's contents aroused fear and threatened old securities.

The fact that Davidson had played little or no part in denominational affairs, that he had taken an active role in the peace movements of the 1850s (whereas Robert Vaughan took a contrary attitude), and that he was a supporter of secular education, may not have helped. Neither did his tendency to caustic dismissal of those who disagreed with him, nor his scorn for those ignorant of Greek and Hebrew, make for mutual understanding. A significant factor underlying this debate was the fact that subscribers would withdraw financial support from an institution accused, rightly or wrongly, of heterodoxy. The situation was not helped by the furore within the denomination over Thomas Toke Lynch's *Hymns for Heart and Voice: The Rivulet* (London 1855) – a volume which many found to be symptomatic of a general lapse from orthodoxy and which had prompted a debate in which John Kelly was involved.[63]

By this time, reports, not always accurate, were beginning to appear in the press, and at a meeting on 2 March 1857 the Committee felt it necessary to draw up a circular to be sent to all subscribers. When Samuel Davidson's explanations[64] were put before the Committee on 1 June, John Kelly moved a resolution proposing that the explanations were 'far from satisfactory ... the most formidable objections are rather passed over than fairly met.' Long discussion failed to produce agreement, and the meeting was adjourned. Ten days later, after further extended discussion and the rejection of two amendments, the resolution was carried by 18 votes to 16.

[62] The crisis is well documented in both the College Council Minute Book III 1856–73 and MS record of the subcommittee, NCA.

[63] See Albert Peel, *These Hundred Years: A History of the Congregational Union of England and Wales 1831–1931* (London 1931) 221–35.

[64] Published as *Facts, Statements and Explanations Connected with the Publication of the Second Volume of the Tenth Edition of Horne's Introduction to the Scriptures* (London 1857).

Nineteen days later, on 29 June, Samuel Davidson's letter of resignation was read out at the Committee meeting:

> Having patiently waited to witness your exemplification of that Christian truth and liberty which I once thought you had advocated and allowed; having been refused in writing the precise grounds on which a vague resolution of want of confidence in me may be supposed to have been based: and having long ago resolved to remain in no situation where I could not freely express, without annoyance from such as have a little brief authority over me in this world, opinions at variance neither with *expressed* formularies of Independents, nor with the *recognized* doctrinal formularies of the Established Church, I now respectfully resign into your hands the office which I have held for the last fourteen years, in the Lancashire Independent College.[65]

No doubt this was a great relief to most of the Committee at the time. They were gracious enough to allow him to live in his college house until the end of the year. On 13 July, Davidson was presented with a testimonial and silver plate and gold pencil case by 32 of his former students, and later in the summer he was presented with £1,500 (which was soon doubled) by a public meeting of sympathisers. One of his former students, Thomas Nicholas, who was professor of Biblical Literature and Mental and Moral Science at the Presbyterian College, Carmarthen, later published a substantial pamphlet in which he aimed 'to defend the interests of reverent and free Biblical enquiry, and the injured reputation of a gentleman and scholar'.[66] Another, James Allanson Picton,[67] contributed a chapter on 'The College Crisis' to Dr Davidson's autobiography in 1899.

Another two former students, initially writing under the heading of 'two graduates' but later identified as Enoch Mellor and James Guinness Rogers, published a rather cruel pamphlet on *Dr Davidson: His Heresies, Contradictions and Plagiarisms* in the autumn of 1857. It is noteworthy that Guinness Rogers made no mention of this in his autobiography of 1903.

In the end, Davidson had to go because the College was 'hardly prepared for this kind of teaching yet'.[68] But there was an uncomfortable

[65] LIC Committee Minute Book 1856–63.

[66] Thomas Nicholas, *Dr Davidson's Removal from the Professorship of Biblical Literature in the Lancashire Independent College, Manchester, on account of Alleged Error in Doctrine. A statement of Facts, with Documents; Together with Remarks and Criticisms* (London and Edinburgh 1860). Thomas Nicholas had entered the Blackburn Academy, but moved to the new college at Whalley Range to complete his course. See *DNB*.

[67] James Allanson Picton (1832–1910) spent the first part of his career as a Congregational minister, then entered political life and was MP for Leicester 1884–94. See *DNB*.

[68] John Kelly, *An Examination of the Facts, Statements and Explanations of the Rev. Dr. Samuel Davidson* (London 1857) 25.

feeling that justice had not been done, and when its jubilee was celebrated 36 years later, in 1893, there were several apologetic references to the crisis, and the college's historian, Joseph Thompson, did his best to make amends.[69]

Davidson had only recently passed his fiftieth birthday, and was to live another 40 years. He soon moved to London, where he was able to do some examining and occasional writing. He never held another academic post, and the last years of his life were very lonely. He did not live to see his estate contribute towards the endowment of the Samuel Davidson Chair in Old Testament Studies in the University of London, a chair which was occupied by distinguished Old Testament scholars from 1926 until 1992, and again since 1997.

Within a month of Davidson's resignation, Robert Vaughan (who seems to have played no decisive role in the crisis) had sent in his own resignation. Recent events, he wrote, 'have done something towards strengthening the inclination [to resign],' which had been circulating in his mind for the previous two or three years. The College crisis had been compounded for him by the premature death of his brilliant eldest son, and the murder of his son-in-law and former pupil, Carl Buch, in India in 1857. He returned to London, and settled in St John's Wood after a brief pastorate in Uxbridge. Here he continued with his literary work and published a substantial three-volume work on *Revolutions in English History* (London 1859–63). In his last year he moved to Torquay to take charge of a new congregation but died after a few months in 1868.

Thus by the end of 1857 none of the founding members of staff remained, and the Council were in search of a new principal.

'A Period of Prosperity and Tranquillity' 1858–75

This is how James Gwyther, honorary secretary of the College Committee, looked back on the years of Henry Rogers's principalship from two decades later.[70] Henry Rogers,[71] invited to succeed Robert Vaughan, had

[69] See Joseph Thompson, *Lancashire Independent College, 1843–1893* (Manchester 1893) 127–145.

[70] J. H. Gwyther, 'The Past History of the College' in *Memorial of the Opening of the New and Enlarged Buildings of Lancashire Independent College* (Manchester 1878) 32.

[71] For Henry Rogers (1806–77) see *DNB* and R. W. Dale's 'Memoir of Henry Rogers' in the eighth edition of Henry Rogers, *The Superhuman Origin of the Bible* (London 1893). Dale was a student of Rogers at Spring Hill. For a recent discussion of Henry Rogers, see Alan P. F. Sell, 'Henry Rogers and *The Eclipse of Faith*', *JURCHS* 2/5 1980 128–143, reprinted in Sell, *Dissenting Thought* (1990).

an eirenic temperament which helped to settle the College after the recent controversy and his lack of interest in German biblical criticism gave Davidson's critics no cause for alarm. His literary interests and achievements and his wide contacts added further lustre to the College's reputation.

Like Vaughan, he had held a chair at University College, London, during the 1830s. He was born in St Albans, and after a brief period of study with a surgeon entered Highbury College in 1826, and remained for three years. He then went as assistant to Thomas Durant at Poole, but a persistent throat problem and consequent weakness of voice soon indicated that teaching and writing were more appropriate than pastoral ministry. After a variety of part-time teaching assignments, including lecturing at Highbury and at University College, he was appointed professor of English language and literature and intellectual philosophy at the newly-founded Spring Hill College in Birmingham.[72]

As lecturer and teacher at Spring Hill he outshone his two colleagues, Thomas Barker and Francis Watts, being able to inspire his students with intellectual excitement and to instil a lifelong love of literature and philosophy. Unusually for those days, when lectures often consisted of dictated notes, Rogers encouraged discussion, and his voluntary philosophy class was always well-attended. Simultaneously with his teaching he was contributing to journals such as the *Eclectic Review*, the *Edinburgh Review* (of which he was twice invited to be editor), and the *British Quarterly Review*, and therefore in correspondence with significant literary figures such as Thomas Babington Macaulay, James Stephen and Richard Whateley, Archbishop of Dublin. His reading was wide-ranging; he knew the work of the great thinkers of the past almost as he knew his own friends, and this intellectual dialogue was shared with his brightest students. His own particular 'hero' was John Howe, the seventeenth century ecumenical Puritan, whose biography he wrote and whose works he edited.[73] He engaged seriously with the intellectual challenges of his generation, particularly those represented respectively by the brothers John Henry Newman and Francis William Newman.[74] R. W. Dale remembered 'his delight in vigorous discussion, his quick wit, graceful fancy, and alert memory', together with his readiness to be diverted by a question relating to one of his favourite writers 'as a hungry trout, in the

[72] Founded by the Mansfield family, and forerunner of Mansfield College, Oxford. See Elaine Kaye, *Mansfield College: Its Origin, History and Significance* (Oxford 1996).

[73] *The Life and Character of John Howe* (London 1836) was published before he went to Spring Hill. The *Works* of John Howe he edited and published in five volumes in 1862–3 while he was in Manchester.

[74] See his articles published in *Essays on Some Theological Controversies of the Time* (London 1874).

dusk of evening, rises to a favourite fly'.[75] And on reading Rogers's most famous and most stimulating work, *The Eclipse of Faith* (London 1852), written in response to F. W. Newman's *Phases of Faith* (London 1850), Dale detected 'traces of the very real and ardent debates in which they had tried their strength against their tutor.'[76] It is not surprising to learn that several of his students won the Gold Medal for Philosophy in the London University MA examinations.

Rogers took up his position in Manchester as College president and professor of theology and moral philosophy in April 1858, joining Theophilus Dwight Hall (who taught classics) and Alfred Newth (mathematics, philosophy and Hebrew) to form the complement of staff. The committee, still reeling from the Davidson affair, did not appoint another professor of biblical studies; for the next 35 years the study of the Bible was restricted to detailed examination of the Greek and Hebrew texts, with special attention to passages which presented a challenge to apologetics. Henry Rogers himself took a conservative view of biblical criticism, as was revealed after his retirement in his *The Superhuman Origin of the Bible Inferred from Itself* (London 1873).[77]

Rogers had not previously taught systematic theology, and preparation for his classes took up most of his time. The Committee's *Report* for 1863 gives some idea of the range of his teaching. The senior class read Joseph Butler's *Analogy of Religion*, John Davison's *Discourses on Prophecy* and John Pye Smith's *Four Discourses*, while the junior class studied Richard Whately's *Elements of Rhetoric* and Paley's *A View of the Evidence of Christianity* and *Horae Paulinae*. Though he was 'far more a literary critic than a professional divine', his students realised that 'there was the undescribable mark of genius on all that he did'.[78] One of his old students wrote, 'His style is as clear as crystal, and sparkles ever and anon with spontaneous outbursts of wit.'[79]

There was now a steady increase in the number of students. By 1862 there were 42, and by 1875 the number had reached 47 and was continuing to grow. The increasing list of exhibitions and scholarships/fellowships available added to the attraction of the College. To two exhibitions financed by Lady Hewley's Charity, the three Shorrock Fellowships and a Hadfield scholarship were now added in the 1860s a Raffles scholarship, endowed in 1861 in honour of Thomas Raffles'

[75] Dale, 'Memoir', xxiv, xxv.

[76] R. W. Dale, 'The History of Spring Hill College' in *Mansfield College, Oxford: Its Origin and Opening* (London 1890).

[77] Congregational Lectures which Rogers was unable to deliver in person, but which were subsequently published.

[78] G. S. Barrett (student at LIC 1863–6), 'Address' in *Lancashire Independent College Jubilee 1893* (Manchester 1893) 55.

[79] Parrish, *From the World to the Pulpit* (1863) 172.

Liverpool jubilee, a Prince Albert Fellowship in 1862,[80] a Woodward scholarship endowed by the College Treasurer in 1863 and a Ramsay-Gilbert scholarship, endowed by Miss Ramsay of Nantwich in 1867.

Thomas Raffles did not long survive his jubilee, but died in 1863 at the age of 75. He had been chairman of the College Committee since 1839, and a supporter of the Blackburn Academy for many years previous to that.[81] He had steered the College through the process of new building and fund-raising, and latterly through the Davidson crisis. He was a great collector of books, and it was fitting that a special collection of books, known as the Raffles Library, was now added to the existing library.

There was already a feeling among the more perceptive members of the Committee that too much responsibility was being placed on a staff of three professors, who had to teach basic language, literary, classical and mathematical subjects as well as theology. G. S. Barrett (LIC 1863–6) wondered in retrospect how Alfred Newth managed to teach the range of subjects required:

> He would begin his work by lecturing on Church History in the morning then he would go on to the Binomial Theorem, the next hour you would hear him discussing the quantification of the predicate with a logic class, then in the next he would be deep in the unutterable mysteries of Khateph Kamets, and Furtive Pathakh; and, last of all, by way of diversion, he would finish the day by lecturing on 'Berkeley's Idealism,' or 'The Nature and Manufacture of Hydrogen Gas.'[82]

In January 1861 the Education Committee had resolved that 'it is desirable that as soon as circumstances will admit of the change, Lancashire Independent College should become exclusively a theological institution,' reflecting a concern in several colleges and in the Congregational Union itself, that colleges were failing to provide an adequate standard of theological education because they had to give so much time and effort to preliminary education.

Henry Allon[83] had challenged the denomination in his Chairman's address to the Congregational Union's Autumn Assembly to think more seriously about ministerial education, and called for a colleges' conference. He cited evidence quoted in *The Patriot* that 450 out of 1,738

[80] The *Report of the Committee* for 1862 noted that 'certain gentlemen' had raised funds for this object, 'thereby to give an additional proof to posterity of the loyalty of Nonconformists to the throne of these realms, and testify in an appropriate manner their great respect for the character of this highly-cultured and liberal minded Prince'.

[81] After Thomas Raffles retired from the chair of the Committee, future chairmen were elected for a period of two years only.

[82] G. S. Barrett, *Jubilee*, 54–5.

[83] Henry Allon (1818–92) was minister at Union Chapel, Islington. See *CYB 1893* 202–5 and *DNB*.

ministers had 'no known specific education for their work'.[84] He raised the issue again in a paper on 'The Amalgamation of the Colleges' at the autumn assembly of the Congregational Union in 1871 (the year in which university tests at Oxford, Cambridge and Durham were abolished, thus enabling Nonconformists to study at those universities without discrimination – except for divinity degrees at Oxford), and challenged the colleges to separate the curricula in arts and theology and to require graduation in arts before allowing admission to a theological course. He recognised that some ministers, 'drawn from the higher ranks of Nonconformist social life' would take advantage of the opening of national universities, but believed that 'the best staple of any ministry consists of men who have had personal experience of the hardships and struggles of common life, and who by strength of purpose, indomitable industry, and severe self-discipline, have risen above their circumstances.'[85] His vision was of two Nonconformist universities, each a federation of five or six colleges, one in London and one in Manchester.[86]

To the colleges and their supporters he made a direct plea:

> Is it not a reckless waste of tutorial power to have sixteen independent institutions, each maintaining a miscellaneous and fragmentary course of teaching, and necessitating sixteen classes of three or four students each, when the teaching would be much more effective were the whole combined into one or two large classes, and when each of our thirty-seven professors might occupy with unspeakably greater advantage to himself and to the whole his own distinctive chair?[87]

Amalgamation was to be a theme of discussions over the next 100 years, arousing all the jealous feelings of independence latent in Congregationalism.

Some change was forced on the Lancashire College because of the ill-health of the president. By the end of 1864 Rogers had proffered his resignation. But the Committee was reluctant to let him go, and early in the new year an arrangement was made by which he would continue to teach, but as a non-resident president. A new resident member of staff would take charge of administration and share in the teaching of philosophy and church history. Rogers limped on for another six years, until a serious fall led to his final retirement in 1871.[88]

The new member of staff appointed was Caleb Scott,[89] son of the former principal of Airedale College, Bradford, Walter Scott. Caleb Scott

[84] A conference was held, but had little practical effect. See *CYB 1865* 46–72.
[85] *CYB 1872* 105.
[86] Ibid 112.
[87] Ibid 111.
[88] He retired first to Silverdale, then finally to Machynlleth. He died in 1877.
[89] Caleb Scott (1831–1919). See *CYB 1920* 112–13.

was to give long and devoted service to the College for almost 40 years. He was educated at Silcoates School and Airedale College and served as minister in Lincoln for eleven years before moving to Manchester in 1865. His first brief was to teach New Testament criticism and exegesis. When Henry Rogers withdrew further from his responsibilities in 1869, Scott was appointed president, a position he held until 1902. He published no books, but provided a solid and wise presence in the College as others came and went. His experience in business in Bradford for a few years before entering Airedale College was to prove invaluable in the succeeding years of expansion and financial difficulty.[90]

With the resignation of Theophilus Hall in 1867 to become principal of the Collegiate School, Bowdon, came the opportunity to renew contact with Owens College, an arrangement made more attractive by the fact that plans were afoot to erect new buildings for Owens on a site in Oxford Road, more accessible to Whalley Range. A tutor (Revd W. C. Russell) was appointed to provide informal tuition at the College to complement formal lectures and support new students who arrived with little experience of study. Though the students were not to take the whole of their non-theological studies at Owens College, as some members of the Committee wished, the link now forged became permanent, and the move towards becoming a purely theological college was set on course.

Expansion 1875–93

The College report for 1875 indicated that there was no more room for resident students, and the Committee was faced with the choice either of admitting non-resident students, or of extending the building. The argument for extension was strengthened by the recognition that the living conditions were spartan; the studies were very small and cold, and the roof over the bedrooms leaked. The library was not only cold but damp, so that 'some of our most valuable works in divinity were fast becoming of interest rather to the students of natural science, on account of the large growth of fungus which they displayed.'[91] With rising numbers of students (47 in 1875 and 53 in 1876) the Committee felt

[90] This experience may also have contributed to an interest in mathematical games, which he seems to have played with his family, and which apparently gave his daughter Charlotte useful experience for her future academic career as a distinguished mathematician, after winning a scholarship to Girton College, Cambridge. See Patricia Kenschaft, 'Charlotte Angas Scott' in L. S. Grinstein and P. J. Campbell, *Women of Mathematics: A Bibliographic Sourcebook* (New York and London 1987).

[91] T. K. Higgs, Senior Student, at the opening of the extended buildings, 1878. See *Memorial of the Opening of the New and Enlarged Buildings of Lancashire Independent College* (Manchester 1878) 50.

confident enough to decide on extension. There was the added possibility that the amalgamation of colleges might bring yet more students to Manchester.

They turned to the architect whose new Town Hall for Manchester was almost reaching completion, Alfred Waterhouse.[92] Joseph Thompson,[93] a leading member of the College Committee, was not only a member of the subcommittee responsible for the Town Hall building, but also a personal friend of Waterhouse, whom he had already employed to build two new Congregational churches.[94] Waterhouse came from a Quaker family in Liverpool, had been apprenticed to a firm in Manchester, and was known to have attended an Independent Chapel.[95] His brief now was to enlarge the students' rooms, to provide a new assembly room-cum-library and a new staff house, and to re-arrange the domestic department. His plans were presented to the Committee, and accepted, at a meeting on 27 March 1876. The first estimate of the cost was between £10,000 and £12,000, but that rose dramatically before the end of the year, and the eventual cost was £20,315.[96] Further improvements, including the purchase of extra land, brought the total expenditure to over £22,000.

For the next eighteen months the College was the scene of building works. By using spare space on the ground floor of the wings, the number of both studies and bedrooms was increased to 60, and the studies themselves were enlarged, re-windowed and redecorated. By a skilful addition to the NW corner of the main front, a spacious new president's house was provided, including nine bedrooms (it was assumed that a college president would need to provide for domestic servants as well as a family). A new wing was added to the south of the main building, providing three new lecture rooms on the ground floor, and above them the *pièce de résistance*, an assembly room/library 60 feet in length and 30 feet wide.

The reopening ceremony was planned for September 1878. With Gladstone's campaign against the Bulgarian atrocities of 1876 (widely supported among Nonconformists) still fresh in their minds, and knowing of his good relations with Nonconformists, the Committee felt

[92] Alfred Waterhouse (1830–1905). See C. Cunningham and P. Waterhouse, *Alfred Waterhouse 1830–1905: The Biography of a Practice* (Oxford 1992).

[93] Alderman Joseph Thompson (1833–1909) was the third generation of his family to serve the College. He was one of the earliest students of Owens College, whose first history, *The Owens College* (Manchester 1886) he wrote. He was Treasurer and Chairman of the Council of Owens College 1887–1904.

[94] Ancoats Congregational Church, 1861–5 (which had to be pulled down not long after its construction to make way for a new railway line) and Broadheath Congregational Church, Altrincham, 1866.

[95] Cunningham and Waterhouse 10.

[96] Cunningham and Waterhouse 249.

that he was the most appropriate person to open the new buildings;[97] the president and two members of the Committee were deputed to visit Gladstone to issue the invitation. They had 'a long and interesting conversation on the training of students for the work of the ministry, in which Mr Gladstone urged strongly that Nonconformists should have a college at Oxford',[98] but their appeal was in vain; 'it was announced that Mr Gladstone did not regard the re-opening ceremony as sufficiently exceptional to warrant his coming.'[99]

The celebrations on 25 September therefore were of a more parochial kind than originally hoped, but distinguished nevertheless. Two important speeches were delivered, each representing significant future developments, and each impressing upon the assembled company the importance of an educated ministry. The first, on 'The Relation of University Training to our College,' was delivered by Professor A. S. Wilkins,[100] Professor of Classics at Owens College and distinguished Congregationalist. He emphasised the mutual benefit which the connection between the two colleges, Owens and Lancashire Independent, had brought to both since 1867, and added his voice to those who wanted the Lancashire College to become an exclusively theological institution, with professors able to specialise in one field only. The second lecture was delivered by one of the College's earlier students David Worthington Simon (student 1849–54), on 'Theological Training for Ministerial Students'. Simon had spent several years in Germany since leaving college, and was now introducing stimulating new forms of teaching as principal of Spring Hill College, Birmingham. He was one of the strongest advocates of a graduate ministry. He warned of the danger of exaggerating 'Christian individualism' at the expense of reasoned convictions; 'the thorough philosophical and theological training of the ministry' was the best safeguard against a sentimental and superficial understanding of Christian doctrine.[101]

These two speeches were delivered less than a year after the controversial 'Leicester Conference' of October 1877, at which two

[97] On the afternoon of 18 April 1878 Gladstone had spoken for an hour to a meeting of Nonconformist ministers at Memorial Hall. In his diary he noted, 'Never did I address a better audience.' See *The Gladstone Diaries vol IX*, ed. H. C. G. Matthew (Oxford 1986) 307.

[98] J. Thompson, *Lancashire Independent College 1843–1893* (Manchester 1893) 179.

[99] LIC Committee Minute Book VI 1875–82, entry for 9 September 1878.

[100] Augustus Samuel Wilkins (1843–1905). He had won many prizes at St John's College, Cambridge, but was disqualified from holding a fellowship, first as a Nonconformist, then after 1871 because he was married. He was Professor of Classics at Owens College 1869–1903, an influential supporter both of the Lancashire College and of women's education.

[101] See *Memorial of the Opening of the New and Enlarged Buildings of Lancashire Independent College* (Manchester 1878) 78–92.

former Lancashire students, James Allanson Picton and Thomas Gasquoine (contemporaries of Simon) had been the main speakers.[102] Picton spoke on 'Some Relations of Theology to Religion', arguing that religious feeling rather than theological creed was what bound Christians, while Gasquoine's subject was 'Freedom of Theological Thought and the Spiritual Life'. The conference was actually an unofficial meeting during the Congregational Union's Autumn Assembly, but the publicity it received conveyed the impression that it was a Union-sponsored meeting. It was advertised as 'a public conference of those who feel that agreement in theological opinion can no longer be held to be essential to religious communion', and its proceedings raised a furore within the Congregational Union and in the Congregational press. Simon was one of those who was particularly critical. A rigorous theological education was, more evidently than ever, urgently needed.

In the College, student life was a little more comfortable, and the purchase of extra land at the back of the College made the provision of a cricket pitch possible. A College cricket team now had a good fixture list, as did the football team. A fives court provided an alternative sport. One aspect of life which the students felt had not improved was the catering. The diet was monotonous, especially at supper, which every evening consisted of milk, bread and cheese, and treacle; jam and marmalade at breakfast were considered luxuries, and had to be provided by the students themselves.[103]

Before the formal opening had taken place, £13,000 had been raised towards the cost of the improvements, leaving a debt of over £9,000, which coincided with another severe depression in Lancashire trade. The large-scale fund raising now deemed essential resulted in two remarkable bazaars, one in Liverpool and the other in Manchester, which not only eradicated the debt but produced a generous surplus. Support was rallied from the local Congregational churches, and all the artistic and imaginative skills of the members were drawn upon. The Liverpool bazaar in March 1882 consisted of stalls set in 'a Chinese city' and raised nearly £3,000. The Congregationalists of Manchester took over St James's Hall for ten days in May 1882 and transformed its appearance into that of a late mediaeval German town. The ambitious design was the work of the architect Alfred Darbyshire, while the actual construction was carried out at the cabinet works of James Reilly at Cornbrook.[104] Special excursion trains, with reduced fares, were laid on from the surrounding towns. This too was a great success, and not only raised

[102] See Mark D. Johnson, *The Dissolution of Dissent 1850–1918* (New York and London 1987) chapter 2 for a detailed account of the conference.

[103] See J. P. Kingsland, 'Lancashire College Sixty Five Years Ago' in *TCHS* 14/3 (1943) for an account of student life 1878–84.

[104] The Official Handbook to the bazaar survives in the College Archive.

over £12,000, but brought a closer relationship between the churches and the College.

The large sum raised not only wiped out the debt on the extensions but averted a threat to the staff salaries and possible redundancies. The Education Committee now saw the opportunity to propose the establishment of a proper theology faculty in the College, with six chairs in New Testament, Old Testament, philosophy, church history with systematic theology, philosophy of religion, and pastoral work with homiletics. This ambition was never realised, but they revealed the greater aspirations of the College. A quarter of the students were now graduates, and the association with Owens College,[105] and after 1871 occasionally with Cambridge (where W. H. Bennett won all three theological prizes in 1881), made it more realistic to seek to confine the College to theological education. Many of the students were now entered for the examinations of the Senatus Academicus, a body representative of nine Nonconformist theological colleges, whose first examinations were held in 1880.

At the time of the bazaar, there were three members of staff in addition to Caleb Scott. When W. C. Russell, the tutor, had moved to Scotland in 1875 he had been replaced by James Muscutt Hodgson, a former student (Lancashire 1862–5, after graduating and winning prizes at Glasgow) who returned after a ten-year pastorate in Uttoxeter.[106] For the first seven years he combined the role of tutor with some administrative work for the denomination in Manchester, until in 1882, after a brief threat of redundancy, he was appointed to a chair in the science of religion and apologetics. He was a scholar whose position in the College was never quite secure, and whose gifts were not properly recognised until he moved to Edinburgh in 1894 as principal of the Theological Hall of the Congregational churches of Scotland.[107]

Alfred Newth had died suddenly in the autumn of 1875. Most of his work was taken over by Thomas Martin Herbert,[108] a former student of Spring Hill. After three pastorates, made difficult by problems with his voice, Herbert's appointment as professor of philosophy and church

[105] In 1880 the Victoria University was constituted as a degree-giving body alongside Owens College as a teaching body. University College, Liverpool was incorporated into Victoria University in 1884, and Yorkshire College, Leeds in 1887. There was no theology faculty at the Victoria University until 1904.

[106] James Muscutt Hodgson (1841–1923). See *CYB 1924* 97–8.

[107] He was awarded the degree of D.Sc. by Edinburgh University in 1882, and the honorary DD degree in 1888 by the University of Glasgow. In 1887, during a reorganisation of teaching responsibilities, his post was under threat, and the Committee was divided over his re-appointment. He continued on a somewhat unsatisfactory basis until his move to Edinburgh in 1894. He published *Theologia Pectoris: Outlines of Religious Faith and Doctrine Founded on Intuition and Experience* (Edinburgh 1898) and *Religion and the Quest of the Ideal* (London 1911).

[108] Thomas Martin Herbert (1835–77). See *CYB 1879* 320–1.

history at Manchester seemed to open up new and more fulfilling opportunities for his gifts. But his sudden death a year later put an end to those hopes. Hebrew and Old Testament, which Alfred Newth had also taught, were put in the hands of Alexander Thomson,[109] current (1875) Chairman of the Congregational Union and minister of Rusholme Road Chapel, who combined teaching and pastoral ministry until his death at the age of 80 in 1895. He too was a former student of Spring Hill, having previously graduated at Aberdeen, and having spent 13 years as professor of biblical literature at the Congregational Theological Hall in Edinburgh before coming to Rusholme. He was an enthusiastic linguist – 'the reading of Arabic was for many years his favourite diversion during his summer holidays'[110] – but not an advocate of German biblical criticism. Though he was much respected as a minister, 'he drove in class with very slack reins, and his mind was hermetically sealed against modern scientific views in criticism.'[111] It was said that he kept the College Library copy of Wellhausen's *Prolegomena to the History of Israel* permanently in his own study so that it might do no 'harm' to any enterprising and intelligent student. His long years at the College began when he was 60 and did not coincide with his most energetic period.

In 1880 George Lyon Turner[112] of Hackney College was appointed professor of philosophy and church history. There was no doubt about his interest in early Nonconformity, as his transcription and editing of *Original Records of Nonconformity Under Persecution and Indulgence* (three volumes, London 1911–14) revealed, but he was not a very successful teacher, and in 1884 the Committee received complaints about the presentation of his lectures.

By 1885 concern was being expressed about the supply of candidates for ministry. The peak year of 1879, with 61 students on the roll, had now passed. In 1884 the number had fallen back to 42. This led to the first suggestion that Lancashire Independent College should invite representatives of Rotherham and Airedale Colleges, now in process of amalgamation, to consider joining Lancashire in a triple union (in Manchester). But local loyalties were only to be overcome by the severest of financial crises. It having taken the two Yorkshire Colleges 35 years to reach this stage, it was not surprising that Principal Scott reported to the Committee that feeling in Yorkshire was averse to such a suggestion. The opening of Mansfield College as a Nonconformist theological hall in Oxford in 1886, after long debates about the desirability or otherwise of a Nonconformist presence in one of the two ancient universities, which

109 Alexander Thomson (1815–95). See *CYB 1896* 241–3.

110 Caleb Scott, *In Memoriam: Alexander Thomson MA DD* (Manchester 1895) 9.

111 Robert Mackintosh, quoted in L. S. Peake, *Arthur Samuel Peake: A Memoir* (London 1930) 132.

112 George Lyon Turner (1844–1920). See *CYB 1921* 119–20.

were still dominated by, though no longer exclusive to, Anglicanism, was to change the context of Congregational ministerial education. Mansfield was a national rather than a provincial college. There were many generous subscribers to Mansfield's building fund in both Manchester and Liverpool, and this had an effect, temporarily, on financial support for the Lancashire College.

When the College Jubilee was celebrated in 1893, there was much cause for pride, as well as some for regret. The number of students had risen again to 43. The principal had been awarded an honorary DD by the University of St Andrews in 1890, and he was regarded as a wise and trusted counsellor as a governor of Owens College. 310 students had completed the College course. At least five former students[113] had been elected to the chair of the Congregational Union, and a sixth (G. S. Barrett) was elected for the year 1894.

Joseph Thompson was invited to write a history of the College to date, and this was published in 1893 as *Lancashire Independent College 1843–93*. The memory of the Davidson affair was still vivid for many people, and not all wounds were healed. Thompson gave a good deal of space to the affair, and some readers felt that in his anxiety to make amends to Davidson he had been unfair to other participants in the controversy.[114] Several speakers at the Jubilee celebrations spoke apologetically of the events of 1857.

The main address at the Jubilee celebrations was given by Andrew Martin Fairbairn, principal of Mansfield College, Oxford, the towering intellectual figure of English Congregationalism (apart from R. W. Dale, who by then was already in his final illness). He had a deep belief that 'of all the things we know and possess, the greatest institution is the Christian ministry', and made a passionate plea to the churches 'to supply us with their choicest sons,' and to the college to 'make theology able to live amid the sciences that command and that exercise the intellect of man'.

New Horizons 1893–1914

While the number of students in the College never reached a total of 50 again, and after a peak of 48 in 1895 fluctuated between 37 and 20, the intellectual horizons of the College were expanding as links with the new University became stronger. In 1894 the Committee was able to report that all but two of the students were either graduates or undergraduates.

[113] Enoch Mellor (1863), Alexander Raleigh (1868), J. Guinness Rogers (1874), J. A. Macfadyen (1882) and John Brown (1891).

[114] See entry for 20 November 1893, LIC Committee Minute Book VII 1882–94, NCA, JRL.

When James Hodgson left for Edinburgh in 1894 his place was taken by Robert Mackintosh,[115] who was to teach in the College for the next 36 years under four different principals. Mackintosh was born in Dunoon, the son of a minister who left the Church of Scotland for the Free Church at the time of the Disruption. After gaining a first class degree in philosophy and several prizes at the University of Glasgow, where he was much influenced by Edward Caird, he entered New College, Edinburgh, to prepare for the ministry. Here he was disappointed that 'we had no breath of modern theological life in the system of doctrine taught us. Our Professor was an arch-Calvinist, and one who loved to put a keen edge of paradox upon his statements of doctrine.'[116] There followed a period of further study in Jena and Marburg (he was only the third Lancashire professor – after Davidson and Robert Halley – to have studied in Germany) and a very brief period as assistant minister in Dundee followed by a visit to New Zealand to improve his health. His first book, *Christ and the Jewish Law*, was published in 1886. He then moved south to Manchester as assistant to the Presbyterian minister at Withington. During this decade he was 'fighting for life as a Christian, and for liberty as a preacher from the fetters of a seventeenth-century creed'.[117] This 'ordeal of religious doubt' led him towards Congregationalism, and his article on 'The Genius of Congregationalism' in *Essays Congregational and Catholic* (ed. A. Peel, London 1931) reveals to what extent he had integrated this church polity into the core of his Christian faith. In 1890 he returned to Scotland as minister of Irving Street Congregational Church, Dumfries, and it was from here that after four years he was invited back to Manchester to the Lancashire College.

He was appointed to teach ethics, Christian sociology and apologetics; later he taught the philosophy of religion (as well as acting as Dean of the Faculty) in the University. Teaching was not his forte: 'Mac had no faintest idea of the art of teaching,' wrote one of his old students, who then added that 'we did at length get some inkling of the meaning of his lectures and some insight into one of the finest minds in all the realms of British scholarship.'[118] He gave rather a different view, when at the end of his life his recollection of his first years at the College was of the Lancashire students complaining that he did not dictate notes as others did, but expected them to write their own from his discursive lecturing, and that when asked to repeat something, he did so in 'different language'. When the senior students refused to attend his lectures, a

[115] Robert Mackintosh (1858–1933). See Alan P. F. Sell, *Robert Mackintosh: Theologian of Integrity* (Bern 1977), and 'The Life and Work of Robert Mackintosh 1858–1933' in *JURCHS* 1/3 (1973) 79–90.

[116] R. Mackintosh, 'My Experiments in Authorship' in *CQ* 9 (1931) 279.

[117] R. Mackintosh, *Christianity and Sin* (London 1913) 107.

[118] B. G. Theobald in the College Magazine for October 1933.

compromise was reached whereby they were to submit sociology essays to him for discussion in class, a system which he felt worked well.[119] His many books and articles were in the fields of both apologetics and biblical studies.[120] He contributed to the eleventh edition of the *Encyclopaedia Britannica* (including a long article on 'theology'), and to Peake's *Commentary* in 1919. Despite the alleged deficiencies of his teaching methods, he was much respected. His later colleague as principal, A. J. Grieve, wrote of him as 'a man whose heart and mind, saintliness and scholarship, Congregationalism too largely overlooked: it would have honoured itself indeed in calling him to the Chair of the Union.'[121]

When Alexander Thomson died in 1895, the way was open for more critical biblical teaching. The College was now able to benefit from the teaching of one of the early twentieth century's most distinguished biblical scholars, Arthur Samuel Peake.[122] Peake was the son of a Primitive Methodist minister and throughout his life remained loyal to his Methodist roots at the same time as developing deep ecumenical sympathies. At St John's College, Oxford, he gained a first class honours degree in theology. He was greatly influenced by three fine biblical scholars who were then teaching in Oxford, William Sanday, T. K. Cheyne and S. R. Driver, and by the church historian Edwin Hatch; but most of all by A. M. Fairbairn, Principal of the new Mansfield College. 'I regard his lectures as the most powerful formative influence which I received from any of my teachers,' he said, adding later, 'It was a wonderfully steadying thing that a man who knew the whole range of theological and philosophical literature, who had thoroughly sounded the worst that could be said against Christianity by its ablest opponents, nevertheless believed wholeheartedly and with intensity of conviction in the truth of Christianity.'[123] He won a fellowship at Merton College and thus became the first Nonconformist to hold a theology fellowship at Oxford, and combined this non-teaching role with a lecturership to which Fairbairn invited him at Mansfield College. In 1892 he was

[119] R. Mackintosh, 'My Experiments in Authorship', *CQ* 9 (1931).

[120] They included *A First Primer of Apologetics* (London 1900), *Hegel and Hegelianism* (Edinburgh 1903), *Albrecht Ritschl and his School* (London 1915), *Historic Theories of the Atonement* (London 1920) and a commentary on Thessalonians and Corinthians in the Westminster Commentary series (London 1909).

[121] Quoted in C. E. Surman, *Alexander James Grieve: A Biographical Sketch* (Manchester 1953) 51.

[122] Arthur Samuel Peake (1865–1929). See L. S. Peake, *Arthur Samuel Peake: A Memoir* (London 1930), J. T. Wilkinson, *Arthur Samuel Peake: A Biography* (London 1971), and *DNB 1922–30*.

[123] 'Some Reminiscences of Dr Fairbairn' quoted in Wilkinson 27. It was a source of great pride to him to be able to present Fairbairn to the Chancellor of Manchester University to receive the University's first honorary DD in 1908.

induced to leave Oxford for Manchester in order to take responsibility for the curriculum at the new Primitive Methodist college established by Sir William Hartley (Hartley College), where he did much to raise the educational standards of the ministry of the Methodist churches. For many years, until pressure of work compelled him to withdraw in 1912, he was able to combine this post with teaching at the Lancashire College. 'Had he been a Congregationalist outright he could have done no more for us,' wrote Robert Mackintosh.[124] He was also to play a leading role in the Theology Faculty when this was established in the University in 1904.

The first proposal for a Faculty of Theology in Manchester was put forward by A. S. Wilkins and the principal of Owens College in 1890. But the University, which at that time had to take account of opinion in Leeds and Liverpool as well as Manchester, was divided; John Owens had felt strongly about the injustice of 'university tests' and suspicion of ecclesiastical domination lingered on. There was a new openness to the proposal, however, when the Victoria University of Manchester, alongside separate universities in both Leeds and Liverpool, was founded in 1903, incorporating Owens College a year later; the Faculty of Theology was created in the same year (1904), and the new (postgraduate) degree of Bachelor of Divinity instituted.[125] Three new professorial chairs were established, and Peake was appointed to the Rylands Chair (endowed by Mrs Rylands) in Biblical Criticism and Exegesis, the first Nonconformist to hold a chair in theology in any English university. In due course he was appointed Dean of the Faculty. He brought great distinction to the task, and helped to lay the foundation for one of the foremost English university theological departments. 'Peake's knowledge of current literature, both native and foreign, in the field of biblical studies, was as nearly exhaustive as one man's knowledge can be,' wrote his successor in the Rylands Chair, C. H. Dodd.[126] He was not a radical, but a judicious interpreter of new biblical scholarship.[127]

From the first, it was the theological colleges of Manchester which in effect formed the Faculty. There were eight: Lancashire Independent College, Didsbury Wesleyan College, the Baptist College at Rusholme, Hartley Primitive Methodist College, the Moravian College at Fairfield,

[124] Quoted Wilkinson 66.

[125] See Edward Fiddes, *Chapters in the History of Owens College and of Manchester University 1851–1914* (Manchester 1937) 155–9, and *Inaugural Lectures Delivered by Members of the Faculty of Theology* (edited A. S. Peake, Manchester 1905).

[126] C. H. Dodd, 'A. S. Peake' in *DNB 1922–30* 658.

[127] His best-known work was the *Commentary on the Bible* (London 1919) which he edited, but he produced many other influential works, including *The Problem of Suffering in the Old Testament* (London 1904) and *The Bible: Its Origin, its Significance, and its Abiding Worth* (London 1913).

the Unitarian Home Missionary College, Victoria Park United Methodist College and the Anglican Egerton Hall. Their lectures were to be included in those of the Faculty, on condition that they were open to all members of the Faculty, and that they were given by their own members of staff. Much was therefore now studied ecumenically; thus for example, students from Egerton Hall and Hartley College came to lectures at Whalley Range. In order to avoid any charge of indoctrination, comparative religion was to be an obligatory subject, and it was laid down that no examination question was to offend any conscience. It was decided in the spirit of John Owens' rule that 'nothing will be introduced in the matter or mode of education in reference to any religious or theological subject which shall be reasonably offensive to the conscience of any student.' The teaching was divided between the University and the theological colleges in more or less equal proportions.

One of the less satisfactory results in practice was that systematic theology was not properly taught in either College or University; the emphasis in teaching doctrine was entirely historical. 'With an altogether unwarranted confidence in student human nature, our pastors and masters seemed to take the view that, having been presented with the historical and philosophical material, we might be safely left to work out our own theological salvation, instead of being turned out to machine-made pattern.'[128]

On the eve of the creation of the new Faculty, Caleb Scott, who had taken part in the discussions about its foundation and who had been a much respected member of the Court of Governors of Owens College, began to decline in health, and it was agreed that the time had come for him to retire – he was now 71. He had been elected chairman of the Congregational Union for the year 1902 but was not well enough to deliver his chairman's addresses. The Committee agreed to seek to replace him by a man with practical experience of preaching and pastoral work who could occupy a chair of pastoral theology and homiletics, and they turned first to R. F. Horton, minister of Lyndhurst Road Congregational Church, Hampstead, since 1883, and previously the first Nonconformist fellow of an Oxford college. He refused this as he had refused many other invitations, partly on grounds of health and partly because he believed his church still needed him. The Committee then modified their requirements and turned to Walter Adeney,[129] tutor in New Testament and church history at New College, London, who had previously held a pastorate in Acton for 17 years. He was a member and elder of Horton's church in Hampstead. He accepted, and for the next ten years presided over the College, lectured in the University and acted

[128] E. J. Price (student at the Lancashire College 1903–10), 'The Place of Systematic Theology', *CQ* 1945 122.

[129] Walter Frederick Adeney (1849–1920). See *CYB 1921* 102.

as Dean in the Theology Faculty, and contributed a weekly article on the Free Churches to the *Manchester Guardian*. He was editor of the Century Bible commentaries. One of his innovations at the College was to hold regular staff meetings. While he was in Manchester he published his most important book, *The Greek and Eastern Churches* (Edinburgh 1908), and was elected Chairman of the Congregational Union for the year 1912–13.

The question of college amalgamation had not disappeared, and there was further negotiation with the Yorkshire college, when Walter Adeney announced his wish to retire in 1913. The first collaboration had begun in 1904, when George Currie Martin was appointed New Testament professor at both colleges, dividing his time almost equally between them. This arrangement lasted for five years until Martin left to take up a post with the London Missionary Society. He was a lively presence. The students much appreciated the conversations when he, the principal and A. S. Peake, all dined in college together: '... those memorable jousts [of A. S. Peake] with Adeney and Currie Martin made tolerable the worst meal ever served.'[130]

The growing co-operation between the denominational colleges through the University Theology Faculty coincided with the beginnings of the ecumenical movement, and with the university element in that movement, the Student Christian Movement (SCM). The SCM was strong in Manchester, and one of the Lancashire students, McEwan Lawson, was president of the British SCM and attended the International SCM conference in Constantinople in 1911. It was also a time of growing awareness of social responsibility, and the students had begun a settlement in Hulme, which was handed over to an interdenominational committee in 1913. But few could foresee the disaster which was about to engulf most of Europe and bring sharp challenges to Christianity.

A later proposal, in 1913, that Manchester should provide arts courses and Bradford theological courses was not approved. The Committee therefore sought a new principal. They approached first J. D. Jones, minister of Richmond Hill, Bournemouth, and then Douglas Mackenzie of Hartford College, Connecticut. Both refused. They therefore turned to W. H. Bennett,[131] a brilliant former student who had gained a first class degree at Cambridge and a fellowship at St John's College after studying at the Lancashire College. He had spent four years at Rotherham as professor of biblical literature and church history before that college closed, then spent 25 years as professor of Hebrew and Old Testament at Hackney College, where he was also Dean of the Theology Faculty of the University of London. By the time he moved to Manchester he was the

[130] Lancashire Independent College Students' Newsletter, autumn 1929, on the occasion of Peake's death.

[131] William Henry Bennett (1855–1920). See *CYB 1921* 103.

author of several works on the Old Testament, a few of them in collaboration with his predecessor W. F. Adeney, and had an international scholarly reputation. There could have been little awareness as he began his principalship of the forthcoming disaster, which was seriously to disrupt the work of the College.

7
Yorkshire

Mid-Victorian Bradford

In 1833, when Airedale College opened on the outskirts of Bradford, across the Pennines from Manchester, the surrounding area was one of rapidly growing prosperity and population. Bradford was now not only the centre of the British worsted industry, but of the world's, and was to be called 'Worstedopolis'. It had overtaken East Anglia as the predominant English centre by 1800, and improved transport facilities and plenty of coal and iron provided the conditions for rapid growth. In 1801 there was just one mill; 50 years later, there were 129, employing almost a quarter of the population. At the same time the growth of the population was phenomenal, even more rapid than that of Manchester. In 1801 it was just over 13,000. In each of the decades from 1811 until 1851 it increased by at least 50 per cent, so that by 1851 it had reached 104,000. By 1911 it was over 288,000.[1] Yet it was not incorporated as a borough until 1847 (in the face of considerable opposition) and did not become a city until 1897. It became the centre of an Anglican diocese in 1919. Bradford survived its rapid industrialisation with remarkably little civil disorder (apart from a strike of woolcombers and handloom weavers in 1825).

The centre of the town lay near the Aire valley, and from its mills smoke rose to blacken buildings and pollute the air in the surrounding hilly areas such as Undercliffe, where the College stood. There was a stark contrast between the rows of back-to-back houses where mill-workers lived and the large stone houses which the mill-owners built for themselves away from the smoke. Yet little was done to improve housing and working conditions until incorporation in 1847.

It was a proud town which vied with Leeds (only eight miles away, but always a quite distinctive community) to build the most impressive buildings. St George's Hall was built in the early 1850s, the 'Venetian Gothic' Wool Exchange a decade later, and the Town Hall, with its echoes of the Signoria in Florence, in 1873.[2]

[1] 1 These figures are for the area which was included in the borough of Bradford in 1847. They are taken from the Parliamentary Papers, Census of England and Wales 1801, 1851, 1911, quoted in D. G. Wright and J. A. Jowitt (ed), *Victorian Bradford: Essays in Honour of Jack Reynolds* (Bradford 1982) 37.

[2] See the chapter on Leeds in Asa Briggs, *Victorian Cities* (London 1963) for a discussion of the differences between Leeds and Bradford.

Figure 4: Airedale Independent College, Undercliffe, Bradford
Source: W. Scruton, Pen and Pencil Pictures of Old Bradford *(Bradford 1889)*

Nonconformity was very strong in Bradford; in 1851, according to the Religious Census of that year, Bradford had the highest proportion of Nonconformists in any English urban area, except for Rochdale and Dudley.[3] And among the Nonconformists, the Congregationalists were the most influential, though the Wesleyan Methodists were the most numerous, and the Baptists had a notable preacher in J. P. Chown[4] at Sion Chapel. The presence not only of the Airedale College but also of Horton Baptist College[5] strengthened the position of the Nonconformists. In the middle years of the century, the most influential local paper, the *Bradford Observer*, founded in 1834 under the editorship and later the proprietorship of the Congregationalist William Byles, was an influential and effective forum for the middle-class Liberalism of most Nonconformists. One of the paper's first campaigns was to support the parliamentary candidature (unsuccessful) of George Hadfield as a disestablishment candidate in the election of 1835, when Bradford returned a Member of Parliament for the first time. Byles's influence

[3] Wright and Jowitt, 37.

[4] Joseph Parbery Chown (1821–86). See D. Milner, 'J. P. Chown 1821–86' in *Baptist Quarterly* 25 (1973) 15–40.

[5] Horton Baptist College was founded in 1804. Later in the century it moved to Rawdon.

extended further as a founder member of the Bradford Reform Society (amalgamated with the Bradford Radical Association to form the Bradford United Reform Club in 1841). He was a member, deacon and trustee of Horton Lane Congregational Church,[6] where the cultured Jonathan Glyde was minister from 1835 until his early death in 1854, and was the first layman to be elected chairman of the Yorkshire Congregational Union, in 1877. Four of his fellow members were among the first seven mayors of Bradford.[7]

The second mayor of Bradford, and the most wealthy Bradford Congregationalist of the nineteenth century was Titus Salt,[8] alpaca and mohair manufacturer, who was created a baronet in 1869. 'It was said that he made a thousand pounds each day before other people were out of bed.'[9] Having discovered a method of using alpaca and mohair in worsted fabrics in 1836, he made his fortune. His great achievement was the establishment not only of a very successful business, but of the model village of Saltaire (strictly outside Bradford, but on the outskirts) for his employees, with an unusual and elegant Congregational church in classical style. He was MP for the town 1859–61 and a generous benefactor to religious causes, including Airedale College.

In the late eighteenth and early nineteenth centuries the work of Anglicans such as William Grimshaw in Haworth and Henry Venn in Huddersfield had created a climate of co-operation between the denominations. But the coming of William Scoresby as Vicar of Bradford in 1839 put an end to this. Scoresby[10] was determined to assert the primacy of Anglicanism in the town, and clashed with the Nonconformists over church rates, parochial schools, factory hours, and through his sponsoring of a Church Institute in response to the Nonconformist-dominated Mechanics Institute. The confrontational atmosphere, in which religion and politics were inseparable, continued after Scoresby left, and in the 1860s Bradford experienced four 'vitriolic elections'; the Liberal candidate at three of them was Edward Miall, editor of the *Nonconformist* and leading figure in the Anti-State Church Association.[11] He was finally elected in 1869, and it was as MP for Bradford that he moved the

[6] The church was founded in 1781. Its new building of 1863 seated 1500.

[7] Robert Milligan (the first, in 1847), Henry Forbes, Samuel Smith and Henry Brown.

[8] Titus Salt (1803–76). See R. Balgarnie, *Sir Titus Salt* (London 1877, reprinted Settle 1970), J. Reynolds, *The Great Paternalist: Titus Salt and the Growth of Nineteenth-Century Bradford* (London 1983), Clyde Binfield, 'Titus Salt' in J. O. Baylen and N. J. Grossman, *Biographical Dictionary of Modern British Radicals* vol 2 1830–70 (Brighton 1984) and *DNB*.

[9] Asa Briggs, 157.

[10] William Scoresby (1789–1857), Vicar of Bradford 1839–47. See R. E. Scoresby-Jackson, *The Life of William Scoresby* (London 1861) and *DNB*.

[11] Edward Miall (1809–81). See *DNB*.

disestablishment of the English Church in the Commons in 1871. The other Bradford MP, who sat from 1861 until 1886, was W. E. Forster, who was felt to have 'betrayed' the Radical cause with his Education Bill in 1870.

Airedale College at Undercliffe was thus close to a town of lively controversy, radical sympathy, social problems, great wealth and great poverty, and was well supported by the predominantly Liberal, Nonconformist worsted manufacturers of Bradford.

Airedale Independent College: Undercliffe 1834–76

Twelve students moved into the new building at Undercliffe on 3 March 1834, eleven of them from Idle, together with one new student. Ten days later, William Vint, the aging tutor who had reluctantly agreed to move from Idle, died. The committee, after an abortive approach to George Redford,[12] had already appointed a new resident principal to open the college in October 1833, Walter Scott.[13]

Walter Scott was minister of Rothwell (then usually known as Rowell), Northamptonshire. He was a native of the same part of Northumberland as Vint, and had grown up in the same church. After studying at Hoxton Academy in London under Robert Simpson (a former Heckmondwike student) from 1808 until 1812, he settled at Rothwell, where 'his once empty chapel became filled, even inconveniently,' despite 'a husky and monotonous voice'.[14] During 15 years at Rothwell, he took students (about 70 altogether) into his home for tuition preparatory to entering Hoxton (Highbury after 1826) Academy.[15] Thus he arrived in Bradford with considerable experience of dealing with students. He was to teach divinity, biblical criticism, philosophy and Hebrew. One of his successors, A. M. Fairbairn, described him as 'a Puritan if ever there was one, stern, upright, severely conscientious, yet with a quaint humour of his own'.[16]

He wished to continue combining tutorial work with pastoral charge, and therefore College Chapel was built for him nearby in Church Bank and opened in 1839. It held 800, and was added to Horton Lane and Salem churches as the third Congregational church within the township. Once a week it was used for 'sermon class'.

The principal was to have an assistant to teach classics and mathe-

[12] Minister of Angel Street Congregational Church, Worcester.

[13] Walter Scott (1779–1858). See *CYB 1859* 218–21. His eighth child was Caleb Scott, later principal of Lancashire Independent College.

[14] *CYB 1859* 219.

[15] See G. F. Nuttall, 'Training for Hoxton and Highbury: Walter Scott of Rothwell and his Pupils' in *JURCHS* 5/8 (1996) 477–83.

[16] *CYB 1903* 34.

matics, Thomas Rawson Taylor,[17] a native of Bradford who had attended Leaf Square School in Manchester, and, after a few years in business, Idle Academy. A brief pastorate in Sheffield was followed by a period of ill-health before he began work as tutor at Airedale. Sadly, his promise was cut short with his death exactly a year later. He left much of his library to the college.

His successor was William Benton Clulow,[18] one of Walter Scott's early students at Rothwell before entering Hoxton Academy in 1819. He was a devoted and able scholar of independent thinking, whose theological exploration was to bring him into conflict with some of the college subscribers. Members of the College staff had to sign a declaration that they would teach the doctrines contained in the Shorter Catechism of the Westminster Assembly of 1643. In August 1842 some concern was expressed about his views on 'the Christian Sabbath', though Walter Scott did his best to defend him. 'Some opinions are held by Mr Clulow not entirely in accordance with those generally received by our Churches, but these were not deemed of so much importance as to affect his retaining his office as Classical Tutor,' reported the Minute Book.[19] However, he must have been left feeling uncomfortable, for he resigned six months later, and spent the rest of his life, first in Bradford and then in his birthplace, Leek, as a private scholar, thus depriving the Congregational colleges of an unusual and gifted man of considerable literary gifts. While the support of local churches and prominent laymen was a great strength to theological colleges, dependence on their financial support sometimes threatened the proper independence and intellectual integrity of the theological teachers and scholars.

Two further tutors served with Walter Scott: Daniel Fraser and Henry Brown Creak. Fraser (appointed in 1843 to succeed Clulow) eventually followed Scott as principal and he will be considered later. Creak's appointment in 1848 as a third tutor, in philosophy, was made possible by a further generous gift of £8,000 from Mrs Mary Bacon. Creak, the son of a Congregational minister in Yarmouth, was an early student at Spring Hill, and came to Airedale at the age of 27 after a short pastorate at Atherstone.[20]

There was now a regular system of written examinations, marked by outside examiners, who were usually scholarly Congregational ministers in pastoral charge. The linguistic study of biblical texts still played a large

[17] Thomas Rawson Taylor (1807–35). See W. S. Matthews, *Memoirs and Select Remains of Rev Thomas Rawson Taylor* (London 1836) and *Congregational Magazine* 1837, 327.

[18] William Benton Clulow (1802–82). See *CYB 1883* 269–71 and *DNB*.

[19] Airedale Independent Academy Committee Minute Book 1831–48, entry for 28 December 1842. NCA.

[20] Henry Brown Creak (1821–64). See *CYB 1865* 230–2.

part in the curriculum. In 1840, for example, the students were examined in 32 chapters of Isaiah in Hebrew (which they collated with the Greek Septuagint); in Ezra in Aramaic; in Matthew and six chapters of Mark in Syriac; and in most of the New Testament epistles in Greek. They also studied Greek and Latin classical texts, Hugh Blair's *Lectures on Rhetoric*, parts of Euclid, Mosheim's *Ecclesiastical History*[21] and works by Fénelon. Doctrinal studies were based on the lectures by the principal. By the 1850s the works studied for doctrine were listed in the *Annual Reports*. They included John Pye Smith's *Scripture Testimony to the Messiah* (two volumes, London 1818), Joseph Bellamy's *True Religion Delineated* (London 1841), and Ralph Wardlaw's *Systematic Theology* (three volumes, Edinburgh 1856, 1857).

The somewhat ostentatious stone building in which the comparatively small community of students (ranging in number between 12 and 20) and staff worked was in the Grecian style with a large portico, high above the steep hill out of the Aire valley, with views for miles beyond.[22] But the stone was soon blackened by smoke rising from the valley below, and its exposed position left it open to battering by wind and storm. It was very cold. The students, each of whom was provided with a study ten feet by eight, with a fireplace, on the ground floor, and a bedroom, ten feet square, on the floor above, were required to provide their own coal, candles and soap, and to clean their own rooms. The principal's house was at the front of the main building, and students who were not away preaching had tea there on Sundays.

The College was surrounded by lawns, gardens and shrubberies, and not far away was the ground which was to become Peel Park in 1854. At first it was a pleasant ambience, apart from the smoke. But after 20 years, the opening of the 26 acre Undercliffe Cemetery adjoining the College in 1854 created a rather different environment, and increased doubts about the suitability of the site for a college. One architect who was consulted gave it as his opinion that the site was better adapted for a castle of defence than for an educational institution. Charles Berry, however, who was a student from 1870 until 1874, thought the site had advantages: 'I studied theology in full view of the busy industrial city of Bradford, lying at the foot of the hill on which the college stands, and this gave an intensely practical turn to my thinking, forcing me to regard all problems from the standpoint of actual life.'[23]

[21] Johann Lorenz von Mosheim (c.1694–1755) was a Lutheran scholar. The book used at Airedale was probably a one-volume English version of extracts from the original German version of five volumes published in 1726. In 1838 a volume of examination questions and answers on Mosheim's work for the use of 'students in divinity' was published in London.

[22] The building has disappeared, but is still commemorated by Airedale College Road and Airedale College Terrace.

[23] J. S. Drummond, *Charles A. Berry DD* (London 1899).

About 80 students were educated in the College while Walter Scott was principal, and many of them were able to take the degrees of London University, with which the College was affiliated in 1841. While the students did regularly go out preaching, the earlier evangelical motivation behind the work of the Idle Academy was moderated by the growing recognition of the need now for *educated* ministers. The Report for 1837–8 had reminded the subscribers of 'the growing importance of Academical Institutions for the Christian ministry, and the necessity of redoubled efforts to elevate their standard, both literary and intellectually' and continued:

> The history of the church seems to show, that while in every epoch some theological novelty has been in the ascendant, the victims of the delusion have commonly been those least disciplined by careful study, applied, in humble dependence on divine illumination, to the sublime doctrines and discoveries of the sacred records.[24]

The Report for 1844–5 referred to 'the apostate spirit of popery in the form of Puseyism' as a further sign of the need for a properly educated Congregational ministry.

Walter Scott resigned in 1856 at the age of 77.[25] Some time before he left, discussions about a possible amalgamation with the Rotherham College to form one Yorkshire college had taken place. An approach was made from Rotherham early in 1850, and representatives of the two colleges had met on 20 February. The advantages of such an amalgamation – more tutors and greater financial resources in one college – were generally accepted, and the majority agreed that Bradford, as an important commercial railway centre (the railway had arrived in 1846), should be the location. But the absence of 'a thorough cordiality and unity of opinion' on Rotherham's part decided the Airedale committee against immediate agreement.[26] Negotiations dragged on intermittently, and it was to be another 38 years before a united Yorkshire Independent College opened in 1888. In the meantime and until then, an inordinate amount of time and energy was spent on frustrating discussions.

Walter Scott's successor as principal and theological tutor was Daniel Fraser,[27] classics tutor since 1843. Fraser was brought up and educated at school and university in Glasgow (where he won several prizes) and studied under Ralph Wardlaw at the Theological Academy. When one of his brothers, who was minister of Chapel Street Congregational Church

[24] *College Report 1837–8* 8.

[25] He accepted an honorary pastorate at Shanklin on the Isle of Wight, but died in 1858.

[26] Airedale College Minute Book 1848–55, entry for 3 April 1850.

[27] Daniel Fraser (1820–1902). See Lucy A. Fraser (ed) *Memoirs of Daniel Fraser* (London 1905) and *CYB 1903* 175–6.

in Blackburn, was asked on a visit to Yorkshire whether he knew of a suitable candidate to succeed W. B. Clulow at Airedale, he recommended his brother. The result was that Daniel Fraser came south to Bradford as classical tutor in 1843. He was not appointed principal immediately after Scott's departure, but in 1858, after another round of negotiations with Rotherham.

He was a normally quiet and reserved person, though fire could be drawn when he was called on to defend Nonconformist principles in public, 'not by any means venturesome in the domain of Theology,'[28] but 'possessed by an overmastering sense of duty'.[29] His regime was one of order and regular routine. One of his former students described the regular timetable of study with Dr Fraser. When the first bell went at 6.30 some students rose while others waited until the bell for prayers was rung at 6.55, dashing in to the library at the last minute to attend prayers taken according to a rota by both principal and students. After breakfast at 8.00, classes began at 9.00 and continued until 2.00; on one day a week sermon class took place from 1 until 2 p.m. Those who were taking a three-year course had one year of study in classics and mathematics, followed by two years of theology; those who were following a five-year course had two years of study in classics and mathematics, and three years of theology. After dinner at 2.00, the students were free to walk or, in the summer, play cricket in Peel Park; there were regular cricket matches against Rawdon Baptist College and Headingley Wesleyan College. Tea was served at 5.00, followed by private study and sermon preparation, or visits to meetings and lectures in the city centre. On Sundays the principal and his wife entertained students to tea, and it was not unknown for those who were going to preach in some outlying village in the evening to secrete some extra lumps of sugar to enhance their energy.

At first, Fraser was assisted by H. B. Creak (who died in 1864) as tutor in mathematics and philosophy, and by R. G. Hartley,[30] who came straight from the Lancashire College and Owens College, combining his tutorship with pastoral ministry at a new church in Windhill, Shipley. He left in 1863 to serve with the London Missionary Society in Madagascar, where he was involved in revising the Malagasy translation of the New Testament. These two tutors were in turn replaced by W. C. Shearer and Robert Harley. Shearer[31] was a diffident scholar who played little part in Bradford life, but who served the college faithfully as tutor in classics (later in philosophy and logic) over many years until 1902. Robert

[28] T. Willis, quoted in Fraser 91.
[29] D. Johnstone, quoted ibid 93.
[30] Richard Griffiths Hartley (1836–70). See *CYB 1871* 316–17.
[31] William Campbell Shearer (c.1832–1907) was a Scotsman, educated at Edinburgh University and Cheshunt College.

Harley[32] was a former student of Airedale, who achieved distinction in being elected as a Fellow of the Royal Society while minister at Brighouse. For four years he combined pastoral ministry with the post of mathematics and logic tutor at Airedale. He had a varied later career, in both teaching and pastoral ministry. Mathematics was his life-long interest, and he made distinguished contributions to the *Memoirs* of the Manchester Literary and Philosophical Society.

While Daniel Fraser may not have been particularly distinguished academically, had no substantial book to his credit, and did not regard it as part of his responsibility to deal with contemporary intellectual challenges to the Christian faith, he took a very active part in Bradford life. He was a Director of the Mechanics Institute, where he lectured frequently, a member of the Bradford School Board after 1870, and of the Bradford Library Committee, and one of those who helped to promote the Technical College. He was frequently to be heard on the public platforms of Bradford, notably during the education controversy of 1870, when Anglicans and Nonconformists battled over the issue of sectarian control of public education.[33] One of his students, James Drummond, recollected how, on the public platform

> our own Principal, called upon to voice the convictions of his stalwart fellow-townsmen on some burning public question, or to represent the Free Churches, did so with a stately grace, a chaste and dignified eloquence, a clearness, a cogency, a fire, together with a readiness and keenness of retort when challenged, that made us prouder of him than before.[34]

By the early 1860s, dissatisfaction with the building was being widely expressed, and in April 1863 the decision was taken to erect a new one. The first question to be resolved was whether or not a new site was to be chosen. Advice was sought from Dr William Burnie of Eldon Place. His report, dated 1 November 1864, concluded that the existing location was quite unsuitable for an educational institution for three reasons, which were, in order of significance: the bleakness of the position, the smoke, and the juxtaposition of a cemetery. 'I believe that much of the sickness which has prevailed in the College has been due to the original ill-construction of the place, in respect of drainage, ventilation and the admission of light.'[35] Another report from W. H. Crosland, architect, of Leeds, agreed that while the potentiality of the site for architectural display was unsurpassed, it was quite unsuitable on most other grounds. A new location was therefore sought, with the expectation that the new building might well house a joint college with Rotherham.

[32] Robert Harley (1828–1910). See *CYB 1911* 207 and *DNB*.

[33] W. E. Forster, promoter of the 1870 Education Act, was MP for Bradford.

[34] Quoted in Fraser, 104–5.

[35] MS Report on the Site of Airedale College in a Sanitary Point of View, NCA, JRL.

In 1870 the Committee heard that Sir Titus Salt was prepared to give £2,500 towards a new building, and that a site near Saltaire was thought to be appropriate. A complicated series of discussions, often but not always involving representatives from Rotherham, took place. Finally a site near Manningham Park, in Emm Lane, above the main Bradford–Shipley road, was purchased in 1873. A competition for plans was held, and the design of Messrs Lockwood and Mawson[36] was chosen in December.

The new college was to be non-residential for it was now felt more desirable that the students should not be separated from the life of the town during the week. Advice was sought from Samuel Newth, principal of New College, London, the only other non-residential Congregational college at the time. In the light of his advice, it was decided that the new building should include an assembly room to hold 300, which could be of use to the Congregational churches of the area, a muniment room for college and local church archives, a library, five lecture rooms, a dining hall, council room and principal's house.

The foundation stone was laid by Titus Salt (son of the alpaca manufacturer) on 16 October 1874. The land had cost £5,000 and the building and its fitting were to cost £21,000. These expenses were eventually covered through the sale of the old building and its adjoining land, and the £13,000 which was raised through subscriptions. While the new building was being completed, classes were held in the nearby Salem Chapel. The formal opening took place in June 1877.

The most difficult problem facing the Governors (as now constituted under the new Trust Deed) was that of the principalship of the newly-constituted college. Dr Fraser, who was now in his mid-fifties, was aware that he did not have the whole-hearted confidence of the education subcommittee, and this was confirmed when he attended a meeting at which, without prior warning, a minute was read stating that 'in order to [ensure] the success of the new College, it will be necessary to obtain the services of a new Theological Professor and President'.[37] It was understandable that when he was invited to assume the title of Principal Emeritus, to occupy the resident professor's house, and to continue to teach but not as theological professor, he refused, and offered his resignation. The committee was evenly divided over whether to accept it or not, but the chairman's casting vote determined the matter, and his resignation was accepted on 24 May 1876.

[36] Henry Francis Lockwood (1811–78) and William Mawson (1828–89) were in practice together in Bradford until 1874, when Lockwood moved to London. They were responsible for designing Bradford's Town Hall, Exchange and St George's Hall, and for several buildings in Saltaire, including the Congregational Church. See *The Builder* 36, 27 July 1878 and *Building News* 56, 3 May 1889, 639.

[37] Fraser 191.

Figure 5: Airedale Independent College, Emm Lane, Bradford (later the Yorkshire United Independent College)
Source: Congregational Year Book 1878

At the same meeting, five names were proposed as suitable principals: Eustace Conder, Henry Reynolds (principal of Cheshunt College), John Radford Thomson (minister at Mount Pleasant, Tunbridge Wells, and a tutor at New College, London), Robert Ainslie Redford (minister at Streatham Hill, and a tutor at New College) and John Brown Paton (principal of the Nottingham Congregational Institute). All refused. In August eight more names were put forward, and it was not until the last name was reached, and that not an English one, that an acceptance was received, from Andrew Martin Fairbairn, a minister of the Evangelical Union Church in Aberdeen. It proved to be the boldest and most forward-looking decision they could have made, for Fairbairn was set to become the greatest Congregational theologian of his generation, and indeed one of the outstanding British theologians and theological educators of the century. His nine years in Bradford transformed the status of the College, brought it into the forefront of Bradford life, and raised the whole standard of Congregational theological education.

Airedale Independent College: Emm Lane 1876–88

Andrew Martin Fairbairn[38] was minister of St Paul's Evangelical Union Church in Aberdeen, where he had not only established a fine reputation for preaching, but written his first book, *Studies in the Philosophy of Religion and History* (London 1876), contributed the first of his numerous articles to the *Contemporary Review*, and drawn large congregations of students to his Sunday evening lectures.

He was born to a family which belonged to the United Secession Church in Inverkeithing, Fife, but in his youth followed James Morison into the less strictly Calvinist Evangelical Union. Despite a very sparse early education, he entered the Evangelical Union Academy in Glasgow in 1857 at the age of 19 and attended some classes at Edinburgh University. Three years later he became minister of Bathgate Evangelical Union Church. Here he tried to make up for his earlier lack of education and worked prodigiously hard. But the more he read of the theology of his tradition the less could he accept it. He confessed to a friend that 'he had not an inch of ground beneath his feet'. In desperation and in a crisis of faith, he set off for Germany in 1865 in search of a theology which he could accept, realising that he might have to leave the ministry and make his way in future by journalism and writing. During a year spent listening to German university lectures and in conversation with other students he

[38] Andrew Martin Fairbairn (1838–1912). See W. B. Selbie, *The Life of Andrew Martin Fairbairn* (London 1914), *DNB 1912–21*, and Alan P. F. Sell, 'An Arminian, A Calvinist and a Liberal' in Sell, *Dissenting Thought*.

found a theology in which he could believe, 'a larger and nobler Christianity,' and returned to Bathgate a wiser and more mature Christian.[39] In a land 'seething with controversies' he learned from the professors 'that doubt was not sin but rather a growing pain of the soul, a means to a wider outlook and a clearer faith'.[40] For him, theology had now changed from 'a system doubted' to 'a system believed'; but 'the system believed was not the old system which had been doubted'.[41]

The theological system which he now began to create ultimately found expression in *The Place of Modern Theology* (London 1893), which was published after he had moved from Bradford to Oxford. We can however assume that the themes of that book were already being worked out in Fairbairn's teaching in Bradford. It was an attempt to provide the groundwork for a theological system through the historical records of the life of Jesus, now thought to be more accessible than ever before through the fruits of German biblical scholarship. Fairbairn tried to make a distinction between the historical Jesus and the Church's interpretation of Christ, and so, instead of taking the Church's creeds and traditions as a starting point, he attempted to construct a theology through the consciousness of Christ's relationship to God as Son of the Father. It has to be said that the first part of the book, a brilliant critical survey of Christian teaching about Christ, was more successful than the second, more constructive part, but altogether it revealed a fine, fearless theological mind.

Fairbairn's first public appearance in Bradford was in June 1877, when he gave an impassioned inaugural address on 'The Christian Ministry and its Preparatory Discipline'.[42] Immediately, Bradford Congregationalists knew that they had 'entered on a new dispensation'. By contrasting the concepts of priestly and prophetic ministry, he laid out his theology of the Christian ministry and of the way in which men should be prepared for it: 'Through the priest man seeks God, but through the prophet God seeks man; the essential aim of the first is by gifts and sacrifices to propitiate God, but the essential aim of the second is to make man so see and feel the divine truth and righteousness as to be lifted into fellowship with the Eternal.'[43]

A few years later, while he was still in Bradford, he brought the Congregational Union Assembly to its feet with a rousing address on 'The New Puritanism and the New Sacerdotalism,' contrasting the two opposing conceptions of the Christian Church which claimed allegiance

[39] See A. M. Fairbairn, 'Experience in Theology: A Chapter of Autobiography', *Contemporary Review* 91 (April 1907) for his later reflections on the experience.

[40] Selbie, 37.

[41] A. M. Fairbairn, 'Experience in Theology', 568.

[42] Published under that title (London 1877).

[43] Ibid 4–5.

in late nineteenth century England. The great challenge to 'the people called of God' was 'the creation of the new Puritanism'. Congregationalists, heirs of the Puritan tradition, were now free to realise their particular conception of the Church.[44] The medium of prophetic ministry was preaching, and men could become preachers only through long, patient study of biblical languages and texts, systematic theology, apologetics and ethics. Such study required the utmost concentration, and could only be pursued single-mindedly, not alongside other basic studies.

From the first, Fairbairn sought to separate the arts courses from the theology course, and to confine the teaching in his college to those who were already graduates. 'Theology ought not to be a first, but a final study,' for its study required a well-trained and well-equipped mind.[45] His determination to end the concurrent study of theology with general subjects was boundless. His colleague, Archibald Duff, reported: 'Dr Fairbairn's first vigorous blows were aimed at the removal of that fatal system. He spoke of it in season and out of season. He pleaded with the Governors; he lectured to the churches and the County Union. Within five years he had prevailed.'[46] He had had to persuade the practical and sometimes blunt Bradford businessmen among the governors that this scheme was viable as well as desirable. In 1882 the Governors agreed to the stipulation that no student could begin the theology course until he was either a graduate or could at least show a high proficiency in arts subjects. It may be that attempts to lure Fairbairn away from Bradford convinced the Governors that it was better to retain Fairbairn and bow to his ideas than to risk losing him. He was greatly tempted by an invitation to become principal of the Congregational Theological Hall in Edinburgh, and it was to the great relief of the Governors that he finally decided that it was his duty to remain in Bradford for the time being.

In 1884, by an official vote of the subscribers, it was agreed formally to separate the arts and theology courses, and the following year it was reported that 14 of the enrolled students were at universities – eight at Glasgow, five at Edinburgh and one at Cambridge (T. H. Martin, who actually continued at Mansfield College, Oxford, instead of returning to Bradford). In achieving this separation of the two aspects of the course before he left Bradford, Fairbairn had succeeded where the denominational colleges committee had so frequently failed.

He had a high view of theology, and as one greatly influenced by Hegel, laid an emphasis on philosophy as a basis for theological thinking.

[44] Address delivered to the autumn assembly of the Congregational Union at Hanley on 7 October 1885. Published as 'The Sacerdotal and the Puritan Idea' in A. M. Fairbairn, *Studies in Religion and Theology* (London 1910).

[45] Ibid 27.

[46] Quoted Selbie 90–1.

This was one reason for encouraging his students to take degrees in Scottish universities, where philosophy was an important subject in any arts course, before beginning the study of theology. The necessity for the agreement of faith and reason was one of the great principles underlying his thought: 'In every controversy concerning what is or what is not truth, reason and not authority is the supreme arbiter; the authority that decided against reason commits itself to a conflict which is certain to issue in its defeat.'[47] He set new intellectual standards for Congregational ministers. He would not allow his Bradford students to take the examinations of the Senatus Academicus because he thought the standard was too low. Edinburgh recognised his achievements by awarding an honorary DD in 1878 (the first of seven honorary degrees he was to receive), and by inviting him to give the first Muir Lectures in the Science of Religion in the years 1878 to 1882.

Under Fairbairn, much greater attention was given to systematic theology than previously, and a very full syllabus was worked out. The fact that one of the main textbooks was August Hahn's *Bibliothek der Symbole und Glaubens Regeln* (1842) gives some idea of the depth and seriousness of the study.

Fairbairn's two colleagues were W. Campbell Shearer, who moved from Undercliffe as philosophy tutor, and Archibald Duff.[48] Although Fairbairn was not a wholehearted supporter of modern biblical studies, he demonstrated his recognition of its significance by recommending Duff's appointment. Duff joined the College from a teaching post at McGill College, Montreal, as professor of Hebrew, Old Testament exegesis and (until such teaching was redundant) mathematics. Duff's career had been unusual in that although born in Scotland, he had received his education in Canada, whence his family moved when he was eleven, in the United States at Andover Newton Theological Seminary near Boston (then sometimes called 'the home of heretics'), and in Germany.[49] In Halle he had lived in the private hostel run by August Tholuck, and studied Hebrew, Arabic and Syriac. In Göttingen, he attended Ritschl's lectures on doctrinal thought. At the end of this period of study in Germany he first met Fairbairn on a visit to Aberdeen in 1875. He had acquired a thorough grounding in Semitic languages and an understanding of German critical methods, and on his arrival in Bradford he was considered 'advanced' in his opinions, but his patent evangelical faith and enthusiasm saved him from uninformed criticism. His inaugural lecture on 'The Use of the Old Testament in the Study of the Rise of

[47] A. M. Fairbairn, *The Philosophy of the Christian Religion* (London 1902) 18.

[48] Archibald Duff (1845–1934). See *CYB 1935* 272–4.

[49] See Archibald Duff, 'A Theological Professor's Training in the Nineteenth Century', *CQ* 14 (1936) for the posthumously published first part of an unpublished autobiography.

our Doctrines' was published in 1879. Within two years he was awarded an honorary doctorate by the University of Montreal. He achieved a fine reputation as a critical scholar of the Old Testament, and evoked great admiration and affection from many of his students. John Henry Jowett, who studied at Airedale 1882–3 and 1888–9, and was later recognised as one of the great preachers of his generation, wrote that 'Dr Duff made Hebrew literature as fascinating as a romance', and always spoke of his teacher as one of the deepest influences of his life.[50] Though Duff's later students may not have universally agreed with his contention that Hebrew was 'the simplest and easiest language one can learn', there was no doubting his enthusiasm and scholarship. His enthusiasm for German scholarship led him to organise a class to read works by Schleiermacher and Lessing in the original. He proved a most loyal member of staff, kindly and courteous.

The College was now more central in its location adjoining Manningham, at the time an attractive area for middle-class Bradfordians. At first a congregation met at the College as Airedale College Congregational Church, but when it disbanded in 1887 the members distributed themselves among the three local churches, Frizinghall, Salem and Greenfield. Many new Congregational churches had opened in Bradford since the middle of the century, and the formation of the Bradford Congregational Association in 1884 indicated the confidence and strength of Bradford Congregationalism, as did the fact that the Congregational Union held it autumn meetings in Bradford on three occasions in the second half of the century.[51]

It did not take long for Fairbairn to have an impact on the local community. He was a regular contributor to the *Bradford Observer* and helped to revive the Bradford Philosophical Society. He and Duff founded the Bradford Athenaeum, a discussion group which met monthly. Fairbairn gave a most successful series of lectures to working men in Horton Lane Chapel, later published as *Religion in History and in the Life of Today* (London 1884). 'I felt bound, as a student and teacher of the Christian religion, to speak to my fellow-townsmen, especially those of the industrial classes, concerning questions they were discussing and honestly trying to understand.'[52] His early experiences of employment in childhood and adolescence left him with an innate sympathy for working men which he never lost, despite his intellectual eminence. He was elected chairman of the Yorkshire Congregational Union in 1880, and three years later of the Congregational Union of England and Wales – a remarkable achievement for one who had only been in England for six years. He found time somehow for his own scholarly work. Apart

[50] See Arthur Porritt, *John Henry Jowett CH MA DD* (London 1924).
[51] In 1852, 1876 and 1892.
[52] Quoted in Selbie, 113.

from his lectures to working men, he published two other books, *Studies in the Life of Christ* (London 1880), which was a collection of essays previously published in *The Expositor* and ran to 14 editions, and *The City of God* (London 1883), which ran to ten editions and was translated into several languages.

As a teacher he was demanding because his ideal of ministry was so high. He 'could not tolerate idleness, pretension or flippancy. . . . Not for any man would he abate one jot of his ideal of what a fully equipped minister of the Gospel should be,' wrote W. B. Selbie, one of his Mansfield students.[53] F. H. Stead, a former Bradford student, wrote, 'As some of his old students recall (not without a cold shudder at times) the freedom of discussion which he granted, and which they took to the full, they begin to understand how it is that the meekest of men are the makers of men and of nations.'[54] Another Bradford student, Matthew Stanley, wrote of the sermon class, in words that seem to echo Fairbairn's own: 'Ignorant dogmatism, superficial sentimentality, puerile and unworthy handling of the sacred Scriptures, dependence on pulpit helps and every other substitute for hard work he could not endure. Upon them he poured torrents of burning, blistering scorn with such fierceness that the memory of his look and tone no years can efface.'[55]

It was not surprising that Fairbairn's name should have occurred to R. W. Dale once he had determined that Spring Hill College should move from Birmingham to Oxford as the first Nonconformist theological hall in one of the ancient English universities. Fairbairn had expressed his own approval of the idea in an address he gave to the Oxford University Nonconformists' Union in May 1883, and in the following December he had explained his proposal in some detail in a letter to Dale.[56] By April 1885 Dale and Fairbairn were again in correspondence, this time with a view to Fairbairn's becoming principal of the proposed college, and the invitation and its acceptance were confirmed in October. Fairbairn finally left Bradford in the spring of 1886, to begin what proved to be the greatest work of his life, the establishment of Mansfield College in Oxford.[57]

For the Yorkshire College, this was a great blow, though it cannot have been altogether unexpected. It precipitated more decisive negotiations with Rotherham College, with the result that Fairbairn's successor was principal not of Airedale Independent College, but of the Yorkshire United Independent College.

[53] Selbie 92.

[54] Quoted Selbie 95.

[55] Quoted Selbie 96.

[56] Quoted Selbie 167–9.

[57] See Elaine Kaye, *Mansfield College, Oxford: Its Origin, History and Significance* (Oxford 1996).

Rotherham Independent College 1834–88

Rotherham's new principal in 1834, William Hendry Stowell,[58] had come to the notice of some of the subscribers to the College through a sermon he had preached to the West Riding Auxiliary of the London Missionary Society on 'Christian Zeal'. The favourable impression was confirmed when he paid a visit to the College to discuss the possibility of taking up the position, for one of those present remembered it as 'like a refreshing shower on the parched garden of the Lord'.

Stowell was born in the Isle of Man but moved to Liverpool with his family when he was ten. His family was Anglican, but he soon came under the influence of Dr Raffles, as a result of which he entered the Blackburn Academy to prepare for the Congregational ministry in 1816. From there he was recommended by his principal, Dr Fletcher, as minister of a church in North Shields which had just moved from Presbyterian to Independent allegiance. Here he remained for 21 years.

In Rotherham he was the last principal to combine teaching with the pastorate of Masbro'. In both capacities he was, like most of his predecessors, exceedingly energetic. Within five years he had built up the congregation of Masbro' church to 270 members, and extended its influence in the surrounding neighbourhood. He built up the Sunday School until 300 pupils attended regularly, taught by almost 70 teachers. Each deacon was given a geographical district for pastoral care and evangelism. Every Sunday, Stowell would conduct three services, not only preaching to his own congregation but to small outlying ones as well. His concern for evangelism resulted in his participation in 'missions to working men', not only in the surrounding area but also in other parts of the country; he took part in the working men's Sabbath services in Liverpool organized by Nathaniel Caine. He was also active in the West Riding Home Missionary Society and the local LMS auxiliary.

He worked equally hard in the College. It was his custom to rise before 5 a.m. and spend the first part of the day in private study. He would give his first lecture at 7.00, followed by communal worship, and then spend another four hours lecturing until 1 p.m. After a walk with one or two students, he would preside over a college meal at 2.00 p.m., and then use the rest of the day for private study and lecture and sermon preparation.

[58] William Hendry Stowell (1800–58). See William Stowell (ed), *Memoir of the Life and Labours of William Hendry Stowell* (London 1859), *CYB 1859* 222–3 and *DNB*. He was a cousin of the Evangelical Anglican priest, Hugh Stowell. W. H. Stowell was in the first of four generations of Congregational ministers. See Clyde Binfield, 'The Story of Button Hill: An Essay in Leeds Nonconformity' in A. Mason (ed), *Religion in Leeds* (Stroud 1994).

His son's description of the preparation and delivery of these lectures gives some insight into collegiate life at the time:

> The heavy plodding labour involved in the preparation of lectures which were to be copied, studied, and commented on – lectures which would in almost every case remain the standard for reference and appeal through a whole pastoral life – was carried on with so much energy as to scatter precious fragments of intelligence and wisdom – apparently more brilliant from being unexpected, and more precious from the danger of being lost. The hammer plied unceasingly, forging the more solid parts of the theological fabric, and the sparks flying plentifully around settled and kindled in many a watching mind.[59]

Like his predecessor, James Bennett, Stowell's greatest enthusiasm was for languages; alongside his lecturing and preaching he sought further tuition in Hebrew, Arabic and Syriac, and learnt several modern languages, not only French, German and Italian, but Dutch and Spanish as well. He was a contributor to the *British Quarterly Review* and joint editor of the fifth series of the *Eclectic Review*. He published a *History of the Puritans* (London 1849) while he was in Rotherham, and gave the Congregational Lecture in 1849, 'On the Work of the Spirit', in the published version of which 'he ventured to quote a little German in his notes'.[60] His contribution to theology was recognised by the University of Glasgow, which awarded him the honorary degree of DD in 1849, after the publication of his Congregational Lecture. Yet his distinction as a scholar did not outweigh the tedium of his teaching methods, and he did not attract large numbers of students, who numbered only five in 1849.

A serious shortage of funds made the 1840s a particularly difficult period for the College. It was already clear by 1842 that there was a financial crisis. The Jubilee celebrations of 1845 attracted some new subscriptions and brought temporary relief, but the situation became desperate in 1848 with the sudden failure of railway stock, to which funds had just been moved.

The burden of college teaching in arts subjects as well as theology, shared with just one tutor (Thomas Smith) and combined with so much literary and pastoral work, was too much for one man. Some of the subscribers began to complain that the College was behind the times in its educational arrangements. The students themselves complained in 1849 that they were not being properly prepared for the degrees of London University, to which the College had been affiliated in 1841; only one student to date had been able to take such a degree. In response the

[59] Stowell, 203.

[60] W. H. Stowell, *On the Work of the Spirit* (London 1849). See Stowell, 224. But in a letter to John Angell James in 1850 he rejected German systems of philosophy as 'fundamentally false'. See Stowell, 313.

Figure 6: Rotherham Independent College, Moorgate
Source: Congregational Year Book 1875, *reproduced from* Building News

course was adapted so that every student should be prepared to take the London BA after four years.

In 1849 Stowell had to give up the Masbro' pastorate because of ill-health brought on by overwork. A year later Thomas Smith, the classics tutor, resigned, and Dr Stowell was asked to assume responsibility for all the teaching, classics and mathematics as well as theology. When an invitation to be president of Cheshunt College arrived, he accepted, probably with relief.[61]

The Committee now faced a dilemma. In January 1850 they had made their first approach to Airedale College for possible amalgamation; but the Airedale College representatives were not convinced, with some justification, that Rotherham's supporters were whole-heartedly in favour of amalgamation, and refused to take the matter further. The committee therefore looked for a new tutor. First they turned to a recent former student, F. J. Falding,[62] then minister at Bury, Lancashire. Like Stowell, he came from an Anglican family (of Ecclesfield, near Sheffield), but became a Congregationalist under the influence of John Ely of Leeds. He had entered Rotherham in 1838, then proceeded to Glasgow as a Dr Williams's scholar and was awarded the MA degree in 1845. His first pastorate of three years was in Wellington, Shropshire, after which he moved to Bury in 1849. In accepting the Rotherham College committee's invitation, he imagined that he was taking up the post of tutor as a temporary measure. In fact he was to remain with the College until and after its amalgamation with Airedale in 1888.[63]

The committee then sought a theology tutor and principal. They approached John Kelly of Liverpool, Eustace Conder of Leeds, George Redford of Angel Street, Worcester, Andrew Reed of Stepney, and one or two others. Not surprisingly, in view of the uncertain future of the College, all refused. After eighteen months of fruitless searching, they agreed to invite Falding to preside as well as act as theology tutor, and appointed Thomas Clark[64] as classical and mathematical tutor. The new minister at Masbro' Chapel, Alexander Raleigh, was to teach homiletics and pastoral theology for a few hours a week. This arrangement proved to be a more satisfactory decision than some may have feared, for Falding was able to revive the College's fortunes and conduct its affairs with a

[61] He had also allowed his name to go forward as a candidate for the presidency of the new Owens College in Manchester. His comparatively undistinguished presidency at Cheshunt lasted until 1856.

[62] Frederick John Falding (1818–92). See *CYB 1894* 191–3.

[63] During these years, Dr Falding trained 140 students. Of these, four conformed to the Church of England, two died and two withdrew; of the rest 15 served with the London Missionary Society and almost all the rest worked in pastoral ministry. *Rotherham Advertiser* 30 June 1888.

[64] Thomas Clark (?–1863) entered Highbury in 1837, and served as minister in Bungay for four years. His death is noted in *CYB 1865*.

quiet dignity for the remaining thirty-six years of its separate life. His two colleagues both moved away in 1854, but another former student, Cornelius Curtis Tyte, was appointed in 1854 and served as classics tutor for almost twenty years, until 1873. Falding took a leading part in Rotherham life, serving on its School Board in his later years there. He was an 'advanced Liberal' and was known as a friend of the Wombwell miners.

Within seven years the College had grown to a community of 17 students, the maximum which could be accommodated in the existing building.[65] It was known that the building was unsatisfactory, and at the end of 1860 a boiler explosion – which fortunately did not cause any injuries – once more raised the question of the future of the College. Airedale was considering a new building, and the possibility of one amalgamated Yorkshire college on a new site was again considered. The annual meeting of subscribers on 25 June 1861 approved details of a proposed new amalgamated college building in Leeds. Subscribers were then circularised with a document setting forth the arguments for and against amalgamation and seeking a response; of the 127 replies received, it was reported that 87 voted in favour of the proposed plan, 33 were against, and 8 were neutral.[66] In the following January (1862) a special meeting of trustees and subscribers of at least one guinea was held, at which 64 voted in favour of more detailed proposals, and 26 against, with two abstentions. In the light of this vote, a scheme was prepared for the Charity Commissioners, whose approval was necessary.

The opposition was not prepared to give in without a challenge. They produced a pamphlet advocating the retention of the College in Rotherham, arguing that closure would extinguish 'a tried method of education,' and allow one which was more unsatisfactory (in their eyes) to prevail. 'It is, indeed, gravely doubted, by the more sober, earnest, and intelligent Christians, whether the present tendency towards a University education, in which theological training is subordinate to classical and mathematical pursuits, may not lead rather to coldness and pedantry than to an earnest, conscience-awakening ministry.'[67] They also charged the Committee with acting unconstitutionally, using the Trust Deed of 1812 to over-ride the original resolutions of 1794. Their trump card was an appeal to the Charity Commissioners. Despite the protestations of those representing the majority in favour of the proposal, the Charity

[65] In 1854 16 small rooms had been formed into eight larger ones, thus reducing the total number available.

[66] This information is reported in a pamphlet, *The Yorkshire Colleges: The Amalgamation Question*, reprinted from the *English Independent* c.1872. The observant reader will have noticed that these figures do not quite tally; one of the figures must therefore be incorrect.

[67] *Rotherham College: Its Retention Advocated* (Sheffield 1862), bound with *Rotherham College Annual Reports 1849–76*, NCA.

Commissioners decided, early in 1863, that there was 'too much difference of opinion between the two parties to render it expedient that the Commissioners should (as of their own authority) sanction the amalgamation of the two Colleges.'[68]

By 1867 moves were being made to find another site in Rotherham for a new college building. For the next four years, negotiations for a new site continued while two more abortive attempts to merge with Airedale took place, in 1867–8 and 1871–2. When news of the search for a new site, and therefore for a new building, reached William Gilbee Habershon,[69] a London architect whose family were prominent Rotherham Congregational citizens,[70] he wrote to Dr Falding: 'When the time comes, I am sure you will think of me as Architect. It is everything to be named early, as I should not like to compete.'[71] When a site at Moorgate, 300 feet above the town, was eventually chosen and purchased, Habershon had his wish and was appointed as architect without having to compete. But life was made awkward for him by John Crossley, the Halifax manufacturer who as chairman of the English Chapel Building Society had wanted the College to hold a competition. On the College committee his continuous and detailed criticism forced Habershon into producing five plans altogether.[72]

Not until after the negotiations of 1871–2 with Airedale had foundered yet again could building begin. The foundation stone was laid by James Yates (great nephew of Samuel Walker) on 23 April 1874, six months before Titus Salt laid the foundation stone of the new Airedale College in Bradford. In the intervening period before the formal opening on 20 September 1876, Dr Falding went on a tour round the world, and returned with fresh energy.[73] The new College was an impressive building in 'Collegiate Gothic,' approached from Moorgate by a broad avenue of 200 yards, leading to a flight of stone steps and wide terrace. Above the main entrance rose a tower 60 feet high, from which could be seen a wide expanse of Yorkshire and Derbyshire. One hundred and forty rooms, placed not only in the main frontage but also in rear wings, provided ample room for up to 30 students, staff, common rooms and domestic services. A large waiting room-cum-library was designed to serve as an

[68] *The Yorkshire Colleges: The Amalgamation Question* 4.

[69] William Gilbee Habershon (1818/9–91). See *The Builder* 61, 31 October 1891, 335.

[70] John Matthew Habershon was Rotherham's first Mayor. Many of his relations were deacons at the Masbro' church.

[71] Correspondence relating to the new building for Rotherham Independent College, NCA.

[72] See Clyde Binfield, 'Three Personalities and a Theological College' in *Transactions of the Hunter Archaeological Society* vol 14 (1987).

[73] See T. Coote and F. J. Falding, *Notes of a Journey Round the World Made in 1875* (Sheffield 1876).

area for public worship on Sundays. Local firms supplied the furniture, kitchen fittings and ironwork.[74] The cost of the site, building, architects' fees and furnishings amounted to £23,000, of which £3,000 was offset by the sale of the old premises to a hay dealer who converted them to use as a lodging house.[75] The rest had to be raised through subscriptions, and a partial debt on the premises lingered on for the next few years.

Twenty-two students and the Falding family moved into the new premises. The theology and arts courses were now more clearly separated, and the hope was expressed that students might pursue their classical and literary studies at Owens College in Manchester, or, after its opening in 1880, at Firth College in Sheffield. Cornelius Tyte officially retired just before the move, but he was persuaded to return for a few hours a week to teach biblical criticism. He was joined for four years by former student James Smith,[76] minister at Wicker, Sheffield, and for a longer period by Philip Barker, son of the first resident tutor at Spring Hill, until he left in 1884 for the Church of England. For the final four years of the College's existence, Dr Falding was joined by two outstanding younger Congregational scholars, W. H. Bennett[77] as Professor of Biblical Literature and Church History, and Elkanah Armitage[78] as part-time lecturer in philosophy. Both were prize-winning Cambridge graduates. The number of students began to increase.

But the pressures for amalgamation were growing stronger, from both the Congregational Union and the Yorkshire Congregational Union, and when Fairbairn left Airedale College for Oxford early in 1886 the issue could no longer be evaded. This time, the negotiations between the two colleges proceeded relatively smoothly, and it was agreed to submit all contentious issues to three arbitrators, Alfred Cave (Principal of Hackney College), R. W. Dale and Henry Spicer (chairman of the Colleges Committee). It was left to them to decide which site should be used. The claims of Bradford as a wealthy industrial city with a lively intellectual and cultural life (now owing much to the mid-nineteenth century influx of German merchants) outweighed any advantages claimed by Rotherham for a residential college, and the Manningham site was chosen.

The Charity Commissioners approved the scheme of union on 17 February 1888, and the arbitrators announced their decision about the

[74] A full description of the building appeared in *The Rotherham and Masbro' Advertiser* on 23 September 1876.

[75] The building has since been destroyed, but the road which now replaces it is named Falding Street.

[76] James Smith (1822–1906) was a Scotsman whose ministries were in Germany and England.

[77] Later Principal of Lancashire Independent College.

[78] Elkanah Armitage (1844–1929) was a member of the well-known Manchester Congregational family. He combined teaching at the College with the pastorate of

site in October. It was a great blow to Dr Falding and to most of the College supporters in Rotherham, though not an unexpected one. One of the students present on the day the decision was notified to Dr Falding remembered vividly the scene in the dining room when the principal told the students of the decision and said calmly but sadly, 'I do not know how you feel, gentlemen, but I confess that, were it not for my trust in the over-ruling wisdom and goodness of God, this blow would be heavier than I could bear.'[79]

For two years, there had been considerable interchange of teaching between the two colleges; finally, in January 1889 the Rotherham staff and students moved to Bradford and the Yorkshire United Independent College came into being.

YORKSHIRE UNITED INDEPENDENT COLLEGE 1888–1914

Within a month of the decision to unite the two colleges on the Bradford site, the Governors had elected Dr Falding, in the year of his election to the chair of the Congregational Union, as principal and professor of systematic theology, pastoral theology, homiletics and English Bible. Professor Shearer was to continue to teach New Testament and the Greek and Latin Fathers, and Professor Duff was to teach Hebrew and Old Testament, the history of Christian life and institutions, and German.[80] Rotherham's second full-time professor, W. H. Bennett, had elected to accept an invitation to Hackney rather than to move to Bradford. At the end of 1889 the Governors decided to offer the fourth full-time chair to Elkanah Armitage, who had been travelling weekly to Bradford to lecture on philosophy, and he agreed to accept. He added apologetics, and later economics, to his responsibilities.

Although the work of the College had begun in Bradford in January 1889, it was not until some months later that it was decided to hold a formal inaugural meeting as a way of attracting greater interest among the local churches. Accordingly a large assembly gathered in the College

Doncaster Road Church. His wife, Ella Sophia Armitage (née Bulley, 1841–1931), a granddaughter of Thomas Raffles, was one of the earliest students of Newnham College, Cambridge; became an authority on Norman castles, a hymn writer, and the only woman ever to sit on the Rotherham School Board. See *DNB: Missing Persons*.

[79] Bertram Smith, in *In Memoriam: F. J. Falding MA DD* (Bradford 1893) 25–6.

[80] During the first year he read texts by Duhm, Ritschl and Harnack with his students. See the first annual report 1887–8.

on 4 March 1890 to hear Henry Allon give an address, and many stayed on to hear Dr Falding trace the history of the College. There were frequent references to the courage of men such as Richard Frankland and Timothy Jollie in the dark days of the late seventeenth century, as well as to James Scott of Heckmondwike and William Vint at Idle, and the early years at Rotherham. The audience was aware that only a few months previously a new building for Mansfield College had been opened in Oxford (14–16 October 1889), and there was a general confidence that Nonconformists had now moved towards the centre of English political, cultural and religious life.[81]

Dr Falding was already 70 when he moved to Bradford. His wife[82] had died, and he was content to reside in the College with his daughter. Soon after settling in Bradford he had an accident when leaving a steam tram near the College; although he recovered, this left him frailer. He continued in office for another four years, but died suddenly of a chill while visiting a relative at Christmas at the end of 1892. He had served ministerial education in Yorkshire for over 40 years as a fine teacher and administrator, and his gentle personality contributed much to the eventual smooth process of amalgamation. Though he liked to regard himself as an 'advanced' theologian, his academic duties and involvement in practical affairs left him little opportunity for writing and he published very little.

His successor had less talent for administration, but was a lively and stimulating theologian who wrote a great deal, and had a long-standing interest in German theology. David Worthington Simon[83] had already been principal of two Congregational theological colleges before moving to Bradford in 1893 at the age of 63. The son of a Congregational minister, he was one of the early students at the Lancashire Independent College and had continued his theological education in Germany through contacts arranged for him by Samuel Davidson. Apart from two very short ministries in Manchester, he spent the first years of his professional life translating German theological works.[84] There followed some years in Germany as representative of the British and Foreign Bible Society in Berlin, where Dorner and other theological scholars became his friends.

In 1869 he was invited to become resident tutor (in effect principal) and professor of theology at Spring Hill College, Birmingham. Here he brought a new method of teaching theology, rejecting the traditional

[81] The situation in Wales was rather different.

[82] Ellen, née Plimsoll, sister of Samuel Plimsoll, who was responsible for legislation to improve conditions in merchant shipping.

[83] David Worthington Simon (1830–1909). See F. J. Powicke, *David Worthington Simon* (London 1912) and *CYB 1910* 189–91.

[84] Especially Isaak Dorner's *History of the Development of the Doctrine of the Person of Christ* 5 vols 1861–3.

reliance on works such as Paley's *Evidences*, and encouraging his students to think and argue for themselves.[85] He was a firm advocate of an educated ministry and was eager for Congregationalists to take advantage of the new opportunities offered to Nonconformists at Oxford and Cambridge after 1871. But he failed to persuade either the College Council or the denomination in general to seize this opportunity, and in disappointed mood accepted an invitation to become principal of the Theological Hall of the Scottish Congregational Churches in Edinburgh at the end of 1883.[86] Here he was happy in his work, though its sphere was more limited. When the invitation to Bradford came in March 1893, it promised wider and more influential opportunities.

His inaugural address on 20 September 1893, on 'The Nature and Scope of Systematic Theology', indicated his intention to deal with fundamental issues. Only two years earlier, in an address to the first International Congregational Council held in London in July 1891, he had deplored the lack of interest among Congregationalists in basic doctrine, and pointed out the difficulty this presented to the colleges: 'The theological tone of our colleges, is, I believe, higher than it ever was; but the anti-theological and falsely practical current outside is so strong that even the best students have difficulty in stemming it – the majority prefer to float with it.'[87] His own method of teaching was Socratic – encouraging his students to argue with and question him. The best results of his teaching were 'not that he imposed his own creed upon his students, but that he established in them a method of thinking which issued ultimately in a well-digested theological system of their own'.[88] He told his students that 'If a man wished to complete his theological education, he would have to arrange to continue his studies in another world.'[89] As one whose thinking was continually developing, he published his finest book, *Reconciliation by Incarnation: The Reconciliation of God and Man by the Incarnation of the Divine Word* (Edinburgh 1898) while he was in Bradford.

Simon could not complain about a lack of *interest* in theological ideas, for the preaching of Rhondda Williams[90] at Greenfield Congregational

[85] See Dale A. Johnson, 'The End of the Evidences: A Study in Nonconformist Theological Transition' in *JURCHS* 2/3 (1979). D. W. Simon, *The Bible an Outgrowth of Theocratic Life* (Edinburgh 1886) contains the substance of his lectures both at Spring Hill and Edinburgh.

[86] It was ironic that within three years of his departure, Spring Hill had moved to Oxford as Mansfield College.

[87] Quoted in F. J. Powicke, 166.

[88] Herbert Brook, quoted ibid 302.

[89] Ibid 361.

[90] Thomas Rhondda Williams (1860–1945). See Rhondda Williams, *How I Found my Faith: A Religious Pilgrimage* (London 1938) and *CYB 1946* 456. He moved to Union Church, Brighton in 1909.

Church, expounding 'the new theology', was drawing large congregations, including Elkanah Armitage and Archibald Duff. Williams had come to Bradford at the age of 28 in 1888; increasingly he found that the theology he had learned at Carmarthen College did not equip him to grapple with the issues which faced him and his congregation, and he turned to Dr Duff (a member of his congregation) and to a fellow minister at Horton Lane, K. C. Anderson,[91] for help. Anderson was an original thinker who during his lifetime moved away from the Calvinism of his youth to a version of the Christ-myth theory.[92] He and Rhondda Williams were leading members of a group whose most publicised member was R. J. Campbell, minister of the City Temple in London, and who called themselves the 'New Theology League';[93] they shared a desire to reinterpret traditional Christianity in terms in line with modern thought. Campbell's book on *The New Theology* (London 1907) was produced under some pressure after intense press interest, and brought the movement under suspicion.[94] Although Simon distanced himself from the ideas of the movement, he welcomed it as stimulating thought and discussion: 'Anything is better than the cynical self-complacent indifference and carelessness about the highest problems of life and destiny, which too largely characterised our country less than a quarter of a century ago.'[95]

The members of the New Theology movement shared concern for the Social Gospel and were supportive of the growing Labour movement; Rhondda Williams actively supported the Independent Labour Party, which was founded in Bradford early in 1893. His book, *The Social Gospel* (1902), consisted of sermons preached at Greenfield on social themes. The students at the College helped to found and took part in the work of the Cambridge Place Settlement in the Wapping district of Bradford, and Elkanah Armitage's lectures on economics were an attempt to develop understanding of the social problems which concerned most thinking Christians.

Dr Duff was taken to task by some subscribers in 1893 for his advanced views on biblical criticism, and charged with 'heresy'. The Governors held several meetings for discussion of the issue, and eventually united in supporting four resolutions. The first was as follows: 'We decide that we are not a body of scholars trained in discussion of

[91] Kerr Crunston Anderson (c.1843–1923). Minister at Horton Lane 1885–92, then at Ward Chapel, Dundee 1892–1919. He was a friend of A. M. Fairbairn. See *CYB 1924* 91–2.

[92] See K. C. Anderson, *The New Theology* (London 1907).

[93] See J. W. Grant, *Free Churchmanship in England 1870–1940* (London n.d. [1955]) 131–50.

[94] Campbell soon retracted his more extreme views, and joined the Church of England. See R. J. Campbell, *A Spiritual Pilgrimage* (London 1916).

[95] Quoted in F. J. Powicke, 266.

such questions concerning the Old Testament; we are mostly laymen, and are therefore not qualified to express any opinion on such a field. Therefore we decline to pronounce any opinion of the subject of these complaints.' They went on to express their confidence in Dr Duff's scholarship and Christian character, and therefore 'we bid our Professor go forward, with the help of God, and teach our students what he sees to be right and proper.'[96] The fact that R. F. Horton had met with hostility, not only from some members of his congregation at Lyndhurst Road, but also from some church leaders when he published his *Inspiration and the Bible* in 1888, says much for the courage of the Yorkshire College governors, as well as illustrating the change in attitude which was taking place.

When Simon arrived in Bradford there were 30 students attached to the College, half of whom were studying in various Scottish universities for arts degrees. The numbers slowly increased, so that by 1910 there were 40 students altogether. Early in the new century it was felt that sending off students to different universities just as they were embarking on preparation for ministry, without College support or supervision, was not helpful to them and sometimes resulted in withdrawal. It was therefore agreed that all should go to Edinburgh, and that the principal and occasionally a governor should visit them once a term. In addition, the students could form a nucleus of support and friendship. The link with Edinburgh was strengthened in 1901 when the University recognised the College as a theological school for the degree of BD; thenceforward it was usual for Bradford students to leave the College with two degrees, MA and BD. Some men were accepted at the Yorkshire College who were not sufficiently qualified to begin a university degree course, and in 1908 the College appointed an arts tutor to provide a year's course in preparation for university entrance. Ambrose Pope[97] served in this capacity for 20 years.

Principal Simon offered his resignation in 1905 when he reached the age of 75, but agreed to continue until a successor was found. He finally left in June 1907, after the appointment of Ebenezer Griffith-Jones.[98] Thirty years younger than Simon, and therefore more familiar with modern theological developments, Griffith-Jones[99] was a Welshman whose two dominant interests in life were theology and motor cars, in

[96] Unfortunately the minutes for this period have disappeared, but Duff left an account of the debates in his article in *CQ* 14 (1936), from which these quotations are taken.

[97] Ambrose Pope (1865–1928) studied at Jesus College, then Mansfield College, Oxford, and came to Bradford from two pastorates in Manchester and Bakewell. See *CYB 1929* 226.

[98] Simon and his two daughters decided to settle in Dresden, where he died two years later.

[99] Ebenezer Griffith-Jones (1860–1942). See *CYB 1943* 428.

that order; when he was out driving, any theological issue raised by a passenger immediately assumed priority over considerations of road safety. There was nothing he loved more than controversy with friends, colleagues and students, declaring that 'we must learn to disagree without being disagreeable'. He grew up in Wales during the years of revival in the 1860s – 'my childhood was spent in the afterglow of that fine creative movement, which renewed the spiritual life of my fellow countrymen for a generation.'[100] He had studied first at Carmarthen College, and then at New College, London. He had one short ministry in Wales, and three in London, the last in Balham, where he published his most successful book, *The Ascent through Christ* (London 1899), an attempt to reconcile modern scientific thought with Christian faith.

Professor Shearer had retired in 1903, when he was succeeded for six years by George Currie Martin,[101] whose teaching was shared with the Lancashire College. When he left to become foreign secretary of the London Missionary Society, his place was taken by A. J. Grieve,[102] as professor of New Testament and Church History. Brought up in Wales but of Scottish parentage, he came to Bradford after study at Mansfield College (under Fairbairn) and a first class degree in theology from Oxford, teaching in India, and a pastorate at Romsey, Hampshire. He was a meticulous biblical scholar and church historian, who later spent 22 years as principal of the Lancashire College. 'By his very air [he] made one feel the tremendous importance of his subject,' wrote one of his former Bradford students.[103] His enthusiasm for church history was echoed in his most brilliant student at Bradford, Albert Peel,[104] later editor of both the *Congregational Quarterly* and the *Transactions of the Congregational Historical Society*.

In 1914 there were 32 Congregational churches in Bradford; Greenfield had 426 members (it had 502 in the last year of Rhondda Williams's ministry) and Salem had 324; the general mood was optimistic. No one could have foreseen that the college would be closed in the following year (see Chapters 10 and 13).

[100] Address to the Congregational Union, May 1918. See *CYB 1919* 26.

[101] George Currie Martin (1865–1937). See *CYB 1938* 665.

[102] Alexander James Grieve (1874–1952). See C. E. Surman, *Alexander James Grieve: A Biographical Sketch* (Manchester 1953) and *CYB 1953* 508–9.

[103] D. R. Davies, *In Search of Myself* (London 1961).

[104] Albert Peel (1887–1949) was a prolific writer of reviews, and a noted historian of Nonconformity. See Alan Argent, 'Albert Peel: The Restless Labourer' in *JURCHS* 4/5 October 1989.

8

Nottingham Congregational Institute[1]

Cavendish Theological College, Manchester 1860–63[2]

By the middle of the nineteenth century, the demands for an educated ministry and the need to keep pace with educational standards in the rest of society had led to higher standards of ministerial training, and often to higher standards for entry to training. This meant that many men, unable to satisfy entrance requirements, but experiencing a call to full-time preaching and pastoral work, continued to enter the ministry without any college training.[3] Churches anxious to secure a minister would often call a man who showed promise as a preacher, regardless of college training. Yet the total number of ministers was not keeping pace with the rise in population; many Congregationalists recognised the urgent need for both ministers and buildings, not only for the new urban areas of population, but for villages without Congregational churches. 'English Nonconformity, which once throve so vigorously – striking its roots deep, and throwing its branches wide and high – in the freedom-loving, Puritanic spirit of our rural districts, now droops there in the cold shade of an ascendant Anglicanism, and needs for bare maintenance to be alimented and nursed by the wealth of our town churches.'[4] The larger, wealthier churches were able to call college-trained men, leaving smaller churches to find ministers lacking any formal training.

From the 1840s onwards the perceived danger from the spread of

[1] This chapter is much indebted to the unpublished MS on the Nottingham Congregational Institute of R. R. Turner, and to the privately published *Serve through Love: History of Paton Congregational College, Nottingham* by R. R. Turner and I. H. Wallace, NCA.

[2] See R. R. Turner, 'Cavendish Theological College (1860–63)' in *TCHS* 21/4 (1972).

[3] According to *The Patriot* (18 February 1864) the number of men entering the ministry after training in recognised colleges between 1854 and 1863 was 278, while 249 came through other routes, not necessarily including any formal training.

[4] J. B. Paton, 'Independency in the Rural Districts of England', a paper read before the Derbyshire Congregational Union, n. d., Congregational Library, DWL.

'Puseyite' ideas and practices was a further spur to evangelistic effort. The Home Missionary Society, founded in 1819 as an undenominational society but largely supported by Congregationalists, raised money for evangelistic work, though the increase in need outstripped its capacity to help. The results of the Religious Census of 1851 amply demonstrated the scope for more strenuous evangelism. The religious revival which reached Britain from America in the early 1860s and the plan to open 100 memorial chapels in 1862 as a response to the bicentenary of the events of 1662 made the need for more ministers ever more urgent.

One of those who responded to this need was Joseph Parker,[5] minister of Cavendish Church (successor to Mosley Street), Manchester. Parker himself had had little formal training, apart from a brief period of private study with John Hoppus at University College, London, but his outstanding gifts as a preacher were recognized by the Manchester congregation, who called him from Banbury to succeed Robert Halley in 1858. His energetic ministry soon required assistants to help with all the expanding activities at the church. It was not long before he saw the need for more ministers and evangelists in the area round Manchester, and he began training preachers at evening classes. These classes soon evolved into formal sessions on the church premises, in the daytime as well as in the evenings, and a three-year experimental programme was planned.

Parker perceived certain deficiencies in the existing colleges. While he accepted that they were 'the expression of an earnest desire for a learned, intellectual, refined and powerful ministry,' he saw 'the want of adaptation in our college arrangements to the peculiar circumstances in which many young men are placed.' The comparatively small numbers of students in large college buildings were an illustration of this.[6] He now prepared a prospectus requesting both applications and donations for an institution which would train men for ministry who otherwise would be denied the opportunity. It would have three distinctive features. In the first place, students would be allowed to combine secular work with preparation for ministry; secondly, literary attainments would not be a test of eligibility for admission; and thirdly, the emphasis would be on 'subjects of practical importance'. The chief aim was to produce 'earnest and powerful preachers', and the young men who enrolled were sent out for part of each day to churches and mission stations in the surrounding area, which was divided into districts; two students in each district were to share in visiting, preaching, distributing tracts and giving open-air addresses. They sat with Parker, in turns, while he talked with enquirers and candidates for church membership. At first the programme was designated the 'Operative College', but when the ambiguity of the word

[5] Joseph Parker (1830–1902). See *DNB*.
[6] Joseph Parker, *The Operative College*. NCA.

was pointed out it was changed to the 'Cavendish Theological College'. The initial funds were supplied by the congregation.

Within a year, 20 students had enrolled. Of these, seven came from Parker's own congregation, eight from other parts of England, one each from Wales and Scotland, two from Northern Ireland, and one from Demarara.[7] The College was advertised as 'fundamentally an INDEPENDENT Institution yet, by special arrangement, Baptists, Wesleyans, Presbyterians, and others, may be admitted to that section of the course of study which comprises Theology, Scriptural Criticism, Homiletics, Philosophy, Logic and Elocution.' Two Baptists were among the first students. Parker himself taught homiletics, and invited two ministers from elsewhere to share in the teaching: John Brown Paton from Wicker, Sheffield, who taught theology, philosophy, Christian evidences and Old Testament, and J. Radford Thomson of Heywood, Lancashire, who taught English, Greek New Testament and church history. An unfortunate clash with the deacons of Park Chapel, Blackburn, over a student who was asked to leave led to Parker's withdrawal from most of the work of the College early in 1862. But by this time a number of subscribers, including George Hadfield, Samuel Morley and Abraham Haworth, had formed themselves into a committee, thus enabling the work to continue. The chairman was James Sidebottom, a Manchester textile manufacturer.

Some Congregationalists were suspicious of the new College and its relation to the existing colleges, one of which was only two miles away in another part of Manchester. The first Annual Report sought to pacify this opposition, declaring that the design of the new college was 'the education of young men for the public service of Christ's Church as Home, Town, Congregational and Colonial Missionaries, Evangelists and Pastors. We desire to hold towards existing Colleges the relation, not of a rival, but of an auxiliary.' The first phase of the College's life largely bore out that intention. Thirty men were trained in the College, seven of whom were transferred to Nottingham, and three of whom moved to other colleges; almost all the rest were already engaged in pastoral ministry when the three-year experimental period came to an end.

NOTTINGHAM CONGREGATIONAL INSTITUTE

The need for an institution such as the Cavendish College had been demonstrated by the number who enrolled, but after Parker withdrew it was not self-evident that it should continue in Manchester. A conference of representatives, chiefly from the Midlands and Lancashire, was

[7] Joseph Nicholls Levi, who later transferred to a private college for training men for the London Missionary Society at Weston-super-Mare, run by R. C. Pritchett, before returning to serve with the Society.

summoned at Victoria Street Congregational Church, Derby in June 1863 to discuss its future. It was agreed there that an institution on the lines of Cavendish College was desirable, but in the east Midlands rather than in Manchester; Derby, Nottingham and Lincoln were all to be considered. The proposed institution would work 'side by side with older institutions, holding itself in readiness as in time past, to receive students unfit for their curriculum, and to send on students of this College who show capacities for a longer course.' Invitations signed by both the chairman (Enoch Mellor) and secretary (George Smith) of the Congregational Union were then sent out to a second similar conference in Nottingham on 10 September: '... it is the desire of the promoters of this new Institution to form an agency which will have special faculty and adaptation for laying hold upon the masses of the working classes in our land and in our colonies, who, alas! are so neglectful of religion, and so neglected by the Church'.[8] At this meeting, the decision was taken in favour of Nottingham, because it was the furthest distance from the existing colleges in Birmingham and Manchester, and because it had four strong Congregational churches.[9] Another factor in favour of Nottingham was the influence of Samuel Morley, the Congregational hosiery manufacturer, whose factories employed thousands in the area. The formal title was to be 'The Congregational Institute for Theological and Missionary Training.'[10] The full course was to be two years, and two tutors would form the staff. James Sidebottom[11] continued as chairman of an executive committee, which was to meet monthly. The chief function of the members of a larger general committee was to raise funds in their own areas; that, and the work of a series of travelling secretaries seems to have worked well, for the Institute was never in severe financial difficulties.[12] The long lists of subscribers from many parts of the country indicates both good organisation, and a recognition of the importance of the Institute's work.

The Committee could have chosen no one better than John Brown Paton[13] to be the first and founding principal of the new Institute. He remained at the helm for 35 years. An outstanding scholar and public

[8] Circular letter 21 August 1863, Nottingham Congregational Institute Archive, NCA.

[9] Castle Gate (founded 1655), Friar Lane (1827), St James Street (1824) and Sneinton (1856).

[10] The Gloucestershire Institution for the Education of Home Missionaries, on similar lines, opened in Bristol in the same year.

[11] He did a good deal of travelling round the country to raise funds, and personally contributed £1,000 to the cost of the new building.

[12] The principal also did a great deal of fund raising.

[13] John Brown Paton (1830–1911). See J. L. Paton, *John Brown Paton: A Biography* (London 1914), James Marchant, *J. B. Paton: Educational and Social Pioneer* (London 1909), and *DNB*.

figure, ecumenical in outlook, deeply concerned for both the study and the practice of the Christian faith, he was one of the great educationalists and religious leaders of the nineteenth century.

Paton was brought up in Scotland, the son of a handloom weaver who took charge of the first co-operative in Newmilns, near Kilmarnock. The family belonged to the United Secession Church, but were influenced by James Morison and sympathised with the Congregational polity; when they moved to Glasgow in 1846 Paton's father became a Congregationalist. Meanwhile the young Paton had spent a good deal of time with his uncle, Morton Brown, who was a Congregational minister in Poole, Dorset. When the uncle moved to Cheltenham, Paton, who had left school at the age of ten to work on the *Kilmarnock Herald*, went for a prolonged stay, working as an usher at a school in Gloucester. At his uncle's house, he met the charismatic Henry Rogers, then a tutor at Spring Hill College. That meeting, as well as his uncle's example, inspired him to seek training for the Congregational ministry himself. By the time he was 16 he was a student at Spring Hill, working for the London University matriculation. A year later R. W. Dale entered the College, and the two became life-long friends. Both had distinguished careers as students; Paton won the gold medal in the London University MA philosophy examinations.

In 1854 he was called to a new church at Wicker, Sheffield, where he became a life-long friend of William Booth. Within six years he had built up the membership to 240, trained 56 teachers for a large Sunday School, and founded a Village Preachers' Society for evangelism in the rural areas outside the city. He combined this ministry with the main editorship of the *Eclectic Review* (assisted by Dale) and teaching at Cavendish College (which necessitated an overnight stay in Manchester). Not for the last time, overwork eventually forced him to take a long rest.

He was appointed principal of the Nottingham Institute on 2 October 1863, with a salary of £350 p.a. His assistant, as residential English tutor and later also financial secretary, was to be Frederick Smeeton Williams,[14] a genial man who was editor of the *Christian's Penny Magazine* from 1865, and former minister at Birkenhead. Williams's great interest outside his work was railways, on which he wrote two highly-regarded books.[15] The two men were to collaborate happily for the next 23 years. Henry Ollard of Derby was appointed secretary and came over weekly to

[14] Frederick Smeeton Williams (1829–1886). He was the son of a Congregational minister, and was educated at University College and New College, London. See *CYB 1887* 250–1, and *DNB*.

[15] F. S. Williams, *Our Iron Roads: Their History, Construction and Social Influences* (London 1852), and *The Midland Railway: Its Rise and Progress* (London 1876). He also published an attractive illustrated book on *Nottingham Past and Present* (Nottingham) in 1878.

take a class in church history. The opening service of the new Institute was held in Friar Lane Chapel on 25 November, and a few days later, on 1 December, the first session opened in rented premises on the corner of Shakespeare Street and North Sherwood Street, with 24 non-resident students, who were boarded out with families approved by the principal. A year later the Institute moved to the corner of Waverley Street and Portland Road.

The men who entered the Institute were often those who lacked sufficient basic education to be accepted by one of the recognized colleges, or men to whom the call to ministry had come at a more mature age, when a long college course was not possible. The first Annual Report gave an outline of the course of study. Literary and theological studies were combined in each of the two years. In the first year, students attended classes in English, geography, history, natural philosophy and Greek grammar in the literary course, and 'Christian Evidences' (using

Figure 7: Nottingham Congregational Institute
Source: Congregational Year Book 1869

Paley's work), biblical criticism and interpretation, doctrinal theology,[16] church history, homiletics and pastoral theology in the theological course. In the second session, they added Greek New Testament to the theological subjects, and studied English, natural science and more wide-ranging history in the literary course. For a student who chose to stay for a third year, a more advanced course was available. It proved impossible to cover this adequately in two years, and by 1877 the course had been lengthened to four years. The chief difference from the curriculum of other colleges was that much less attention was given to linguistic study. The teaching of Hebrew was actually forbidden in the Trust Deed, but later it was possible for a student to elect to join a Hebrew class in the University College.

Six supervised hours a week were devoted to evangelistic work in the surrounding area, in addition to Sunday preaching engagements, and accounts of such mission work were provided in some detail in the early Annual Reports. The Nottingham Enclosure Act of 1845 and consequent availability for building of the common land which had encircled the town led to a wave of new development and areas ill-provided with churches, and there was a rapid increase in population between 1851 and 1881. When the surrounding hamlets were incorporated into the town in 1877, the population immediately increased from 90,000 to 140,000.[17]

The rapid increase in the number of students (there were 50 by 1866) made the Committee sufficiently confident to consider a new permanent building. A site was found on the corner of Forest Road and Mount Hooton Road, with a fine view over the surrounding countryside, and R. C. Sutton,[18] architect of the newly-built Castle Gate Congregational Church, was engaged to prepare the design. The foundation stone was laid by James Sidebottom on 26 June 1867, followed by a banquet for over 100 guests in the George Hotel. A year later, on 17 June 1868, the new building was opened, most of the total cost of £7,112 having been raised. Thomas Binney came from the King's Weigh House in London to give the main speech, in the presence of the Mayor of Nottingham, John Barber, and Paton's uncle, Morton Brown, took part in the opening session. The new building was of red brick, in fourteenth century Gothic style. A fine lecture room, 60 feet by 30, took up the upper floor, while underneath

[16] The textbooks included Ralph Wardlaw's *Systematic Theology*, and *Outlines of Theology* (London 1863) by the Princeton professor, Archibald Alexander Hodge.

[17] By 1911 it had reached 260,000, according to the *Congregational Union Assembly Handbook 1911*. See also R. A. Church, *Victorian Nottingham* (London 1966) and W. H. Wylie and J. P. Briscoe, *A Popular History of Nottingham* (Nottingham 1893).

[18] Richard Charles Sutton (1833/4–1915) had begun practice in Nottingham in 1857, and designed numerous churches (both Anglican and Nonconformist), schools and factories there in the later nineteenth century. See *The Builder* 109, 12 November 1915, 345.

were a class room, reception room and library. Tutors' houses stood at either end. As was the custom, the Institute had no chapel; weekday services were held in the library or lecture room, and on Sundays staff and students were out taking services in local churches and missions.

Samuel Morley was one of the chief benefactors of the Institute.[19] His family hosiery business, which together with lace formed the chief occupations of the borough, was based in Nottingham, though Morley himself lived in London, maintaining close connections with his home town. In 1865 he was elected MP for Nottingham, but was soon unseated because of charges of corruption among some of his supporters (though no charge was made against him personally).[20] As treasurer of the Home Missionary Society he had a particular interest in the Institute, and for a time was chairman of the Committee. When the Institute's premises were extended in 1886, the new large classroom was named 'The Morley Hall' in recognition of his support.

Paton was greatly beloved by his students, and had a warmer and more relaxed relationship with them than most college principals of the time.[21] In addition he was an effective fund-raiser and a much-respected public figure in the town. It is not surprising that Airedale College should have thought of him when they sought a new principal in 1876. Their invitation to him caused him much heart-searching, for the skills he possessed were much needed to help the two Yorkshire colleges to unite amicably.[22] He realized that as principal of one of the colleges he would be in a better position to persuade his colleagues to respect the work at Nottingham more generously. Eventually, however, the pleading and the commitment of the Institute's Committee to raise more money for the support of poor students prevailed, and Paton remained in Nottingham.

For Paton, preaching was the most important ministerial task, and his aim was to prepare men to preach with conviction and understanding. His sermon class 'has been spoken of all over the world by ministers and missionaries and others whose privilege it was to belong to it'.[23]

> The distinguishing mark in the Nottingham training has been the sermon class. The first ambition of the Institute, to supply preachers and pastors, has never been forgotten, and the sermon class is designed specially to bring out the points that are most necessary to the work. It was in this class that Dr Paton was at his best. His old students tell that it was here that they

[19] Samuel Morley (1809–86). See Clyde Binfield, 'Samuel Morley' in J. O. Baylen and N. J. Grossman, *Biographical Dictionary of Modern British Radicals* vol 2 1830–70 (Brighton 1984) and *DNB*.

[20] He was elected MP for Bristol in 1868 and settled there for the rest of his life.

[21] See L. S. Hunter, *John Hunter DD: A Life* (London 1922) 13–16, and Marchant 82–98, for appreciations by some of his students.

[22] See Paton 332–6.

[23] H. F. Sanders, tutor at the Institute for 40 years and one who knew Paton in his later years, in Marchant, 78.

> got their visions of their calling, and first realised the greatness of the task to which they had given themselves.[24]

The 'Sermon Class Canons' which Paton adopted were used throughout the whole life of the College (though with certain modifications), and were one of its special features – so much so that it is worth quoting them here in full:

Exegesis
1. Was the text correctly read?
2. Did the sermon show that the preacher understood the context?
3. Did the sermon come NATURALLY out of the passage from which the text was taken?
4. Were the passages of scripture QUOTED in the sermon rightly used?

Plan
1. Had the sermon an INTELLIGIBLE form?
2. Was the introduction calculated to arouse INTEREST?
3. Was there LOGICAL COHESION of EFFECT in the conclusion?
4. Was there proper CULMINATION OF EFFECT IN THE CONCLUSION?
5. Can you suggest a better conclusion?

Composition
1. Was the GRAMMAR correct?
2. Were the sentences JUDICIOUSLY MIXED?
3. Did any sentences end with a preposition? If so, was it JUSTIFIABLE?
4. Were the interrogations reasonably abundant and JUDICIOUSLY used?
5. Were the figures of speech, especially the SIMILES and METAPHORS, appropriate and well expressed?
6. Were the paragraphs well built and clearly marked?

Words and Phrases
1. Were the words used too elaborate, or too simple?
2. Were the words rightly pronounced?
3. Were the words so spoken as to bring out the essential MEANING in the positive word?
4. Did each syllable have its proper weight?
5. Were all the vowels properly sounded?
6. Were the final CONSONANTS duly brought out?

Delivery
1. Was the delivery too rapid or too slow?
2. Was the delivery MONOTONOUS?
3. Did the preacher stand FIRMLY and EASILY?

[24] Sanders, op cit 61. See also J. L. Paton, 98–106.

General Estimate

1. Was the SUBJECT suitable for treatment in the pulpit?
2. What classes of persons are most likely to benefit by considering the subject?
3. In the treatment of the subject, was there any OBJECT obviously and continually kept in view?
4. If so, was the treatment likely to accomplish the OBJECT in VIEW?
5. Did the preacher show a real knowledge of HUMAN NATURE, AND A SYMPATHY with it?
6. Did he press home the truth wisely and AFFECTIONATELY?[25]

The methods which Paton adopted in the Institute were so much admired that when the Bishop of Lincoln (Christopher Wordsworth) planned a theological college to be linked to his cathedral, it was to the Nottingham Institute that he turned for ideas.[26]

In 1884 the Institute celebrated its twenty-first anniversary, and invited A. M. Fairbairn to come over from Bradford to preach for the occasion. Four hundred students had now been admitted to the Institute for the full course. Of these, 100 had moved on to other colleges, 200 were in pastoral ministry, 50 were in lay service or retirement because of ill health, and 50 were still studying. The celebrations spurred those who returned for the occasion to form an association for former students, which continued to flourish. The numbers increased steadily; by the time the 1885–6 session opened, there were 70 students.

'I am a Nonconformist because I am a Catholic,' Paton once wrote;[27] and on another occasion, 'I am a Nonconformist because I am a Churchman.'[28] Only in Nonconformity did he find two significant elements of catholicity: the recognition of the position, responsibilities and rights of all members, and the duty of fellowship between churches. On the other hand, he recognized that Nonconformity was often too local and too denominational.[29] His Nonconformity was never aggressive, and his vision was ecumenical.[30]

He was so much impressed by meeting a group of Old Catholics in

[25] These Canons are quoted in the *Annual Report of Paton College 1960*, 14–15, NCA.

[26] See *Annual Report* for 1875.

[27] Quoted Paton 480. Canon Rawnsley called him a 'Churchman of all Churches'. Ibid 521.

[28] Quoted Marchant 287.

[29] J. B. Paton, 'Dr Wordsworth on the Church of England', a response to Christopher Wordsworth's speech at the Church congress in Nottingham 1871, extract from an unknown book, 282, DWL.

[30] An example of the good relations which the Institute enjoyed with other denominations was a series of lectures given there in the session 1895–6 by the Revd E. Sell of the Church Missionary Society in India on 'Islamism', which was attended not only by Anglicans and by other Nonconformists, but also by the Rabbi of the local synagogue.

Germany in 1870 that he attended their second Congress in Cologne in 1872. Three years later he was in Bonn, attending the meeting of Old Catholics and representatives of Eastern Churches. It was he who persuaded the Bishop of Lincoln (Christopher Wordsworth) to give expressions of sympathy, on behalf of the English churches, to the position of the Old Catholics.[31]

He was fortunate in his collaboration with Canon Francis Morse (1818–86), Vicar of St Mary's Church from 1864 until 1886. They worked together on many projects, and ensured that the bitter divisions over the Education Act of 1870 in so many areas of the country found no place in Nottingham. The two of them organised meetings in the town in order to propose and support the idea of undenominational state schools, with undenominational biblical teaching. Together they were instrumental not only in the foundation of Nottingham High School for Girls as a school of the Girls' Public Day School Company, but were prominent among those who promoted the movement for extension lectures, which gradually led to the establishment of a University College in Nottingham, opened in 1881.[32] Some of the Institute's students were then able to attend classes at the new college.

Paton loved to travel in vacations, especially to Germany. He often visited Friedrich Tholuck in Halle, and met other German scholars such as Ritschl, Harnack and Dorner. On these visits to Germany he encountered several social and educational experiments which inspired him to similar work in England. Chief among these was the work of the 'Inner Mission', begun by Dr Wichern of Hamburg at the Rauhe Haus in 1848. The idea of the 'Inner Mission' – missionary work at home – was to become a constant theme of Paton's, and inspire a whole range of inter-denominational social projects.

These travels and his social and educational work in Nottingham left little time for scholarship,[33] but they were not allowed to interfere substantially with the work of the Institute, which continued to develop. An additional part-time tutor, W. R. Stevenson, a Baptist minister who also lectured at the Chilwell Baptist College,[34] was appointed in 1877 to

[31] Marchant 289.

[32] It became the University of Nottingham in 1949.

[33] '... he had to make a choice between theology and philanthropy, and he chose the latter', wrote P. T. Forsyth somewhat regretfully (Marchant 150). His extensive writings were mostly pamphlets and articles relating to the social projects in which he was interested. However the University of Glasgow recognised his achievements in awarding him the honorary degree of DD in 1882.

[34] Chilwell Baptist College was founded by the New Connexion of General Baptists in 1770, and moved to Chilwell, four miles from Nottingham, in 1861. In 1882 it was moved to Nottingham, almost opposite the Congregational Institute, as the Midland Baptist College. See W. J. Avery, 'The Late Midland College' in the *Baptist Quarterly* I/5, 1923.

teach the large number now seeking preparatory training at the Institute; he was able to offer extra help during Paton's absence in 1878. He left after four years, when he was one of the first to be appointed to the staff of the new University College. No successor was appointed immediately, but several changes occurred after the death of F. S. Williams in 1886. James Mitchell, minister at Friar Lane and Paton's eventual successor, taught church history from 1886. Frederick Bumby came from Oxford, where he had worked with Sir James Murray on the Oxford Dictionary project, as English tutor. Neither of these tutors was resident in the Institute, and it was therefore decided to turn the tutor's house into a residential hall which could accommodate 14 students.

During the years 1889–91 Paton had another period of enforced rest because of ill-health, to which overwork must have contributed, and went abroad (mostly to Florence) to convalesce. Local Congregational and Baptist ministers[35] shared in the teaching during the principal's absence, and R. A. Redford (a contemporary of Paton's at Spring Hill) came from Putney for two days each week. There was also a certain amount of shared teaching with the Midland Baptist College. T. Witton Davies, the Baptist principal from 1892 until 1899, who was a close friend and admirer of Paton, taught Old Testament to the Congregational students, while the Baptist students came to the Congregational Institute for New Testament and church history classes. Paton was well enough to return full-time in 1892, but it was clear that retirement was now not far off.

Paton's retirement in 1898 was marked by a large public meeting in the Exchange Hall on 26 October 1899, at which his portrait, by Arnesby Brown, was presented to the city[36] by the Bishop of Hereford, John Percival, who had been a friend of Paton's ever since they met on a walking holiday in the Alps in 1864. The list of contributors bore witness to his ecumenical standing, for they included the Archbishop of Canterbury (Frederick Temple) and the Bishops of Durham, Ripon and Southwell, as well as the Unitarian scholar, James Martineau, and many others.[37] Paton's own gift to the Institute was the endowment of a John Brown Paton and a Jessie Paton scholarship.

The man chosen to succeed Paton was James Mitchell;[38] like Paton he was a native of Scotland who moved to England as a boy. He was a former student of New College, minister at Friar Lane for 15 years,

[35] One of these was J. D. Jones, then the young minister of Newland Church, Lincoln.

[36] Nottingham became a city in 1897.

[37] The inscription read: 'The Rev John Brown Paton MA DD: For thirty-five years Principal of the Nottingham Congregational Institute. Presented to the City of Nottingham by public subscription on the occasion of his retirement to commemorate his distinguished service as a Christian Minister, Philanthropist, and Educationist.'

[38] James Alexander Mitchell (1849–1905). See *CYB 1906* 227–30.

followed by four years at St Helen's. He had returned to Nottingham in 1897 in order to work with Paton for one year before assuming the responsibilities as principal alone, and the teaching of Old and New Testaments. Like Paton, he was active in the city and was liked and respected by local Anglicans.

Frederick Bumby had left the Institute in 1897 to become Lecturer in English Language at the University College. His successor, who was to be responsible for teaching English, New Testament, elementary science, and all teaching of the preparatory class, was H. F. Sanders,[39] who had been the new principal's assistant at St Helen's for two years. For him it was the beginning of a forty-year association with the Institute and its successor, Paton College.

Principal Mitchell's tenure of office was comparatively short, for in 1903 he was appointed as Secretary of the Congregational Union, a recognition of his intellectual and administrative gifts. Sadly he died suddenly in 1905.[40] His successor in Nottingham was David Lakie Ritchie, minister of St James's, Newcastle upon Tyne, yet another Scot, who received his ministerial training at the Congregational Theological Hall in Edinburgh, and held a pastorate in Dunfermline before moving to the north of England. He was a very keen educationalist, was elected to the Nottingham Education Committee, and published several books on religious education.[41]

Principal Ritchie was able to take up residence in the Institute after Paton's death in 1911. On the other hand, residence for the students was abandoned. It was more expensive than a non-residential system, and the tutors told the Committee that they saw no appreciable advantage in a residential system.

The Institute's Jubilee in 1913 was marked by further improvements to the building, designed by Paton's son-in-law, T. P. Figgis. A conference on 'The Ministry of Today' was planned for September 1914 as part of the commemorations. In the event, this had to be cancelled.

[39] Harold Freer Sanders (1868–1956) was a former student of Lancashire Independent College. See *CYB 1957* 522–3.

[40] The extended library was named the Mitchell Memorial Library in his memory.

[41] David Lakie Ritchie (1864–1951). See *Who Was Who 1951–60*.

9
Western College

PLYMOUTH

'If the Schools of the Prophets be closed ... whence are these champions of truth to be obtained?' With these words, together with warnings about the widespread efforts 'to disseminate anti-scriptural principles', 'vigorously directed against the very foundations of our pure protestantism' and emphasis on the need for 'sanctified learning' in order to resist these efforts, the writers of the College's Annual Report of 1844 appealed for more generous subscriptions from their supporters. Debt now threatened the continuing existence of the College, for expenditure exceeded income each year.

The Committee now began to consider moving from Exeter to another West Country centre where more support might be found. Three places were considered: Taunton, Bristol and Plymouth. Enquiries revealed that the ministers of Taunton and Bristol were unwilling to assume responsibility for a theological college, but the response from Plymouth was more positive. Plymouth also had the most rapidly growing population of all the towns in the south west. Its population grew from just under 50,000 when the College moved there, to 209,000 in 1914. Samuel Newth, who was tutor from 1845 until 1854, gave it as his opinion that 'the College would have been given up had not the ministers and churches of Plymouth and its neighbourhood come to the rescue, expressed their willingness to receive the College and do their best to revive it.'[1] Thus the College moved south to Plymouth at Christmas 1845, to temporary premises in Wyndham Square. The *Evangelical Magazine* commented:

> We think the committee have acted wisely in resolving on this step, as the new site will be more central, both to the Congregational churches in Devonshire, and to the masses of the people generally in the county; while it will bring the college into more ready communication with the counties of Cornwall, Somerset, and Dorset, and lay open to its labours the channel islands, with their seventy thousand inhabitants.[2]

A few months later the Congregational Union held its autumn assembly

[1] Samuel Newth, MS Autobiography, DWL.
[2] *Evangelical Magazine* March 1846, 140. There is no record of a connection with the Channel Islands.

in Plymouth. The chairman for the year was Robert Vaughan of Lancashire Independent College, and he took pride in referring to the fact that it was to Plymouth Harbour that the Pilgrim Fathers had come when storms forced them to take refuge before their final voyage across the Atlantic.

Plymouth[3] had an unusual religious history during the 56 years that Western College was situated there, in that there were fourteen non-Anglican groups with congregations there, with no one of them dominant.[4] It was very different from Exeter, which was to be one of the models for Trollope's Barchester. The Plymouth Brethren took their name from the first English congregation established there by J. N. Darby, among others, in 1831; the movement soon spread and flourished in surrounding villages. One of its best-known members was the biblical scholar, Samuel Prideaux Tregelles, who settled in Plymouth in 1846. A strong influx of Irish immigrants after the famine of 1845 meant that there was a comparatively large Roman Catholic population, for whom a cathedral was built in Cecil Street between 1856 and 1858 to serve the diocese founded in 1850 for Cornwall, Devon and Dorset. The new Vicar of St Peter's appointed in 1848, George Prynne, was an ardent Puseyite, and aroused great opposition among Evangelicals. He remained there until his death in 1903. In the same year, Priscilla Lydia Sellon, the daughter of a naval officer, was inspired by an appeal from the Bishop of Exeter (Henry Philpotts) to work among the poor of neighbouring Devonport, and was actively supported by Pusey. Others joined her in a community life, and in 1856 she became abbess of one of the first Anglican communities of Sisters since the Reformation, the Society of the Sisters of Mercy of the Holy Trinity, for whom Prynne celebrated Holy Communion daily.

Dissent had reached a low ebb in Plymouth in the previous century, and owed its revival at the end of the century mainly to the Wesleyans and other Methodists. By the middle of the nineteenth century, the Congregationalists and Baptists had become more confident, and built new churches away from the centre (whereas the Anglicans and Wesleyans established new missions in the overcrowded slum areas of the centre[5]). In 1845 there were two Congregational churches in Plymouth itself: Norley

[3] The three towns of Devonport, Stonehouse and Plymouth were one conurbation, but were not united until 1914. For an account of Plymouth during the nineteenth century, see Crispin Gill, *Plymouth: A New History* vol 2 (Newton Abbot 1979).

[4] See the chapter on nineteenth-century Nonconformity by Bruce Coleman in N. Orme (ed), *Unity and Variety: A History of the Church in Devon and Cornwall* (Exeter 1991).

[5] The overcrowding in the centre was much worse than the national average. It was the work of a Unitarian minister, W. J. Odgers, *A Report on the Sanitary Condition of Plymouth* (1847) which led to a government inquiry and a gradual improvement.

Chapel (which moved to Tavistock Road as Sherwell Congregational Church in 1864)[6] and Batter Street Chapel, whose origins went back to the seventeenth century. Two years later, George Payne delivered the address at the laying of the foundation stone of a new Union Chapel in Courtenay Street, sponsored by the Batter Street Chapel; it was opened the following year. The 1851 Census revealed that Plymouth had by that date more Nonconformist worshippers (30,900) than Anglican (23,761).[7]

George Payne, who was 64, moved with three students to Plymouth, where they were joined by five new students. He survived for another three years, but died in 1848. Thomas Dobbin left Exeter to become Principal of Hull College, and his place as resident tutor of classics and mathematics was taken by Samuel Newth,[8] who travelled to Plymouth with his wife, two children and a nursemaid on Christmas Day, ready to begin teaching in the new year. Newth was proud of the fact that through his mother he was descended from Thomas Garrett, who was burned at Smithfield in 1540 for his radical Protestant opinions. His father assisted Rowland Hill at the Surrey Chapel in South London for 30 years. He himself studied at Coward College and University College, London, before becoming minister at Broseley, Shropshire, where he claimed to have reconstituted a 'disordered' church. It was after three years there, when still only 24, that he moved to Plymouth as tutor, and, for two years, as minister of Stonehouse Congregational Church.

He found the Committee's expectations for the College too low and set out to raise them. With his knowledge and experience of the University of London he entered three men for matriculation, all of whom were placed in the first class. When 'at last the leading men on the Committee began to take heart,' he persuaded them to seek, and achieve, affiliation with the University of London. During his time at the Western College he published two textbooks on natural philosophy, which were widely used by students preparing for matriculation. Although he did not make any significant contribution to theology during his subsequent career, his status as a Greek scholar was recognised in his appointment as one of the Revisers of the New Testament in 1870. After the death of George Payne in 1848 he had sole charge of the College for a year, and then worked happily with the new principal, Richard Alliott,[9] until he was invited to

[6] See S. Griffin, *The Sherwell Story* (Plymouth 1964).

[7] C. Gill, 163. See also E. Welch, 'Dissenters' Meeting Houses in Plymouth to 1852' and 'Dissenters' Meeting Houses in Plymouth 1852–1939' in *Transactions of the Devonshire Association* XCIV (1962) and XCIX (1967).

[8] Samuel Newth (1821–98). See *CYB 1899* 195–7 and *DNB*. See also his MS Autobiography in Dr Williams's Library.

[9] Richard Alliott (1804–63). See *CYB 1865* 217–18, and *Evangelical Magazine* 1864, 129–35.

become tutor in mathematics and church history at New College, London.[10]

Payne's successor 'entered very heartily' into Newth's ideas for improving the standard of the College, and the number of students gradually increased. Richard Alliott was the son of a former minister of Castle Gate, Nottingham, who died in 1820. After education at Homerton and Glasgow University, he followed his father as a minister at Castle Gate, then moved to London as the first minister of York Road Congregational Church in Lambeth, founded by the Metropolis Chapel Building Society, where the membership increased from 99 to 279 within six years. During his eight years at the Western College, the number of students increased from 12 to 29. The latter number included eight lay students, to whom the College had been opened, on a non-resident basis, in 1850. The second significant development was the opening of a Centenary Fund to raise money for a new college building.

Before the Fund had raised sufficient money, Alliott was invited to be president of Cheshunt College, and moved there, with six of his students, in 1857. He had given the Congregational Lectures in 1854, and they were published a year later as *Psychology and Theology, or Psychology Applied to the Investigation of Questions Relating to Religion, Natural Theology and Revelation* (London 1855). The year after his move to Cheshunt he was elected to the chair of the Congregational Union.[11]

There then began a partnership of 20 years between John Charlton[12] as principal and Frederick Anthony[13] as tutor. Charlton, who was a former student of Highbury, had fourteen years' experience of pastoral ministry (in Totteridge and Masbro', where presumably he had contact with Rotherham College), while Anthony was a very recent alumnus of Western. Neither made any significant academic contribution to theology, but both were devoted to the College and its interests. Frederick Anthony also served the town as a JP and as a member, and later chairman, of the Plymouth School Board for 32 years. He was church secretary of Sherwell Congregational Church for 33 years.

Great efforts were now made, especially by John Charlton, to increase the Centenary Fund to the point at which a new site could be sought and an architect chosen. By 1858 a site had been chosen at Mannamead, an

[10] He was subsequently principal of New College from 1872 until 1889, and chairman of the Congregational Union in 1880. His older brother, Alfred Newth, taught at Lancashire Independent College for nineteen years.

[11] He resigned after three years at Cheshunt because of his wife's ill-health, and then spent the last three years of his life as a professor at Spring Hill College and minister at Acocks Green.

[12] John Moon Charlton (1817–75). See *CYB 1877* 350–3.

[13] Frederick Evans Anthony (1832–1908). See *CYB 1909* 158–9. He was preceded for three years by William Henry Griffiths, who then became headmaster of Taunton School.

estate recently sold by the Culme-Seymour family for development, with a fine view over the Sound, and James Hine[14] was engaged as architect. The foundation stone was laid in April 1860, and the Gothic building opened in 1861, by which time almost all the £6,500 needed had been raised.

The succeeding 30 years were apparently uneventful apart from a change of principal. John Charlton died in 1875 at the age of 58, and was succeeded by Charles Chapman,[15] who remained at the helm until his retirement at the age of 82 in 1910. He was a former student of Western under Richard Alliott, and returned to the College in 1876 after pastoral ministry at Chester and Bath, and five years of lecturing at McGill University, Montreal. He played a leading role not only in Congregational church life, but also in the Devonshire Association for the Advancement of Science, Literature and Art, of which he was President in 1881. No doubt he also shared in the life of the Plymouth Athenaeum.[16] Frederick Anthony continued as tutor in classics and mathematics, also

Figure 8: Western College, Plymouth
Source: A. W. Sims, Western College: An Outline History *(Bristol 1952)*

[14] James Hine (1829/30–1914) was one of the best-known architects in the West of England, and principal partner of Hine and Odgers, Plymouth. He designed several schools and churches in Plymouth, as well as the Guildhall, Law Courts and Municipal Offices. See *The Builder* 106, 27 February 1914, 277.

[15] Charles Chapman (1828–1922). See *CYB 1923* 102–3.

[16] The destruction of their records in the Second World War has removed the evidence.

playing an active role on the School Board. They were joined later, in 1886, by a third tutor, in Hebrew and logic, Thomas Macey,[17] another former student.

A list of 'Rules and Regulations' of the College in Plymouth has survived among the meagre records of this period of the College's history, and gives some insight into the communal life.[18] A resident tutor was in overall charge, while domestic arrangements were the responsibility of a matron, supervised by a House Committee. Every student was to attend 'Family Worship', conducted by students in the morning and the Tutor in the evening; the Student Monitor had to keep a register of attendance. The matron presided at meals, unless a tutor was present. The front door was locked at 10 p.m., when all students had to be indoors unless they had special permission to be out late. Preaching engagements were arranged by the tutors. It seems that some students remained in the College during vacations. There is no mention of sport, though one hopes that there were some opportunities for recreation (there were extensive grounds behind the building). It sounds like an orderly, controlled regime.

Meanwhile in Bristol a Theological Institute for training home missionaries had been opened, with 13 students, parallel to that established in Nottingham in the same year. It was the idea of Edwin Hartland,[19] minister of Brunswick Chapel, Bristol, who in his capacity as honorary secretary of the Bristol and Gloucestershire Congregational Union, had drawn attention to the urgent need for more evangelists and rural pastors. The suggestion was approved by the Union, and he was invited to become the first principal. Thomas Knight,[20] a former Western student, was engaged as tutor in 1867 and remained until 1890. When Hartland left to become secretary of the Church Aid and Home Missionary Society in 1879, his place was taken by John Allen,[21] yet another Western student.

It was difficult for the Congregationalists of the south west to maintain two colleges, and by 1891 the supporters of the Bristol Institute sought amalgamation with the college in Plymouth. This was agreed, on condition that for the time being work continued in Plymouth, and that committee meetings should alternate between Bristol and Plymouth. Two courses were now offered, one of six years (which included an arts course leading to a London University degree), and one of three or four years for

[17] Thomas Stenner Macey (died 1926) was a Western College student until 1880, when he began a six-year ministry in Wiveliscombe. He was associated with the College for the rest of his life.

[18] Western College records, NCA.

[19] Edwin Joseph Hartland (1821–86). See *CYB 1888* 167–9.

[20] Thomas Broughton Knight (1834–1905). See *CYB 1906* 223–4.

[21] John Petherick Allen (1834–1909). See *CYB 1910* 158–9.

those with good preaching gifts but a lower academic attainment. In order to provide for this more varied curriculum, C. E. Wilson was appointed as Professor of Classics and English, but had to withdraw after four years because of a shortage of funds.

BRISTOL

It was now only a matter of time before the College would move to Bristol. Bristol was now a much stronger centre of Congregationalism in terms of both wealth and numbers, and could be expected to offer considerable financial support. The presence, not only of the long-established Bristol Baptist College, but of the new University College, founded in 1876, was a further attraction. The annual meeting of 1894, knowing of the support of the Bristol Congregational Council for such a decision, voted in favour of a move to Bristol, and appointed representatives to negotiate with the Bristol Baptist College with a view to shared resources.

The Bristol Baptist College[22] was one of the oldest Nonconformist theological colleges in England, and could trace its history back to 1679. In 1894 W. J. Henderson[23] joined James Culross as co-principal and succeeded as sole principal in 1896. He was favourable towards the negotiations already initiated by the Western College representatives concerning the possibility of the two colleges sharing the same site (the Baptists now found their existing site at Stoke's Croft too noisy). The College Secretary, Richard Glover, minister of Tyndale Baptist Church, was also supportive. The Baptists were not yet ready to make a decision about the building, but were prepared to discuss sharing part of the curriculum, and a detailed plan was drawn up. The Western College solicitor then raised problems about the legality of this proposal and prolonged discussions followed. Eventually the Trustees agreed that the teaching would be shared with the Baptist College on a basis 'not fixed and constitutional', and this satisfied the solicitor. The final decision to move the Western College to Bristol was taken at an extraordinary general meeting on 4 March 1901.

A suitable site (formerly 'Mr Exley's School'[24]) for a new college (but not for two colleges) was found at Cotham, at the top of St Michael's Hill, high above the city centre, an area developed in the earlier part of the nineteenth century. Until the building was completed teaching took

[22] See N. S. Moon, *Education for Ministry: Bristol Baptist College 1679–1979* (Bristol 1979).

[23] William James Henderson (1843–1929) was educated at Rawdon, followed by 21 years as minister of Queen's Road Baptist Church, Coventry. He was President of the Baptist Union in 1907. See *Baptist Union Handbook 1930* 320.

[24] Bristol Congregational Council Minute 3 June 1901. Bristol Record Office.

place at a temporary site at Hillside, Cotham. Frederick Anthony, who was now almost 70, and had served as tutor for 44 years, felt that this was the moment to retire; he remained in Plymouth, and was elected 'Professor Emeritus'. It was therefore Principal Chapman and Professor Macey who moved with the College to Bristol. The joint lectures with the Baptist College enabled the syllabus to be covered with only two tutors. Principal Henderson and his colleague F. E. Robinson[25] taught biblical studies and church history, while Principal Chapman and Professor Macey taught theology, philosophy and comparative religion.

The students of both colleges attended the University College for much of their arts courses, and when the University of Bristol was given its Royal Charter in 1909 (largely through the efforts of Quakers and Congregationalists), the two colleges were designated 'Associated Colleges of the University of Bristol,' and their staffs designated as honorary members of the University staff.[26] The University now awarded degrees in theology, within the Faculty of Arts, supervised by a Committee for Theological Studies. Students preparing for the BA in Theology spent the first year attending University classes in general arts subjects leading to the Intermediate Examination, followed by two years attending classes in the two theological colleges.

Bristol was home to some wealthy and influential Congregationalists, among them T. J. Lennard,[27] who was appointed treasurer in 1901 at the time of the move; not only did he actively raise funds, but himself gave £2,000 towards the £17,500 which was the eventual cost of the new building.[28] But it was the Wills family who were the most generous Congregational benefactors at the turn of the century.[29] In 1901 their family business merged with twelve others to form the Imperial Tobacco Company, of which William Henry Wills was appointed Chairman. Sir William Henry Wills, created Lord Winterstoke in 1906, who was Liberal MP for East Bristol from 1895 until 1900, was a Dissenting Deputy and Trustee of the Memorial Hall; he was a benefactor to

[25] Frank Edward Robinson (1859–1947) was a former student of the Bristol Baptist College, with nine years' experience of pastoral ministry. See the *Baptist Handbook 1949*.

[26] For the early history of the University of Bristol, see B. Cottle and J. W. Sherman, *The Life of a University* (Bristol 1959), and J. G. Macqueen and S. W. Taylor (eds), *University and Community: Essays to Mark the Centenary of the Founding of University College Bristol* (Bristol 1976).

[27] Thomas James Lennard (1861–1938), later Sir Thomas Lennard, founded the Bristol business of Lennards. See *Who Was Who 1920–40*.

[28] A certain amount was raised by the sale of the Bristol Theological Institute's premises in Oakfield Grove, and of the Plymouth building, which later housed the Western College Preparatory School, and is now owned by the Co-operative Wholesale Society.

[29] For the Wills family, see S. J. Watson, *Furnished with Ability: The Lives and Times of the Wills Families* (Salisbury 1991).

Mansfield College, Oxford as well as to Western College, to his old school (Mill Hill), and to many other Bristol institutions, especially the University.[30]

The Wills family were closely connected with two of the leading Congregational churches of Bristol: Redland Park and Highbury. Redland Park was founded in 1861 and grew from a membership of 46 to 515 under the long ministry of Urijah Rees Thomas,[31] who was Chairman of the Congregational Union in 1896. Samuel Day Wills,[32] cousin of W. H. Wills, was one of its deacons, and contributed in numerous ways to the life of the church and college. Immediately opposite the new College site stood Highbury Chapel whose minister in 1901 was Arnold Thomas (no relation of Urijah Thomas), whose own father was minister before him. Highbury was founded in 1843, with three members of the Wills family as trustees and benefactors. The first architect was William Butterfield, nephew of H. O. Wills; his later reputation was not for Nonconformist buildings, but for Anglican cathedrals (in Australia), parish churches and the Chapel of Keble College, Oxford. Highbury had three unusual but unrelated features: its architecture would have made it more immediately identifiable as Anglican; its site had been the scene of the gallows on which five Protestant martyrs were executed during the reign of Mary Tudor; and among its members (until the 1940s) were two direct descendants of Oliver Cromwell.[33] These facts, together with the outstanding ministry of Arnold Thomas, made the proximity of Highbury and Western College fruitful.[34] In addition, the work of the Bristol Itinerant Society, founded in 1811 to evangelise the villages near Bristol, offered plentiful opportunities for student preachers.

The Committee held a competition for the proposed new building, as the result of which Henry Dare Bryan (1868–1909) – 'something of a dandy among Bristol architects at the turn of the century'[35] – a young architect of 35 with some elegant houses in Bristol to his credit, was asked to produce a design for the new college. He was the architect of T. J. Lennard's family business premises in Queen's Road. His first plan, for

30 William Henry Wills (1830–1911). See *DNB*.

31 Urijah Rees Thomas (1839–1901) was minister at Redland Park from 1862 until his death in 1901.

32 His sons, Norman and Dr Kenneth Wills, were later closely connected with the College as treasurer and president respectively. A third son, Dr Harold Temple Wills, served in India with the London Missionary Society.

33 Ignatius Jones, *Bristol Congregationalism* (Bristol 1947) 84.

34 For Highbury Chapel, see W. F. Ayres, *The Highbury Story* (London 1963); for Arnold Thomas, see *Arnold Thomas of Bristol: Collected Papers and Addresses*, with a *Memoir* by Nathaniel Micklem (London 1925).

35 A. Gomme in A. Gomme, M. Jenner and B. Little, *Bristol: An Architectural History* (London 1979) 431. See also *The Builder* 96, 19 June 1909.

a residential college (which proved too expensive), was a piece of 'solid Edwardian classicism'.[36] The second plan, for a non-residential college, was quite different, not only from the first, but also from that of any other Nonconformist college: domestic architecture in the style of the arts and crafts movement, making an imaginative use of a corner site. *The Builder* called it 'a very pleasing building' and provided an illustration of the plan in its issue of 9 September 1905. A drawing was exhibited in the Royal Academy. When this was built, the cream Bath stone provided a warm, calm appearance. Inside, a high central hall was decorated with stained glass windows. In one of them, Thomas Broughton Knight, former tutor at the Bristol Congregational Institute, was mistakenly elevated to 'Sir Thomas Broughton'; another was dedicated to Frederick Anthony after his death in 1908. The new building was opened on 27 September 1906; 25 students now moved from the temporary premises into the attractive new lecture and common rooms.

In September 1909 Principal Chapman told the Committee of his wish to retire (he was now 81). It was 58 years since he had first entered the

Figure 9: Western College, Bristol
Source: A. W. Sims, Western College: An Outline History *(Bristol 1952)*

[36] See Sarah Whittingham, 'Dandy Design', in *Nonesuch* (University of Bristol Magazine) Spring 1996.

College, and he had been principal for 33 years. The Committee lost no time in approaching Arnold Thomas of Highbury Chapel. He refused, though he did agree to become President of the Committee, which now changed its name to 'Council'. Some weeks later, this Council interviewed two candidates, and unanimously agreed to appoint Robert Sleightholme Franks, a former student of Mansfield College, Oxford. He was to bring a new scholarly tradition to the Western College, and to make a major contribution to the teaching of theology in Bristol University.

PART THREE

Twentieth Century Challenges

10

The First World War and Its Aftermath

On 4 August 1914 the life of Britain and Europe was changed for ever. The war which many thought would be over by Christmas was to drag on for four long years, with enormous loss of life. The churches had no easy answer to the deep spiritual issues which it raised, and it was many years before the implications of what had happened became evident.

Though the Boer War had for the first time in a century raised the question of Christian participation in war in concrete terms, and had divided Congregationalists, most Christians had not previously been faced with an explicit personal decision. In 1914 the challenge could not be evaded, as young men flocked to join the army, applauded by their elders. Most Congregationalists, anxious with other Nonconformists to demonstrate that they were the equal of Anglicans in patriotic citizenship, shared the general mood. The Congregational Union Assembly meeting in May 1915 carried a resolution proposed by Sir Arthur Haworth, and seconded by the principal of Mansfield College, W. B. Selbie, confirming that, while respecting the sincerity of those who took a different view, 'our Assembly as a whole is of opinion that in view of all the facts now before the nation no other course was consonant with national righteousness save that pursued by His Majesty's Government, and it would assure His Majesty's ministers of its loyal and prayerful support.'[1] It was a small minority, many of whom took part in the meeting in Cambridge at the end of December 1914 which led to the formation of the Fellowship of Reconciliation, who believed that participation in war and Christian discipleship were wholly incompatible.

On the whole those in authority in the colleges adopted the prevailing attitude. At the Western College, the principal was instructed to write to every student conveying the view of the Council that 'while each man must ultimately decide for himself the important issue of his duty to his country at the present juncture, the College will put no obstacle in the way, but will, as far as possible, assist those who wish to serve their

[1] See *CYB 1916* 4.

country either as non-combatants or in the fighting line.'[2] Most of the students either enlisted in the army or joined the YMCA in France. One of them, Evan Griffith Evans, was killed while on service with the RAMC on his twenty-ninth birthday in 1918. The students at the Nottingham Institute were officially left free to follow their own consciences; in practice most served either in the army, the RAMC or the YMCA. The position was much the same at the Lancashire Independent College. The most bellicose College authority was that at the Yorkshire College, where the Governors by 1915 were urging the students to enlist, and where the principal, Ebenezer Griffith-Jones, took a strong public pro-war stance.[3] It was said that he stood on a tank outside the Town Hall exhorting young men to enlist. Three of his students died on active service. For men like Archibald Duff and Elkanah Armitage, who had studied in Germany and had many friends there, the war was heart-breaking.

Conscription was introduced in March 1916. Though ministers of religion were exempt, ordinands were not. This meant that the only students left were either unfit for service, or conscientious objectors (who might be required to do alternative service). The Yorkshire College had already closed in 1915, and the staff took the place of ministers who were serving in France; Griffith-Jones spent much time in Canada and the USA. By 1917 the Western and Nottingham Colleges had also closed, Western being occupied by the cadets attached to the sixth flying school of the RAF. The Lancashire College was the only one which remained open, though the RAMC took over the premises for the accommodation of nurses and the few remaining students were moved to the University's Dalton Hall until 1917, when their work continued in the principal's house. Two of the Lancashire students who enlisted were awarded the Military Cross.

When the colleges reopened in 1918/1919 there were all kinds of problems. Men who returned from the war found it difficult to accept the discipline of study. The communities of students were more disparate in age and experience than hitherto, and there was often tension between pacifists and ex-servicemen. The colleges now had to educate ministers facing a more secular society with less time for religion. Declining resources meant that they had to be used more efficiently, and efficiency demanded more centralisation, which inevitably found resistance in a tradition which had emphasised the autonomy of each local congregation. There was much resistance to the introduction of moderators in 1919, although most Congregationalists wanted a system which could help ministers to move more easily, which was one of the moderatorial

[2] *The Western College Annual Report 1914.*

[3] See his *The Challenge of Christianity to a World At War* (London 1915), which includes an address to the Congregational Union soon after the beginning of the war.

functions. The just sharing of ministerial resources raised the question, once more, of the number and function of so many colleges. A Congregational Colleges Board had been instituted in 1910, with representatives from each of the eleven colleges in England and Wales,[4] and six from the Congregational Union. Soon after the war, in 1921, a Colleges Commission was appointed to consider the whole question of the viability of the colleges. Its interim report to the 1923 Assembly recommended 360 as the number of students required in college at any one time in order to fulfil the needs of the denomination, a number whom they felt could best be educated in a smaller number of colleges. They welcomed the approaching union of Hackney and New Colleges, and the discussions between the Welsh colleges, and invited the Yorkshire and Lancashire colleges to reconsider amalgamation.[5] When their final report came out two years later, it concluded that ministerial training was being carried on in the colleges 'with as much economy and as great efficiency as the actual conditions allow'. Their discussions had foundered on strong local loyalty. The fault, they argued, lay not so much in the colleges as in the lack of support, in terms of both money and candidates, that the churches were offering. They quoted a fall of more than 8 per cent in the number of ministers since 1903.[6] The quest for more ministerial vocations and the need to make the most efficient use of ministerial training resources were to be recurring concerns throughout the twentieth century, and discussions concerning amalgamation took place frequently. Almost every decade saw the appointment of a fresh commission on the ministry and ministerial education and training.

One new source of ministers, though not yet appreciated, was to be found in the slowly growing number of women who felt called to ordained ministry. This was part of that movement of general emancipation and growing self-confidence of women which was greatly hastened during the war, and closely linked with the movement for women's suffrage. The first woman to be admitted to a full theological course in preparation for ministry was Constance Todd, who entered Mansfield College in 1913 and was ordained in September 1917 at the King's Weigh House together with Claud Coltman, whom she married the following day.[7] In April 1918 the Colleges Board had suggested that

[4] In addition to the Lancashire Independent College, the Yorkshire United Independent College, the Western College and the Nottingham Institute, they included New and Hackney Colleges in London, Cheshunt, now in Cambridge, Mansfield College, Oxford and three in Wales: Bala-Bangor, Brecon and Carmarthen.

[5] See *CYB 1924* 16–17.

[6] See *CYB 1926* 55–9. In 1903 there were 2,429 ministers; by 1923 the number had fallen to 2,140.

[7] See Elaine Kaye, 'Constance Coltman – a Forgotten Pioneer' in *JURCHS* 4/2 (May 1988).

women should be received in the colleges on the same terms as men.[8] From that time on, a small number of women candidates began to approach the colleges, some of which were more welcoming than others. It was at least another 50 years before such women could really feel accepted as 'ministers', rather than as (usually inferior) 'women ministers,' by the churches, though this was not always the fault of the colleges. Until the end of the third quarter of the century, when many more women came forward, the presence of one or two women in each college did little to change the essential ethos of either college or ministry.

Even before the outbreak of war, the Congregational churches had begun, imperceptibly, to decline numerically,[9] though at the time it seemed possible that it was only a temporary phenomenon. No one was to know that by the end of the century Congregationalists and Presbyterians together would number less than 25 per cent of their strength in 1914. Some, however (including pre-eminently P. T. Forsyth, principal of Hackney College[10]), had become aware of a certain shallowness of faith, of which R. J. Campbell's rather hastily-written *The New Theology* (London 1907) was regarded as a noteworthy example. Forsyth himself believed that the cause was fundamentally a theological one:

> ... *the chief need of the ministry in all the Churches* is not earnestness, not religion, not ethical interest, not social sympathies, not heart, not work, but *a theology*, an evangelical theology capable of producing all these things, and of making our students as ardent about their truth as young doctors are about theirs.[11]

Many in the denomination were still concerned that the proliferation of colleges with small staffs, who were expected to cover several subjects each, made it very difficult to raise the intellectual standards. It is certainly the case that college staff, principals especially, set the tone of ministerial education, and had great and lasting influence over their students. Kenneth Brown[12] has argued (taking into consideration

[8] Entry for 7 October 1918, Western College Committee Minute Book 1891–1935, JRL.

[9] The peak year for Congregational church membership was 1908. See R. Currie, A. Gilbert and L. Horsley, *Churches and Churchgoers: Patterns of Church Growth in the British Isles since 1700* (Oxford 1977), and statistics in the Congregational Year Books for the first years of the twentieth century.

[10] Peter Taylor Forsyth (1848–1921). See *DNB: Missing Persons* (Oxford 1993).

[11] P. T. Forsyth, 'The Grace of the Gospel as the Moral Authority in the Church', address from the chair to the Congregational Union in autumn 1905. See *CYB 1906* 91.

[12] See K. D. Brown, 'College Principals – A Cause of Nonconformist Decay?' in *Journal of Ecclesiastical History* 38 (1987) and *A Social History of the Nonconformist Ministry in England and Wales 1800–1930* (Oxford 1988), particularly 108–23.

principals of all the Nonconformist theological colleges in the later nineteenth and early twentieth centuries) that the higher proportion of college principals who came from ministerial homes, and who had entered the ministry without previous secular employment, as well as the tendency to hold the position of principal for a longer period, meant that they were less qualified than they could have been to help their students to engage with the intellectual and social problems of their congregations. This was less true of Paton College than of any other being considered here.

One has to set against this the fact that all the colleges now had links with universities or university colleges, in Bristol, Manchester, Nottingham and (in the case of Bradford) Edinburgh. The connection brought mutual benefits, for the college staff contributed to the work of the departments of theology, while through the university lectures, as well as through the Student Christian Movement, students were brought into contact with ordinands from other denominations. Until the later part of the century, it could be assumed that almost all of those who were studying theology were preparing either for ordination or for a career in religious education.

While the college staffs could not escape responsibility for some of the denomination's problems, more positively they played a significant role in the revival of interest in both theology and churchmanship after the First World War. This was foreshadowed by a deeper interest in Congregational history, exemplified by the formation in 1899 of the Congregational Historical Society, whose *Transactions* gave space to well-researched articles on Congregational origins and development. The *Congregational Quarterly*, founded after the First World War in 1923, provided a forum for the discussion of serious theological themes by distinguished scholars, among them theological college staff.[13] It was in the pages of that journal in 1926 that R. F. Horton, the veteran minister of Lyndhurst Road Congregational Church, Hampstead, made a plea for Free Churchmen to come together to formulate a presentation of Christianity, 'neither Romanist nor Fundamentalist', which modern people would find acceptable. The result was a series of annual conferences, in Oxford and Cambridge, in which members of staff of the colleges played a leading role.[14] The members of staff were also in varying degrees involved in the leadership of the ecumenical movement, which gained momentum after the First World War.

The question which faced both the denomination and the colleges was: what kind of ministry did the churches really need? The 'College question', and the debate over how ministers should be educated,

[13] R. S. Franks and H. F. Lovell Cocks, successive principals of Western College, and H.Cunliffe-Jones of the Yorkshire United College, were frequent contributors.
[14] Full reports were given in the *Congregational Quarterly*.

continued to exercise the best minds of the denomination throughout the twentieth century. More emphasis came to be placed on practical and pastoral theology, and the rapidly changing social context was a constant challenge to the curriculum. Those who believed that evangelical conviction outweighed any academic deficiencies sometimes found themselves at odds with those who tried to keep alive the ideals of the learned ministry. The more the colleges could keep in touch with local churches, through opening their doors for special lectures, and through preaching engagements by staff and students, the more it was possible to enlist support for what they were trying to do, though securing sufficient income to keep the colleges viable was a perpetual anxiety.

11

Western College 1919–70

'THE work of a theological college contains nothing very showy; and nothing very new or revolutionary. But it is a time of sowing and planting ...' These were the words of Robert Sleightholme Franks[1] to the subscribers to the Western College in 1925. They epitomise his own years as principal: teaching, thinking and writing theology, providing the groundwork for his students as future ministers. A shy, devout and sometimes absent-minded man, who loved music and the study of botany, he never gained great fame or recognition, and was never elected Chairman of the Congregational Union, but his books reveal him as an outstanding theologian of the twentieth century. Yet for him, to be profound was also to be simple.

He was the son of William James Franks,[2] Congregational minister for more than 35 years at Redcar, Yorkshire, the eldest of four sons[3] who all entered Mansfield College as graduates to prepare for ministry. R. S. Franks attended Sir William Turner's Grammar School in Redcar before being sent to a Congregational minister in Somerset who, as a good mathematician, could prepare him for entrance to Cambridge. He gained an exhibition to St John's College to read mathematics; one of the Redcar deacons helped to pay the fees, though a frugal lifestyle was still necessary.[4] Perhaps partly as a result of eating very economically, and partly owing to the fact that at the same time he was working for a London University degree, he broke down just before taking the final Tripos examinations and was awarded an aegrotat instead of being placed among the wranglers as his ability warranted.

He entered Mansfield College in 1893 and not only took the normal theological course but also worked for the new degree of B Litt (Nonconformists were still excluded from Divinity degrees) with a thesis on 'The Theories of the Atonement of Anselm and Grotius', which formed the basis of much of his later work. He retained a great respect

[1] For R. S. Franks (1871–1964), see *DNB 1961–70* and *CYB 1964/5* 439–40. I am indebted to two of his children for help with this account: the late Lord Franks, in an interview on 17 October 1991, and Mrs Rosalind Fells.

[2] William James Franks (1838–1927). See *CYB 1929* 215.

[3] The others were John Edwin, Ernest William and Richard Lister Franks.

[4] W. J. Franks's salary was only £200 a year. The highest paid congregational ministers were receiving £1,000 a year.

for his three teachers at Mansfield, A. M. Fairbairn (the principal, who taught systematic theology), G. B. Gray (Old Testament) and J. V. Bartlet, the church historian, who described himself as 'a liberal of the Harnack or right-wing Ritschlian type'.

He had a brief spell as a tutor at Mansfield before moving to Birkenhead as minister of Prenton Road Congregational Church. He stayed there for four years, his only period of full-time pastoral ministry. In 1904 he was appointed lecturer in theology at the Birmingham Quaker college, Woodbrooke, and remained there until he moved to Bristol as principal of Western College in 1910. His wife, Katharine Shewell, whom he married in 1903, was a lifelong Quaker, and though as one of a large family she was not able to go to university herself, she had an original mind, and made sure that her daughters as well as her sons could enjoy the educational advantages denied to her, a purpose which her husband fully supported. Franks himself was sympathetic to Quakerism, especially in his later years, and found Woodbrooke's atmosphere and ethos congenial. Here he published his first book, a small volume in the *Century Bible Handbooks* series, *The New Testament Doctrines of Man, Sin and Salvation* (London 1908).

There were 20 students in Western College when Franks arrived in 1910. That number increased somewhat before the war started, was then reduced during the war until the College closed,[5] but soon recovered after the war ended. For the first ten years, including the disrupted war years, Franks had Professor Macey as his colleague. The principal taught systematic theology and the philosophy of religion, while his colleague taught Old Testament, Hebrew and comparative religion. Principal Henderson of the Baptist College continued to teach New Testament and ethics, and F. E. Robinson taught church history. The sharing of teaching was made easier when the Baptist College moved to Woodland Road into the new building designed by the Congregational architect, Sir George Oatley.[6]

By the time the war ended Franks had published the first and most substantial of his four major theological works, *A History of the Doctrine of the Work of Christ* (two volumes, London 1918). It gained him the Oxford degree of D.Litt. It was a work of great lucidity, expounding the ideas of theologians who, like him, had 'endeavoured to reduce the doctrine to systematic unity'. Its durability and significance were recognised by its being reissued, in one volume, 44 years later, in 1962. It was an unusual work for a Nonconformist in that it gave close attention to mediaeval scholasticism, alongside Greek theology, Protestant orthodoxy and modern Protestant theology. But then a Noncon-

[5] During the period of closure, Franks preached frequently in chapels in Bristol and the surrounding area.

[6] Sir George Herbert Oatley (1863–1950).

formist who, without the slightest self-consciousness, gave the hens his family acquired during the war the names Aquinas, Alexander of Hales (a theologian with whom Franks had a particular affinity), Bonaventura and Duns Scotus was no ordinary Nonconformist.

In a later work, *The Atonement* (the Dale Lectures delivered at Mansfield College, published by the Oxford University Press in 1934), which was really a sequel to his book on the Work of Christ, he gave a revealing account of his own theological development:

> Brought up in the older evangelicalism, supported as it was by the doctrine of the infallibility of the Bible, I experienced as a theological student the full force of modern Biblical criticism, and had to cast about for a fresh foundation and new statement of the Christian faith. At this stage two books came into my hands, Ritschl's *Justification and Reconciliation*, and Harnack's *History of Dogma*. Mutually supporting each other, together they came to me as a revelation, only describable in the language of a famous sonnet of Keats:
>
> Then felt I like some watcher of the skies
> When a new planet swims into his ken.
>
> I accepted the Ritschlian theology *ex animo*, as it was propounded by the master and illustrated by the disciple; and I rejoiced in my new-found freedom from the vexing problems of historical criticism, and my ability to move easily and naturally in the intelligent use of the different parts of the Bible. I found in Ritschl's *Justification and Reconciliation* the key to Holy Scripture, which Calvin's *Institutes* had been to my evangelical forefathers. . . . As a young minister, I found the Ritschlian theology a theology that could be preached.[7]

The Atonement was a defence of the Abelardian view; in the words of John Huxtable, 'he argued for the Abelardian view of the Atonement and sought to prove it by the method of Anselm.'[8] In later years, particularly as he read Troeltsch,[9] he came to believe that theology needed a metaphysical basis, and the three lectures which he delivered in the University of London in 1928 were published as *The Metaphysical Justification of Religion*. He moved further away from Ritschl and closer to Schleiermacher. Though the publication of his first major work coincided with the publication (in German) of Barth's commentary on Romans, he never accepted Barthian theology, which he regarded as 'altogether unsatisfactory'. By the time his first major work was republished in 1962 he was 'inclined to think that the original impetus of the Barthian revolution has now somewhat spent itself'.

[7] R. S. Franks, *The Atonement* (Oxford 1934) vii–viii.

[8] *DNB 1961–70* 392.

[9] Especially E. Troeltsch, *The Social Teaching of the Christian Churches and Sects* (2 volumes, London 1931). He probably read it in German before the English translation was published.

As a theologian and scholar, Franks overshadowed his three colleagues, though his lack of worldly ambition and quiet demeanour meant that he did not receive the recognition which was his due. However the University of Bristol recognised his worth in 1928 in awarding an honorary LL D (there was no Theology Faculty as yet, and therefore no DD degree). He was an outstanding contributor to the Congregational conferences, and wrote frequently for the *Congregational Quarterly*. John Huxtable, one of his students in the 1930s, felt that he was hampered by having to teach to a restricted syllabus for the Bristol and London theology degrees which many of his students took.[10]

In 1920 T. S. Macey was due to retire, but continued to do some teaching until he was finally forced to retire in 1924 after a stroke. Lack of funds made it impossible to appoint a successor until 1927, when Arnold Sims[11] was appointed bursar and tutor with a particular responsibility for preparing students for matriculation in their first year. He helped many anxious students to develop confidence through his patient teaching, and was able to sympathise with the difficulties of students with a poor academic background. He also took over the duties previously undertaken by the Secretary to the College, W. F. Durant.[12] In this capacity he was a great friend to all local churches, receiving and dealing with their requests for student preachers. Meanwhile there were changes at the Baptist College. When W. J. Henderson retired in 1922, his successor was a layman who had been headmaster of Taunton School for over 20 years, C. D. Whittaker; but ill health forced him to resign after only four terms. His successor was Arthur Dakin,[13] who came with 14 years' experience of pastoral ministry; he remained at the College until 1953, teaching New Testament and church history. Others who had contact with the students were the College officers, especially those who were local ministers. Arnold Thomas of Highbury, who had been on the College Council since 1878, was president from 1910 until his death in 1924.

Franks summed up his aim in teaching his students in his report to the subscribers in 1926:

> It is too often forgotten that the ideal of ministerial education is not to send a man out with some knowledge of every subject he will afterwards find

[10] John Huxtable, *As It Seemed to Me* (London 1991) 11.

[11] Arnold Walter Sims (1887–1958) was a former Western student who had held three pastorates before returning to the College. See *CYB 1959* 430.

[12] William Friend Durant (1858–1937) acted as College Secretary from 1907 until 1927, and gave help to the Bristol Itinerant Society. See *CYB 1938* 430.

[13] Arthur Dakin (1884–1969). He had studied at Rawdon Baptist College, and at Halle and Heidelberg. Like one of his predecessors, W. J. Henderson, he had served for a time as minister of Queen's Road Baptist Church, Coventry. He was President of the Baptist Union in 1945. See *Baptist Handbook 1970* 376.

> useful. It is rather to send him out with a mind that can tackle with success any subject as need arises. The opposite leads to self-confident shallowness.

He used to tell his students that it was better to read big books, even if they disagreed with them, than 'to clutter your minds with pious little books which are like hayforks'.[14] In his Jubilee year at the College in 1935, he told the subscribers that his purpose in teaching and writing had always been 'the formulation of an evangelical theology, which might serve the function in the present which the great systems of the sixteenth and seventeenth centuries served in the past'.[15]

The ever-present financial problems continued to demand much energetic canvassing, especially by the bursar. When Franks was appointed in 1910, he was offered a salary of £350 p.a. together with a house rent-free.[16] It was a hard struggle to make ends meet with a young family of four children to bring up and educate.[17] Owing to financial stringency and even more to the fact that all four children were ill for some time after their arrival in Bristol, Mrs Franks's introduction to the comparatively wealthy Clifton society was to some extent blighted. The salary was raised to £400 after five years, but Franks had to appeal to the Committee, no doubt with embarrassment, for a further rise after the end of the war.

These financial difficulties led Franks to tell the Committee as early as 1923 that they should seriously consider amalgamation with another college. The first proposal was to approach the Baptist College, but the response was not hopeful. The following year Franks and two members of the Committee were called to the Memorial Hall to discuss a possible merger with Paton College, as part of the discussions of the Congregational Colleges Commission. But both colleges successfully resisted the idea.

One of the important factors in considering the future of the College was its role in the life of the churches of the West Country. Many of the students came from the West Country, and many went on to spend their whole ministry there. The staff were in demand for special church functions, and Franks played a role in the educational life of Bristol, not only through the University, but also as Chairman of the Governors of Redland High School for Girls. He lectured for the local WEA in philosophy (to help to pay for his children's higher education). The Bristol Itinerant Society relied heavily on the students, who regularly

[14] Huxtable, 11.

[15] *Annual Report* 1935.

[16] Fairbairn, who resigned as Principal of Mansfield College a year before Franks went to Western, had been paid £1,000 a year.

[17] One of the local Congregational deacons helped with fees in the same way as the Redcar deacons had helped the earlier generation of the Franks family.

preached in the outlying villages on Sundays. A hired car, generally known as 'the Hallelujah Chariot', would collect the students and deliver them to their respective destinations. Some of the village churches were welcoming and produced wonderful meals, and made friendships with their students which lasted for many years. Others were not so generous, and left students to fend for themselves on meagre food between morning and evening services.

Life was not all work for the students. They mixed with other university students in the SCM, and in 1938 were instrumental in forming a Congregational Student Fellowship, which often met at the College. They provided an annual entertainment for local visitors which raised money for the London Missionary Society. There were football matches against the Baptist students and cricket matches against local ministers, and in the summer the minister of Redland Park invited the students to use his tennis court.

There was a long tradition of Western students serving abroad with the London Missionary Society, and this was celebrated by a small missionary museum, housed in glass cabinets at the top of the stairs. On one occasion in the early 1940s one of the exhibits, a stuffed bird which was regarded as the college mascot, was found to be infested. The students arranged a ceremonial 'cremation', during which two of their number were mitred, a curious kind of premonition, since one of the two eventually became an Anglican bishop.[18] The first woman student, Ellen Leaton,[19] was admitted in 1927; she was 39, having already worked as a deaconess in the United Methodist Church. She took the full course of five years. In 1932 another woman made enquiries but does not seem to have been accepted. One does not know exactly what lay behind the Committee's resolution a year later: 'That this College has not the facilities for the training of women students and that it therefore discontinues its practice of receiving applications from women students.' This policy was reversed after the arrival of the next principal.

Just before the outbreak of the second world war Franks told the Committee that ill health forced him to offer his resignation, though for another year he taught in the College for two days each week. He was already 68. The most frequent word which was used to describe him in the many tributes was 'righteous' – 'a righteous man and a true friend'; John Huxtable wrote in the *Mansfield College Magazine* (1964) of 'his keenness for all that is righteous'.

He and his wife now retired to Winscombe in Somerset, where they found a spiritual home with the Quakers. He continued to read and study, though hampered by periods of depression, reverting to an earlier

[18] John Gibbs was Bishop of Coventry 1976–85.
[19] Ellen (Nellie) Leaton (1888–1964). See *CYB 1964/5* 443.

interest in physics and following its recent development, as well as continuing to keep abreast of theology. He produced another historical survey, *The Doctrine of the Trinity* (London 1953), published when he was over 80, and pursued his interest in the relation between theology and science in 'Enigma', a work which was never published. And at the age of 90 he wrote the preface to the second edition of *The Doctrine of the Work of Christ*, admitting however that he had allowed a younger colleague to do the proof reading. He died two years later in 1964.

The Committee found a temporary successor to Franks for the next 18 months in Kenneth Parry,[20] minister at Highbury. The war which had now just broken out disrupted the College in different ways from the earlier war. The College did not have to close, and there was now more respect for the pacifist position, though some of the students did enlist. But the war came to Bristol in the form of severe air raids.[21] The students were required to do fire watching duties once a week in the College and often had to act as air raid wardens near their 'digs' as well. Redland Park Church had been destroyed in a raid in December 1940, and early in 1941 the College and principal's house and Highbury Chapel opposite were damaged by a bomb, though fortunately no one was injured.

Franks's permanent successor at the College was the principal of the Scottish Congregational College in Edinburgh, Lovell Cocks.[22] Lovell Cocks had been trained at Hackney College during the years of the first war, and ever after declared that it was to P. T. Forsyth (his former principal) that he owed his 'theological soul' and 'footing in the Gospel'. The second significant influence on him was Karl Barth, whose theological voice was not dissimilar to that of Forsyth. At the time of his appointment he was in the midst of writing a doctoral thesis, much influenced by Barth, and published as *By Faith Alone* (London 1944). Faced with the problems of another generation, he brought a different standpoint from that of his predecessor, while retaining a great respect for him.

He had begun his ministry with three pastorates, at Winchester, Hove and Headingley, Leeds, before being appointed professor of systematic theology and Christian social philosophy at the Yorkshire United Independent College in 1932. After five years in Bradford he moved to Edinburgh, at the age of 43, as principal of the Scottish Congregational

[20] Kenneth Lloyd Parry (1884–1962) was minister of Highbury Chapel 1933–54. He was an authority on hymnology, and Chairman of the Congregational Union 1942–3. See *CYB 1962* 469–70.

[21] Three members of Redland Park Church were killed in action in the forces, and two were killed in air raids. See Peggy Thomas, *The Story of Redland Park United Reformed Church* (published by the church in 1995).

[22] Harry Francis Lovell Cocks (1894–1983). See *URC Year Book 1984* and Alan P. F. Sell, 'Theology for All: The Contribution of H. F. Lovell Cocks' in *Commemorations: Studies in Christian Thought and History* (Cardiff 1993).

College and a lecturer at Edinburgh University. In 1939, just before the outbreak of war, he had signed the 'Manifesto to Congregational Ministers' drafted by Bernard Manning, J. S. Whale and Nathaniel Micklem,[23] thus identifying himself with the new orthodox group within Congregationalism. Like Franks he had taken an active part in the Congregational theological conferences and contributed many articles to the *Congregational Quarterly*.

He began work in the war-damaged College in April 1941 and was inducted the following month. His manner was more informal than that of his predecessor, who had seemed rather remote to many of his students at first. This was exemplified during his second year when the students gave him a banquet and the 'Freedom of the Common Room' in celebration of the award of his London doctorate. Thereafter he made it a practice to have coffee with the students after lunch in their common room.

For the next ten years he worked happily alongside Arthur Dakin, the Baptist College principal, and G. Henton Davies, who had succeeded F. E. Robinson when the latter retired as Baptist tutor in 1938 at the age of 77. Gwynne Henton Davies was an Old Testament scholar whose later career took him to Durham as Professor and to Regent's Park College in Oxford as principal.[24] In 1953 the partnership continued when L. G. Champion[25] succeeded Dakin as principal and Norman Moon succeeded Davies as Tutor in Old Testament and church history.

Arnold Sims continued as bursar and tutor until after the war,[26] when he was followed by W. J. Downes (generally affectionately known as 'Uncle Bill'), who served in a similar capacity for the next 15 years, teaching Greek language and philosophy and Hebrew as well as general arts subjects. A former student of New College, he came to the Western College after three pastorates, the last at Kingswood on the outskirts of Bristol, so that he was already a familiar figure in Bristol Congregational circles. As a pacifist he believed that one of the greatest obstacles to world peace was the lack of a common language; this led him to study Esperanto, to teaching and preaching in Esperanto in many overseas countries, and to the preparation (though not unfortunately the completion) of a new English/Esperanto dictionary. In later years, after the College had closed, he did not join the United Reformed Church, but joined the Congregational Federation.[27]

[23] The Manifesto is quoted in full in N. Micklem, *The Box and the Puppets* (London 1957) 93–9.

[24] Gwynne Henton Davies (1906–98) was President of the Baptist Union in 1971.

[25] Leonard George Champion was President of the Baptist Union in 1964, and retired from the College in 1972.

[26] In 1952 he produced an *Outline History* of the College on the occasion of the Bicentenary.

[27] William John Downes (1892–1987). See *CYB 1988/9* 28–9.

When Lovell Cocks's appointment was announced, E. H. Jeffs welcomed the combination of his 'deep and instructed loyalty to evangelical truth' with 'a clear-eyed awareness of the actual needs of man and society' in the pages of the *Christian World* (18 July 1940). He was concerned that theology should be what is now described as 'contextual': 'Theology cannot be studied and true sermons cannot be preached in a vacuum. We not only have to give our men a footing in the Gospel but to show them its relevance to contemporary human life and society.'[28] He encouraged his students to study sociology, and in their last year, free from the pressure of examinations, to relate academic work to pastoral needs: 'Many of us remember being pitchforked into a pastorate straight from the hurly-burly of University examinations. It took us a long time to get our bearings, and to acquire the art of laying our minds alongside those of the people in our congregations.'[29]

He was just as insistent as his predecessor on the need for rigorous academic study as a prelude to effective preaching and ministry:

> There is a queer notion, still lingering in some quarters, that a theological college damps down evangelical passion and turns earnest preachers of the Gospel into academic pulpit essayists. What nonsense that is! ... A man's ideas are shaken and sifted, and the process is often unpleasant. But at the end of it all he is more sure of his message than he was at first.[30]

A few years later, he told the subscribers of the harm done by 'well-meaning people' who told potential students that the College course might undermine their faith. 'I do not believe that any man's faith has been destroyed by what he has learned within these walls. But I am quite sure that every man's faith has been tested and strengthened in so far as he has submitted himself to the discipline of the College Course and has not closed his mind against what it has to offer him.'[31]

He was a supporter of women's ministry, and welcomed several women students. In 1949 he told the subscribers that 'our women students are among our best preachers, as they are among our best in the examination lists.' Churches, he said, would be wise to overcome their prejudice in this matter 'in their own highest interest', and 'it will be a happy day for the churches when they recognise it'.

He took a leading role in the life of the churches in the area and, increasingly, in the denomination as a whole. He was elected Chairman of the Congregational Union for the year 1950–1, the first serving principal of Western to hold this position since George Payne in 1836. His address was on the theme, 'A Church Reborn'. Two years later he

[28] *Annual Report* 1946.
[29] *Annual Report* 1948.
[30] *Annual Report* 1948.
[31] *Annual Report* 1957.

addressed the International Congregational Council at St Andrews, and for its first two years served on the committee which eventually drew up the 'Declaration of Faith' of 1967, prior to the formation of the United Reformed Church.

He was a great communicator, to children as well as adults, and was always in demand as a preacher at church anniversaries and other special events. He had a fine baritone voice, and his solos were star items in the annual concerts attended by West Country Congregationalists. He also proved to be an effective broadcaster, and in the 1950s gave series of 'Lift up your Hearts' programmes for the then Home Service of the BBC.[32]

He was thoroughly rooted in his own tradition, as was revealed for instance in his *The Nonconformist Conscience*, one of the 'Forward Books', published in 1943. He was also a great Cromwell enthusiast. In September 1959 he gave the address at the annual service of the Cromwell Association in front of Cromwell's statue in Westminster. When invited to give the Congregational Lectures in 1959 he chose to speak not on what Independency owed to Cromwell, but on what Cromwell owed to Independency; the lectures were published as *The Religious Life of Oliver Cromwell* (London 1960).

Yet he witnessed to the 'catholic substance' of Congregationalism, 'which is never more tragically misjudged than when it is taken to be the apotheosis of religious individualism'.[33] He valued the ecumenical contacts of the College, not only through the Baptist College, but after 1945 with the Methodist College, now merged with Didsbury College which had removed from Manchester, and with the two Anglican colleges in Bristol. Relations between the churches in Bristol were good, and when the College celebrated its bicentenary at a meeting in Highbury Chapel on 11 June 1952, the chair was taken by the University Vice-Chancellor, Sir Philip Morris, and the two principal speakers were the Revd Leslie Cooke, Secretary of the Congregational Union, and Dr F. A. Cockin, Bishop of Bristol.

By the time Lovell Cocks retired in 1960 there were 29 students in the College, almost the maximum number who could be taught. Its future was more hopeful than for a long time. In retirement Cocks was active. In 1962, the tercentenary of the 'Great Ejectment', he was Moderator of the Free Church Federal Council, and preached at the tercentenary service in the City Temple, which was attended by the Anglican archbishops. Two

[32] Several of these were published by the Independent Press.

[33] *The Nonconformist Conscience* 88. Cocks was one of the three Congregational contributors to *The Catholicity of Protestantism* (ed. R. N. Flew and R. E. Davies, London 1950), produced by a group of Nonconformists in 1950 in response to a request from the Archbishop of Canterbury to clarify questions concerning the historic division of Western Christianity. It was in effect a critical reply to the Anglican report on *Catholicity* (1947), which had as its subtitle, 'A Study of the Conflict of Christian Traditions in the West'.

years later it was a proud moment for the College when he gave the charge to the new Minister Secretary of the Congregational Union, John Huxtable, a former Western student.

His successor was Basil Sims,[34] the son of Arnold Sims; he had been minister of the Redland Park Church for the preceding twelve years, overseeing the reconstruction and re-opening of the building. He was brought up in Bristol and educated at Bristol Grammar School before being articled for a short time to a firm of accountants, a useful experience in the light of his later need for fund-raising skills. He went up to Corpus Christi College, Oxford, and then entered Mansfield College as a theological student. Here he not only had a distinguished academic career but also played hockey for the University; like Franks before him, he gained a B Litt degree.[35] Before returning to Bristol as minister of Redland Park, he spent five years as minister at Whitley Bay, Northumberland. His ministry at Redland Park gave him much opportunity for work with young people and students, for which his vitality and sense of humour were assets; he was chaplain to the Congregational Society and took part in 'missions' to the University. He proved to be an effective broadcaster on both radio and television.

The financial position remained 'disquieting'. When the last of a long succession of loyal resident caretakers left in 1961, Basil Sims drew on his close knowledge of local Congregationalists to institute the 'Friends of Western College' – a group of voluntary helpers from Bristol churches, some of whom came into the College each weekday to prepare lunches for staff and students, and to help with other domestic tasks.

Student life continued its busy and lively course, with parties, plays, sports and outings. The annual 'At Home', at which the students presented a play and choral items, was usually attended by coach parties from the West Country, some of them travelling long distances.

Throughout the 1960s the 'Damoclean Sword' of closure hung over the College. During the session 1965/6 negotiations with Mansfield College took place, at the suggestion of the Congregational Church's Colleges Committee, but neither side was prepared to leave its base. In his annual report in 1966 Basil Sims told the subscribers that the number of Congregational theological colleges would have to be reduced, because of the sharp decline in the number of ordinands. A year later he reported that while he and the College Committee had no wish to be obstructionist, 'it would be idle to pretend that our response to the attempt of the Congregational Church in England and Wales to find a mathematical solution to its problem by reducing the number of its

[34] Basil Hudson Sims (1919–83). See *URCYB 1984/5* 200.

[35] The subject of his thesis was 'The Servant of the Lord: The Influence of the Old Testament Conception on the Literature of the New Testament' (1943); his supervisors were H. Wheeler Robinson and A. M. Hunter.

Theological Colleges has not been widely misrepresented.' He also reported 'more in sorrow than in anger' that in the previous November, 'the Council of the Congregational Church voted, by a majority verdict and after insufficient debate, that financial help would not be forthcoming for our Colleges until their number in England . . . is reduced to four.' Perhaps anticipating the closure, Wilson Dennett, the former student who had replaced W. J. Downes as bursar and tutor in 1962, moved to Exeter as minister of Southernhay Congregational Church. The principal then advocated the separation of administrative from academic functions, resulting in the appointment of a full-time Secretary and two part-time tutors for the session 1967–8: David Gaunt, Lecturer in Classics at Bristol University and a deacon at Redland Park, and the Revd John Young of Argyle Church, Bath. This left Basil Sims as the only full-time member of the academic staff, which together with the uncertainty about the future of the College put him under great stress.

The maximum number of students that Western could hope to have in 1968–9 would be 12. A college with 12 students and only one full-time member of staff was neither financially nor educationally viable. In 1966 Western's Education Committee expressed a desire to send two observers to the meetings then taking place between Paton and Northern Colleges, but the representatives of the two colleges concerned felt it was too early in the negotiations for this to be wise.[36]

In December 1967 the principal was placed in a very difficult position on receiving an invitation to become principal of the newly-amalgamated Northern/Congregational College in 1968. After much heart-searching he allowed his name to go forward and early in 1968 he accepted the invitation. Amalgamation with the Manchester college now seemed the only course for the Western College. The death of Kenneth Wills, the College President, in December 1967 at the age of 95, symbolised the end of an era. The College Education and Finance Committees and the College Council met on 15 March and resolved: 'In the light of the needs of the Congregational Church, and of the particular circumstances in theological training, we believe it to be advisable that this College should enter into discussions with the Congregational College, Manchester, with a view to the fullest possible integration of the two colleges.'

It fell to the Chairman of the Council, John Murray, then minister of Mill Hill Congregational Church, London, to steer the negotiations. His diplomatic skills failed to resolve an unfortunate dispute which arose between Basil Sims and the officers of Northern College, and which eventually led to Sims's withdrawal from the proffered principalship. In the end he chose to remain in the West Country, and spent the rest of his

[36] Letters of Gordon Robinson to Basil Sims, 26 October 1966, 18 February 1967, Paton College Archive, NC.

working life as a Lecturer in Liberal Studies at Weston-super-Mare Technical College.

Lovell Cocks returned to preach at the closing service. He took as his text Hebrews 13: 14, 'Here we have no lasting city, but we seek the city which is to come.' There was great sadness not only in Bristol and the surrounding area, but in the whole of the West Country, particularly at the decision to sell the building. It fell to the Gloucestershire and Herefordshire Congregational Union, as Trustees, to arrange the sale, which was conducted by auction (the auctioneer was a member of Redland Park). The library books were also sold off by auction in lots. The purchaser of the College building, who paid £24,000, was the Southern Examinations Board.[37] The principal's house was sold separately to a consultant physician for £9,000.

It was finally agreed that four students would move to Manchester, while the rest would remain in Bristol to be taught by John Young and the staff of the Bristol Baptist College. The funds acquired through the sale of the property and its contents were placed in the hands of a 'Western College Trust', which was to be responsible for using the income to help students (primarily at Northern College), other colleges, and ministers undertaking further study.

[37] Later the building was acquired as a health centre, which retains the name as the Western College Family Practice, and whose staff value and carefully preserve its original character.

12

Paton College 1920–68

At the Annual Meeting of the Committee and subscribers in June 1920 the name of the Nottingham Congregational Institute was changed to 'Paton Congregational College' in honour of the founder. The change from 'Institute' to 'College' was not however intended to indicate any change in the character and purpose of the institution. For the rest of its history (another 48 years) there were repeated affirmations of its special identity and contribution. In 1934, for example, in making reference to the special Commission which was considering the relation between the Congregational Union and the colleges, the Committee stated:

> The only thing that vitally concerns this College is that the door should be kept open to men to whom the call to the ministry comes at a later age than usual, or whose early education has been of an elementary character, but who have intellectual gifts to benefit by a theological course and to render good service to the Kingdom of God in the ministry.[1]

The emphasis on social and educational studies and their relation to preaching and pastoral work gained greater depth in the growing co-operation with the University College.

Towards the end of the First World War the College had had to close. Principal Ritchie went to Canada to lecture at McGill University, and Professor Sanders took a temporary pastorate in Newcastle. McGill recognised Ritchie's gifts by awarding him a doctorate and inviting him to join their staff permanently. At first he refused, and he and Sanders worked among the troops in France with the YMCA during the summer of 1918. But finally he yielded to pressure from Canada and resigned his Nottingham post. He went on to become Dean of Degrees at McGill, and played an important role in the formation of the United Church of Canada.[2]

The person chosen to succeed Principal Ritchie was Alexander Roy Henderson,[3] who was already well-known in Nottingham as minister of Castle Gate Congregational Church from 1902 until 1919; he had served on the College Committee for many years. A very tall man, he was a Scot

[1] *Annual Report* for the year 1934.

[2] He died in 1952. See *Who Was Who 1951–60*.

[3] Alexander Roy Henderson (1862–1950). See *CYB 1951* 512–13.

like Paton, educated at Edinburgh University and the Scottish Congregational Hall under D. W. Simon. He had three Scottish pastorates before moving to Castle Gate. When the invitation to Paton came, he had just moved to Wolverhampton; he felt bound to remain there until the autumn of 1921. By that time he was already 59. Though he wrote no major works of theology, his standing as a preacher and administrator was recognised in his election to the chair of the Congregational Union for the year 1923–4.

Dr Sanders rejoined the College at the end of the war. A third member of staff, also a minister in Wolverhampton until 1921, and a close friend of Henderson, took up a new post funded through a magnificent gift of £10,000 from Sir Jesse Boot (already a great benefactor to the University College),[4] to be used for the provision of teaching in Christian sociology and psychology and allied subjects. John Grant McKenzie (like Henderson, a native of Aberdeenshire) had studied at Aberdeen University and the Yorkshire United Independent College, and held two pastorates, in Halifax and Wolverhampton, before moving to Nottingham.[5] He was something of a pioneer in the teaching and practice of pastoral psychology, following on from the work of William James on *Varieties of Religious Experience* (the Gifford Lectures of 1901–2). His first book, *Modern Psychology and the Achievement of Christian Personality* (London 1923), was published soon after his arrival at the College; this was followed by a number of pioneering books on the relation between religion and psychology. He became well-known as a lecturer, writer and counsellor; his public lectures (published as *Souls in the Making* in 1928) were attended by many local Anglican and Free Church ministers. His own private practice gave him plenty of material for his lectures.[6] His brilliance and charismatic personality shone more brightly when he was prepared to depart from his formal notes and speak of his recent experiences. His teaching role facilitated an arrangement with the University College by which a Diploma in Social Science could be awarded by the two institutions in conjunction to men who passed certain required examinations and carried out particular forms of practical work, including factory visits and work in Dakeyne Street Lads' Club. The University provided the classes in economics, local government, and sanitation and hygiene. Practical work benefited from the co-operation of the city's chief constable, who provided carefully supervised access to 'the lesser known life of a great city' during the hours of darkness. This link gave Paton a more objective validation of its work

[4] Sir Jesse Boot, later Lord Trent (1850–1931) came from a Methodist background, but had always admired J. B. Paton, and took a great interest in his college. See *DNB*.

[5] John Grant McKenzie (1882–1963). See *Who Was Who 1961–70*.

[6] For some years he wrote a regular column in the *British Weekly*.

than hitherto, though all the College's courses were examined by outside examiners, whose reports were published. McKenzie's lectures on sociology in the early 1930s included courses on socialism, fascism and communism, surely unusual for theological colleges of the time.

The fourth, part-time member of staff was the principal's son, Roy Galbraith Henderson, who lectured in voice production and elocution. He was later to achieve fame as a baritone soloist and as the teacher of many outstanding singers of the twentieth century, including Kathleen Ferrier (on whom he wrote the article for the *Dictionary of National Biography*).

It was Principal Henderson who was chiefly responsible for the College's move from Forest Road to Tollerton, a village four miles from the centre of the city. Tollerton Hall, a mediaeval manor house[7] altered in the late eighteenth century in Regency Gothic style, was opened as a country club in 1929, but soon ran into financial difficulties and was put on the market again. Henderson, fully supported by Major Thompson, a leading member of the Committee (who offered £1,000 towards the cost), proposed that it should be purchased for the College, arguing that as it was already well, if not lavishly, furnished and equipped, it would require little extra expenditure, that the ability to offer residence to the students would be an economy measure, and that extra revenue might be raised by accommodating conferences in the vacations. The Committee was persuaded, and when the vote was taken, there was only one dissentient. The Hall was purchased for £16,000, and formally opened on 30 September 1930 in the presence of 400 visitors. The old building in Forest Road was sold to the Nottingham and Nottinghamshire Adult Deaf and Dumb Society for £7000. It was the principal who was mainly instrumental in raising the extra funds needed for this new venture.

There were now 43 students in the College – the number had been steadily rising since the end of the war. The Committee's report at the end of 1931 noted that the best thing about the new location 'is the common life that has now for the first time become possible. The men are no longer separated into little groups within which their friendships were largely confined.'

But there were flaws in the new arrangement, which eventually proved to have been too ambitious a commitment. The maintenance of the estate of 68 acres was expensive and time-consuming. No one could have foreseen that the year 1931 would witness the worst floods in the Midlands since 1875, and that they would break through the retaining wall of the lake in the grounds, turning a large area into a murky swamp; it was two years before the necessary repair work could be completed. By

[7] Earlier known as Troclavestune, or Roclaveston, Manor. For many generations it had been in the hands of the Barry family.

Figure 10: Tollerton Hall, near Nottingham, home of Paton College 1930–41
Source: Nottingham Local Studies Library

the time the College had been on the site for two years there was a serious financial crisis, causing the Committee to ask the professors, bursar and matron to take a temporary 10 per cent reduction in salary.

There were other problems. The original intention had been to build a separate house for the principal and his family, but there were not sufficient funds. There was no clear division in the existing house between the principal's quarters and those of the students, thus causing friction. The distance from the city centre, and from the small churches which the students were intended to help, weakened the links with the community which Paton himself had regarded as so important.

There was now concern that the principal, who was 73, had too much on his shoulders, with responsibility for the estate as well as the teaching and administration. It was decided to appoint a young scholarly minister as tutor, someone of the same generation as the students and able to understand their perspective. The choice fell on Charles Duthie (later principal first of the Scottish Congregational College and then of New College, London), another Scottish graduate of Aberdeen University and the Scottish Congregational College, who had just returned from a year's study in Tübingen. His one-year appointment was extended to two years.

In 1937 Principal Henderson retired after 50 years in the Congregational ministry. As a tribute to his long service to the College, the present and past students raised sufficient money to turn a derelict outbuilding into an attractive chapel, able to hold 50 people.[8] As Dr Sanders was due to retire in the following year, his name too was included in the dedication plaque. An attempt to establish a Sunday School for the children of the village and a Sunday evening service for the adults did not prosper as intended, but the Chapel soon became the centre of College life.

The Committee's first choice as new principal was H. F. Lovell Cocks, then on the staff of the Yorkshire College. But they discovered that he was already committed to moving to Edinburgh as principal of the Scottish Congregational College. An invitation was then issued to T. S. Taylor,[9] minister of Ward Chapel, Dundee and the current chairman of the Congregational Union of Scotland. He accepted, and came to steer the College through what proved to be ten difficult years, including six years of war and several years of his own ill-health. He was a native of

[8] The architect was Frederic Lawrence of Bournemouth. See *CYB 1938* 693 for a description. Lawrence was also the architect of Sherwood and Arnold Congregational churches. See Clyde Binfield, 'Art and Spirituality in Chapel Architecture: F. W. Lawrence (1882–1948) and his Churches' in D. M. Loades (ed), *The End of Strife: Death, Reconciliation and the Experience of Christian Spirituality* (Edinburgh 1984).

[9] Thomas Samuel Taylor (1885–1948). See *CYB 1949* 507.

Staffordshire, educated at St John's and Mansfield Colleges in Oxford, where he had written a B Litt thesis on the Reformer Henry Bullinger of Zurich. His first ministry was in Belfast; his second, before moving to Dundee, in Eccles, Lancashire. Despite the pressures on him, the students always found him to be very approachable and supportive as well as learned.

Dr Sanders' successor was R. R. (Robin) Turner,[10] who was inducted a month after war broke out in 1939.[11] Yet another Scot, he was to remain at the College for almost thirty years until it closed, serving as principal during the final three years. He was the grandson of G. Lyon Turner, historian of Nonconformity, who taught at New College, London and the Lancashire Independent College. His parents were missionaries in China, where he spent the early years of his life. He gained a first class honours degree at Edinburgh University before taking his theological course at Cheshunt College, Cambridge. He served with the LMS in China for a short time, but had to return home in 1930 and worked as Warden of Broad Plain House in Bristol before moving to Nottingham. A quiet meticulous scholar, he particularly excelled in the teaching of New Testament Greek.

The first effect of the war was a reduction in the number of students. Those still in residence had to share in a fire-duty rota, and climb the tower in tin hats whenever the siren sounded. The threat of requisition of the premises hung over the College, and there was a sign of what was to come when the military authorities took over most of the building and established a camp in the grounds for twelve weeks in 1940. In April 1941 notice of requisition was received. Three months later the College building, with the exception of the chapel and the principal's quarters, was taken over by the RAF. The furniture and most of the library was put in store and the Boulevard Congregational Church in the city provided space for teaching while the students were placed in lodgings. By 1942 there were only 20 students, and in the following year only 13, insufficient to provide work for three members of staff. Robin Turner was asked to find temporary alternative employment. Fortunately he was able to fill a vacancy at the Yorkshire College, where he remained for three years, commuting weekly between Nottingham and Bradford. But in spite of these limitations many enquiries were being received from servicemen who wished to prepare for ministry as soon as the war was over. They were encouraged to use any spare time they might have to begin learning Greek. 'It can be said that Nunn's Greek Testament Grammar is being studied for our Entrance Examination, in the desert, in

[10] Robert Reynolds Turner (1901–82). See *URCYB 1983* 265.

[11] New Testament teaching for the session 1938–9 was covered by the Revd J. O. Dobson.

Jerusalem, in Gibraltar, and as far north as the Faroe Islands as well as on the high seas.'[12]

A return to Tollerton was not now envisaged. Just before the end of the war the whole Tollerton estate was sold to the Roman Catholic diocese, who used it to house a boys' secondary school. Now that the College was operating within the city, the advantages of being close to the University College[13] and to the local inner-city and suburban churches were realised. Work continued at the Cottage, Castle Gate, while thought was given to a permanent new location. The social life of the College was concentrated on the Paton Players, which involved not only students but also their families, and which mounted regular productions in the city.

The students were still required to preach on at least half the Sundays of the term. Churches within travelling distance of the College sent in requests for preachers early in the week, and on Thursdays the list was read. In order of seniority the students made their choices, leaving the difficult and the distant churches for the 'freshers'. It was a common experience for students to have a long journey on the Saturday to a remote village, to preach to very small congregations morning and evening, and then to face another long return journey on the Monday.

One former student remembers going to a village in the Lincolnshire Fens, reaching his destination after taking most of the day travelling on a series of buses. Early next morning he was summoned by his host before breakfast to come downstairs. 'Unwashed and unshaven, with no collar or tie, we went down the village street to the chapel, a corrugated iron construction. There he handed me a broom with the instruction to sweep up while he lit the old tortoise stove.' After breakfast they returned to the chapel for Sunday School at 10 a.m. and morning worship at 11 a.m., attended by a congregation of six. The same members of the congregation attended evening worship at 6 p.m., together with another man, 'who put his head against the wall and made no move, apparently asleep, until I gave the blessing when he got up and walked out without a word to anyone'. On Monday morning, as the student caught the bus for his long journey back to College, his host expressed surprise that no student ever came to preach there twice.[14]

Sermon class, usually conducted by McKenzie in the years immediately after the war, was continued, using J. B. Paton's 'canons'. The position of student appointed to preach and conduct the service was known as 'being on the Box'. One of McKenzie's favourite comments was, 'Every sermon should have something in it for the old ladies.' He was now very deaf, and used a small black box to aid communication; when a preacher,

[12] *Annual Report* 1943.

[13] King George V had opened magnificent new buildings in 1928, the gift of Sir Jesse Boot.

[14] I am indebted to the Revd Dr Ken Hibberd for this account.

student or staff, exasperated him, he would lean forward and switch off the box, much to the embarrassment of the preacher concerned.

In 1947 ill health forced T. S. Taylor to resign, and he died early in the following year. Fourteen names were now considered for the post of principal; the choice fell on Maurice Charles.[15] At 45 he was a younger principal than the College had known for a long time, and all his energy was now needed to help it to recover its vitality and direction. Of all Paton's successors, he was the one who most closely shared his vision. He was a Welshman, of a Congregational family well-known in Wales; one of his ancestors was a famous Welsh hymn-writer, and his father had been trained for the Congregational ministry at University College, Cardiff and Brecon College. Though he was largely brought up in England and trained for the ministry at New College, London and Mansfield College, Oxford (where he wrote a thesis under the supervision of A. D. Lindsay, Master of Balliol[16]), he maintained regular and strong contacts with Wales and it was to Wales that he returned to be ordained at Abercarn, and to work with the unemployed in the Western Valley of Monmouthshire (now Gwent). He became involved in the work of the Workers' Educational Assocation, the Council for Social Service in Wales, and Oxford House, Risca (in which Lindsay took a great interest), and had actually lectured at Paton in the mid 1930s about his work with the unemployed. In 1938 he was called to be minister at Walter Road, Swansea, and led the church through the ravages of the blitz.

While he was minister in Swansea he married Elizabeth Phillips, daughter of a Presbyterian minister, and a classics graduate of Cardiff. She was Welsh Officer of the National Association of Girls' Clubs, with responsibility for areas of high unemployment, and had been involved in settlement work, especially with young people, in the Welsh valleys. They formed a dynamic partnership, both idealistic and practical, and the recovery of the College from its depressed state owed much to both of them.

The first task was to find new premises. Within a year, a house on the Derby Road (no. 487) had been selected and purchased; it was well situated, adjacent to the University campus and not far from the centre of the city. It was formally opened in October 1949. From the first Elizabeth Charles took over the domestic side of the College.[17] In an effort to save expense, but also to involve the local churches in the life of the College, she organised teams of women from nearby congregations to prepare lunches for staff and students at the College on weekdays. This helped to

[15] Maurice Charles (1903–64). See *CYB 1964–5* 436–7.

[16] The subject of the thesis was 'The Social Implications of the Gospel of Mark'.

[17] Later, in 1961, her contribution to the College was given some recognition in her appointment as Principal's assistant with a nominal salary.

foster a stronger communal life. Soon a few single students were also taken into residence.[18]

Funding the College was a major concern of Maurice Charles throughout his principalship. In particular he devoted a good deal of time to helping students to find ways and means of covering the cost of their training and the maintenance of their families. He and his wife also instituted an annual garden party, which became an important date in the calendars of the Congregational churches of the East Midlands. Each county was responible for a county stall, and other denominations often participated. This anticipated the need for more funds when maintenance grants for students under the Further Education and Training Scheme ended. The first garden party was held in 1950, attended by 700 Congregationalists from 80 churches in seven counties; it raised £200 for the College funds. Each year more people came and more money was raised – eventually about £1,000 each year, and the whole city gave its support. Elizabeth Charles persuaded local firms to donate gifts for stalls run by different church organisations, so that by 1962 about 100 firms (many of whom had been connected with the College from the beginning) were supporting the event regularly with gifts for sale.

The principal and his wife were appointed joint presidents of the Nottingham Free Church Federal Council in 1957, and in the following year they attended the meeting of the International Congregational Council at Hartford, Connecticut. Elizabeth Charles was made a Justice of the Peace in 1957, and was elected President of the Federation of Congregational Women.[19]

The University of Nottingham was given its charter in 1949, just after Maurice Charles arrived. In the preceding few years, preparations had been made for the founding of a theology department by the appointment of G. D. Kilpatrick,[20] a New Testament scholar, as Reader in Theology; he had regularly lectured to Paton men. The first person to be appointed as Professor of Christian Theology was John Marsh, former chaplain and tutor, and future principal, of Mansfield College, Oxford. The Professor of Adult Education, Robert Peers, and the Professor of Social Science, Arthur Radford, proved to be great supporters of Paton in the college's renegotiation of its status with the new university.

When J. G. McKenzie retired in 1951 and moved to Edinburgh, two

[18] Those who entered the college single were expected to remain so until the course was finished, unless special permission to marry was gained from the College Governors.

[19] Later she was twice elected President of the Women's Council of the National Free Church Federal Council, and represented the Free Churches of England and Wales on the Women's National Commission, in which capacity she promoted exchange visits with women of Eastern Europe.

[20] Later Dean Ireland's Professor of Exegesis of Holy Scripture in the University of Oxford.

part-time tutors, who were also in pastoral ministry, were appointed to share the work he had done: Harold Hodgkins,[21] minister at Buxton, who taught social science and psychology, and David Arafnah Thomas[22] of Leicester (and later of Matlock), who taught logic and philosophy of religion. As the University's Department of Theology developed and expanded, it was able to offer more teaching to Paton students, supplementary to the courses offered by the College.

The years of Maurice Charles's principalship, which were not easy at first, saw a gradual raising of academic standards. In 1949 a Joint Certificate in Religious and Social Studies was initiated; staff in both the University and the College shared in the teaching, and three representatives from each institution formed a committee to validate it. It was a three-year course, which could be taken during the second, third and fourth years of a student's time at Paton. Most students took this Certificate, which was intentionally inter-disciplinary. The principal believed that 'it is in the field of the integration of the subjects included in the course that most urgent issues for the life of the churches, the survival of our country and the advance of human civilisation have to be decided.'[23] Also available to selected students was a Certificate in Youth Leadership, a Certificate in Social Studies, and, for those whose academic attainments were of a sufficiently high standard, a BA degree in Theology. In 1952 eight of the 33 students were working for the degree. It was a proud moment for the College when in 1955 R. J. McKelvey[24] gained both a first class honours degree in theology and a World Council of Churches scholarship to Pittsburgh. Three other graduates went on in the same year to further academic study elsewhere. The principal himself was not neglecting academic study, and wrote a thesis under the supervision of Alan Richardson, John Marsh's successor, on 'The Relevance for Today of St Mark's Interpretation of the Crisis in Jerusalem in the First Century', for which he was awarded a PhD by the University of Nottingham.

In 1959 the University's Social Sciences Department was no longer able to provide the special course for Paton men, but a new Joint Certificate was negotiated, this time in 'Theological and Educational Studies'. This fitted in well with Maurice Charles's definition of the distinctive function of Paton as 'an agency for the redemption of the

[21] Harold Hodgkins (1907–95). He joined the Congregational Federation after the formation of the United Reformed Church in 1972. See the *CYB 1996*.

[22] David Arafnah Thomas (1895–1990) was a native of Wales, educated at Cardiff University College, Merton College, Oxford and Memorial College, Brecon. The year after he retired he was awarded a PhD degree by the University of London for a thesis on 'The Idea of God in the Philosophy of Descartes, Malebranche and Spinoza'.

[23] *Annual Report 1949*.

[24] Later principal of Adams Theological College, South Africa, and of Northern College.

British nation through the training of an ordained and lay ministry by methods akin to those of Adult Education'. He foresaw that churches in the future might be smaller, and less able to support a full-time minister; rather than grouping churches together, he believed that ministers who were not only equipped theologically but were also qualified to work in the community on social projects would best meet the situation. Academic study and ministerial practice were integrated more thoroughly throughout the course than in any other theological college.

The ideals of adult education, and of Paton College, included a belief that opportunities for study should be available to all, whatever their age or intellectual background.[25] In this spirit, a course of preliminary study was drawn up which could be taken by potential students still in full-time jobs; two years of such study successfully completed might then exempt a man from the first year of the full-time course, thus helping an older man with a family to support to lighten the financial burden.[26] These men were known as 'Accepted Students'. A local minister, N. B. Pace, helped with their tuition, as well as assisting the Principal with some of the administrative work. Other students with families to support were sometimes enabled to undertake student pastorates.

As the centenary in 1963 approached, Maurice Charles became ever more convinced of the relevance of Paton's vision to the new Forward Movement of the Congregational churches. There had always been references to Paton's ideals in the annual reports, but he began including passages from the earliest reports in order to demonstrate their relevance to the contemporary world. In the Report for 1957 he stated:

> Whatever be the possibilities of organic Re-union of the Church in England in the next decade, it is now not only possible, but imperative, for the churches in each district to undertake active corporate responsibility for the social redemption of their own locality. Once they do this, then they will find that the aims of the Inner Mission proclaimed by Dr Paton will be effective today for the Unity of the Church in that social leadership and further education which Britain must have to outlive the twentieth century.[27]

He and his wife jointly prepared a booklet on 'The Church's Ministry to the Nation'[28] which had a wide circulation; it drew extensively on Paton's conception of 'the inner mission'.

The actual centenary celebrations were held in December 1963 in Castle Gate church, with addresses from both H. S. Stanley, Secretary of

[25] In 1960, for example, the applicants included a carpenter and joiner, an electrician, an undertaker, a plumber and an insurance salesman.

[26] Of 27 students in the College in 1957, 25 were over 25, 11 over 30, and two were over 40; 21 were married and 10 had children.

[27] *Annual Report 1957*.

[28] Published by the Free Church Federal Council in 1963.

the Congregational Union, and John Marsh, now principal of Mansfield College, Oxford. There were plans for a new building, to include a Lecture Hall to seat an audience of 200, suitable for either university or local church occasions. Sadly, however, the principal became ill within a month of these celebrations, and died in April 1964 at the age of 61, a few months before the meeting in Nottingham of the Faith and Order Conference of the British Council of Churches, in which he would surely have taken part. His widow bravely shouldered the responsibility for the Centenary Garden Party in June (at which a play by Robert Duce on the life of J. B. Paton was performed by the students) and thereafter took up a teaching post in Nottingham. After four years she moved to Swansea as Warden of a University Hall of Residence and Lecturer in Education.

There were now many uncertainties. The number of theological students in the country as a whole was falling (though the number of students at Paton had remained steady at just under 30), and the College Committee of the Congregational Union was at work on determining the appropriate response. Its report, published in November 1965, recommended that Paton and New College, London should amalgamate. While Paton's committee recognised that the number of colleges would have to be reduced, they were not happy about a move to London, which would involve abandoning the work they were doing for churches in the Midlands and the North, and this idea was soon abandoned. A union with Northern College was more attractive, and formal negotiations began in November 1966. Meanwhile, Robin Turner, who had been acting principal since the death of Maurice Charles, was appointed principal on the understanding that this was unlikely to be a long-term arrangement. He completed his many years of loyal service to the College by overseeing the amalgamation of Paton with the College in Manchester, with valuable assistance from two governors, George Marson and Ronald Masser. Governors from Nottingham would continue to serve the new amalgamated College.

Within eighteen months of the opening of negotiations, a draft scheme had been agreed, and the sale of Paton's building to the University for £34,000 arranged. (It now houses the School of Architecture.) Of the five students still in training after the summer of 1968, four were to move to Manchester, while one would stay in Nottingham to complete his course.

On 22 June 1968 the final garden party was held, opened by Mary Wilson, the wife of the Prime Minister; her father, Daniel Baldwin, was at Paton from 1905 until 1909. Three days later John Huxtable, Minister Secretary of the Congregational Church, preached the final valedictory service in Castle Gate.

13

Yorkshire United Independent College 1919–58

TWELVE students assembled for the new academic year in 1919. Their number doubled in the following year and by 1927 had reached 40. There were two new members of staff, both in their thirties, and the principal was at the height of his powers. Bradford Congregationalism was still thriving, and the Yorkshire Congregational Union was one of the most vigorous in the country. After the hard years of war, the outlook was now hopeful.

Principal Griffith-Jones was approaching the age of 60 with his vigour undiminished. He was Chairman of the Congregational Union in the year in which the war ended, addressing the Assembly in May 1918 on 'Congregationalism at the Cross-Roads,' and in October on 'Congregationalism and the Future'. With characteristic Welsh oratory he summoned the audience to renewed hope and action. 'We who have ever led the fight for liberty for ourselves at home must not lose heart, nor allow others to do so, till we have won liberty for all the world.' Congregationalists had, he urged, a duty to take part in shaping the reconstructed society which would follow the end of the war. 'I want to see our Church offering more than its fair share of men who are willing to go on all kinds of public bodies, and to fulfil all kinds of social functions, with a view to tide the nation over the quicksands of revolution, and through the storms of disorder, that may possibly be before us.' He called for a 'clean peace' after the war which was clearly coming to an end, and a League of Nations to keep it. He ended with an appeal 'to bring the whole world to a knowledge of the gospel'.[1]

He was at work on a two-volume book on 'providence', the first part of which was published in 1925 as *Providence – Divine and Human: A Study of the World-Order in the Light of Modern Thought* (London 1925). This was in effect a continuation of the thinking behind his earlier *The Ascent Through Christ* (London 1899), which attempted to investigate the implications of the theory of evolution for theology; the later work was intended for 'the perplexed Christian believer who is anxious to harmonise his faith with the world-view of modern science and philosophy, and to express it, *so far as that can be done without*

[1] *CYB 1919* 25–57.

detriment to spiritual values, in the thought-forms of our day and generation'.[2] A second volume on the human side of the problem of providence was never completed. The published volume never achieved the same popularity as *The Ascent Through Christ*.

Elkanah Armitage had retired in 1914, and his place was taken by E. J. Price,[3] a Mancunian and former student of the Lancashire College, who came to Bradford at the age of 32 after four years of pastoral ministry in Farnworth and spent the rest of his working life in Bradford, the last 15 years as principal. His subjects were church history, comparative religion and the philosophy of religion. A. J. Grieve left the College in 1917 to become principal of the Scottish Congregational Hall in Edinburgh. His successor as professor of New Testament was C. J. Cadoux,[4] who had spent the war years in Oxford as a tutor at Mansfield College, immediately after training there himself, and was able to enjoy reminiscing about Mansfield with the arts tutor, Ambrose Pope.[5] Alexander Duff was still on the staff, though at the age of 74 he was out of touch with the generation of students returning from the war, and the subject of his retirement was of some embarrassment to the College.

Price was a person of equable temperament and quiet learning, an excellent historian with a well-balanced ecumenical understanding and outlook. He never identified himself with any particular 'party' in the denomination. Cadoux, on the other hand, held controversial views which he never tried to hide, and enjoyed stimulating argument. He had taken a strong pacifist line during the war, and his first book, published just before his arrival in Bradford, was *The Early Christian Attitude to War* (London 1919), which remained a standard work for several generations. In it he argued with scholarly thoroughness that until the conversion of Constantine the Church had adopted a consistently pacifist line. Despite strongly held opposing views on the subject of war, Griffith-Jones and Cadoux were excellent colleagues, and they both enjoyed controversy. There was, however, a certain tension in Cadoux's relationship with men who had just returned from several years of fighting in France, especially as he found it difficult to refrain from referring to the subject of war. 'It seemed to us, using the habit of careless judgment we had acquired in the war, that you thought we were a very poor set of Christians and that you were a little puzzled to know why ex-soldiers were in training for the Ministry at all,' wrote one of his former students, Ralph Turner, many years later.[6]

[2] *Providence – Divine and Human* 9.

[3] Ernest Jones Price (1882–1952). See *CYB 1953* 520–1.

[4] Cecil John Cadoux (1883–1947). See Elaine Kaye, *C. J. Cadoux: Theologian, Scholar and Pacifist* (Edinburgh 1988).

[5] Ambrose Pope (1865–1928). See *CYB 1929* 226–7.

[6] Quoted in Elaine Kaye, 76.

These were the years when Cadoux was finding his feet as a scholar; by the time he left Bradford he had published two major works (each of 700 pages) as well as three shorter books and numerous articles. The first major work was *The Early Church and the World: A History of the Christian Attitude to Pagan Society and the State down to the time of Constantine* (Edinburgh 1925), based on his doctoral thesis; it was dedicated to C. H. Dodd, who described it in a review in the *British Weekly* (31 December 1925) as 'a sort of "copec" [i.e., a Conference of Politics, Economics and Citizenship] of the early Church,' in which the thinking of Christians during the first three centuries of the Church's life on these subjects was meticulously and exhaustively recorded. His second major work, in which the question of authority in religion was the dominant theme, was *Catholicism and Christianity: A Vindication of Progressive Protestantism* (London 1928). It was dedicated to the governors, staff and students of the College, who must have felt a measure of pride in opening their copy of the *Christian World* for the last week of October (1928) to find a large photograph of the author alongside a caption, 'Professor Cadoux's Great Book'.

His subject at the College however was New Testament. He had absorbed the biblical criticism of the late nineteenth century and the quest for the historical Jesus was for him an intellectual challenge.[7] In the spring of 1920 the Vice-Chancellor of Leeds University, Sir Michael Sadler, invited him to give a series of public lectures on 'The Life of the Historical Jesus'. Some members of the audience found his liberal views too challenging, and the reports of the lectures in the *Yorkshire Post* gave cause for alarm in the minds of some of the College's wealthier subscribers. One of the Governors complained to the principal, quoting the fact that at least one church in Leeds was threatening to withdraw its subscription to the College. Griffith-Jones, though alarmed and cautious, stood by his colleague, but it was Alexander Duff, who had suffered a similar onslaught a quarter of a century earlier, who gave most comfort to Cadoux.

Cadoux was an exacting teacher, pedantic at times, but always thoughtful for the welfare of his students. He loved to invite them to tea at his home in Shipley or for long walks, 'the main purpose of which was to inspect the furniture of the student's mind'.[8] He was in considerable demand in the West Riding as a preacher and lecturer,[9] and the Fellowship of Reconciliation made ample use of his gifts and learning both locally and nationally.

[7] At the end of his life his conclusions were expounded for a more popular audience in *The Life of Jesus*, published by Penguin in 1947.

[8] Harry Escott to the author 28 February 1982.

[9] With a family of four children to support, he needed to supplement his income with such engagements.

There was a lively intellectual life in the city to which the College staff contributed a good deal. Fairbairn and Duff had been active in the foundation of the Bradford Athenaeum in 1883, and this continued as a stimulating forum during the 1920s. A Leeds and Bradford Theological Circle was formed in 1921 and held its first meeting in December of that year, when Griffith-Jones read a paper on Luke's Gospel. The staffs not only of the Congregational College, but of Rawdon Baptist College and Wesley College in Headingley, and several local Anglican priests, met together regularly to read and discuss papers in turn.[10]

One of the new ventures after the war was to open a hostel for the arts men in Edinburgh. It was more difficult for the students to find satisfactory accommodation after the war, and the Governors took up a suggestion made by one of the College's former students, Henry Parnaby, who had been minister of Augustine Church in Edinburgh in the early years of the century, that a College hostel would provide the men with more support and supervision. Two houses in Royal Terrace were purchased, and Henry Parnaby was appointed Warden and tutor to students taking a preliminary course. The experiment was not a success, and the hostel was closed after three years, involving the College in a considerable loss of money.

The students, however, continued to take first degrees in Edinburgh, despite the proximity of a university in Leeds, which had received its Royal Charter in 1904.[11] The influence of Fairbairn, who demanded a good liberal university education before the study of theology, was still strong. Though the students were usually attached to one of the Congregational churches in Edinburgh, and helped with the church's mission and youth work, the dominating presence of Reformed preaching and teaching within the Church of Scotland introduced them to the demands of theological thinking. Many students remained grateful for the education they received in Edinburgh with its long scholarly, liberal tradition, and its emphasis on rigorous philosophical thinking.

The Lambeth Conference of 1920 issued an 'Appeal to all Christian People,' stimulating a series of ecumenical discussions and conferences in the next two decades. It had been preceded by informal gatherings of Nonconformists and Anglicans, and followed by a series of conferences on reunion. In his address to the Congregational Union Assembly in October 1918 Griffith-Jones had pleaded for inter-communion and the exchange of pulpits as a first step towards reunion. 'Any tampering with the integrity and validity of our Church order, any consent to such humiliation as re-ordination or licence to preach in Episcopal Churches,

[10] The Minutes of the Circle for the years 1935–49 are in the Leeds Archive Office. The Circle was dissolved in 1949, but was replaced by a Leeds Theological Circle.

[11] A Department of Theology within the Faculty of Arts was founded in 1936, and the staff of the United College then became 'recognised teachers' of the Department.

any reunion with the body bought at the expense of credal freedom, or governance by bishops, or surrender to sacerdotal claims on the part of the ministry – all this be far from us now or ever,' he told the Assembly. Congregationalists, he said, had a duty to 'fight to a finish' the campaign for the disestablishment of the Church of England.[12] Just before moving to Bradford, Cadoux had taken part in a conference of Anglicans and Free Churchmen at Mansfield College convened to prepare for the Lambeth Conference. He read a paper on 'The Crux of the Problem of Christian Reunion',[13] the first of many articles from his pen on this theme in the 1920s. Rejecting any credal or moral tests, he believed that the only requirement for acceptance as a Christian was a person's 'simple claim to the Christian name'. Griffith-Jones was a participant in the Anglican–Nonconformist conversations which followed the Lambeth Conferences of both 1920 and 1930, and in 1931 was Chairman of the Free Church Federal Council. Thus members of the College staff were closely involved in the ecumenical movement in the inter-war years.

The College continued until 1932 with only one change in the staff, when Alexander Duff at last retired, aged 80, in 1925,[14] and his place was taken for the next seven years by James Baxter Allan,[15] who came from pastoral ministry in Portobello in Scotland to teach Hebrew and Old Testament in both the Congregational College and the Baptist College at Rawdon. In 1932 Griffith-Jones announced his retirement,[16] and the Governors decided to appoint his colleague E. J. Price in his place.

Price's standing in the denomination was now recognised by his participation in the Oxford theological conferences in the late 1920s, and by his appointment in 1926 to the Editorial Board of the *Congregational Quarterly* (on which he served until his death) and for many years as Review Editor. In 1933 he was invited by the Congregational Union to write a pamphlet on 'Baptists, Presbyterians and Congregationalists', in the light of conversations concerning reunion; he set out the issues at stake with great clarity and fairness, thus indicating the clear, informed and balanced teaching which the students must have been receiving in the College. In 1937 he was elected to the chair of the Congregational Union, and as Chairman attended not only the coronation of King George VI but

[12] See *CYB 1919* 51.

[13] Published in *The Venturer* August 1919.

[14] He continued to attend Governors' meetings at the College almost to the year of his death in 1934.

[15] James Baxter Allan (1873–1932) was a graduate of St Andrews University and the Scottish Congregational Theological Hall in Edinburgh, and had spent a year in Marburg just before the beginning of the century. He had three pastorates in Scotland before moving to Bradford. See *CYB 1933* 224.

[16] He retired to Manordeilo in Wales, where he had oversight of a small church, and continued to enjoy controversy through correspondence. He died in 1942.

also the Life and Work Conference in Oxford in that year. In his second address to the Assembly in October he made a passionate plea for the churches of the denomination to be 'redeemed from our petty parochialisms, and brought to a more ecumenical mind,' and to pursue ecumenical conversations with a view to courageous decision. Independency was not to be equated with isolation or individualism. How many Congregationalists, he asked, had heard of the Savoy Declaration? Were they aware that their seventeenth-century forebears had in the midst of so much turmoil given priority to making a public declaration of their common faith and order?[17]

Within the College he now took on the teaching of homiletics and practical theology as well as church history and comparative religion. Horton Davies, who moved from Edinburgh to Bradford in 1937, was deeply impressed by the Friday afternoon sermon class, and has recorded that it influenced him for life.[18] The students were now all sent to Westhill College, Birmingham, to take a short course in children's and young people's work.

In 1933, a year after Price had been appointed principal, Cadoux was appointed to the Mackennal Chair of Church History at Mansfield College, Oxford in 1933. Despite a yearning to return to Oxford, his years in Bradford had been happy and fulfilling. His responsibility for biblical exegesis (of both Testaments since the death of J. B. Allan) was now given to J. C. Ormerod,[19] a former Mansfield student whose study in Germany before the first war had been followed by pastorates in Scotland and Cheshire. His strengths were as a linguist and historian. He received help from James Stewart, minister of Upper Chapel, Heckmondwike, who took the Hebrew classes.

Though Price was more historian than systematic theologian, he recognised the need for 'a systematic and connected interpretation of the whole body of Christian truth in organic inter-communion'.[20] 'Hence theology must not merely find a place in the curriculum; it must dominate it and shape it from beginning to end.'[21] Concentration on systematic theology in both the first and third years would give the student the best opportunity for this integration. The main teaching of the subject was now entrusted to Lovell Cocks, the future principal of Western College, Bristol. In an attempt to ensure that students were prepared for the contemporary world, he was also asked to teach Christian sociology.

[17] E. J. Price, *Our Churches and the Ecumenical Mind*, Chairman's Address to the Congregational Union (London 1937).

[18] Horton Davies, *A Church Historian's Odyssey: A Memoir* (Allison Park and Grand Rapids 1993) 9.

[19] Joseph Charles Ormerod (1881–1968). See *CYB 1968–9* 438.

[20] E. J. Price, a paper read at a conference of Free Church College Principals in Oxford, in CQ 1945 123.

[21] Ibid 125.

Although a southerner, he soon acquired an understanding of Yorkshire ways, and was in much demand as a preacher.

The links with local churches remained strong, and the College continued to act as a focus for Congregationalists over a wide area. Coachloads would arrive for the annual meeting at the end of the college year, and would enjoy tea and a meeting with old friends on the lawn afterwards. The Heckmondwike 'Lecture', a great festival of Nonconformist preaching, continued to draw both College staff and students and large numbers from West Riding churches. Four different ministers each preached a substantial sermon over a 26-hour period, punctuated by a cricket match between past and present students on the cricket ground behind Heckmondwike's Upper Chapel. Another link with local churches was the Ministers' Summer School in Skipton, organised by the College staff each year from 1925, for the county's ministers.

Many of the students had to supplement their meagre financial resources by preaching to small local churches, and formed links which lasted for many years. These student preachers had a particularly strong influence on the generation a few years younger than their own, many of whom were influenced to seek admission to the College themselves. Life was demanding for the students, especially for those who were preparing for the postgraduate Edinburgh BD degree. The College was able to offer a very thorough education to some men who began their course with very slender academic attainment, through insisting on a good general foundation as a basis for theological thinking, and providing a preliminary arts course for those not yet equipped for university entrance.[22] There were a few diversions in student life. Some students joined Frizinghall Church Badminton Club; some played tennis on the court which occupied part of the college grounds from 1928 until it was dug up for vegetable growing in 1940. The croquet lawn and the billiard table were in constant use throughout the year. There were friendly cricket and football matches against Rawdon Baptist College. And the sense of humour which is an essential quality in ministerial candidates could never be entirely suppressed (sometimes at the expense of the staff), though the atmosphere was formal and discipline strict.

It was during these years that three of the most distinguished alumni of the College (all of whom moved on to Mansfield College) were students: John Marsh, who achieved high distinction during his undergraduate course at Edinburgh University in philosophy, and later became principal of Mansfield; Daniel Jenkins, author of a classic work on *Congregationalism: A Restatement* (London 1954) and other important books and

[22] Ambrose Pope was arts tutor until 1928, followed by Hunter Russell 1928–9, Arnold Mee 1933–5, and Harry Escott 1935–8. After that, the men were sent to Skerry's College in Edinburgh.

Professor of Theology in Chicago and at Princeton Theological Seminary; and Horton Davies, Professor of Religion at Princeton, and author of the multi–volume *Worship and Theology in England*.

In 1937 Lovell Cocks moved to Edinburgh, and from 15 candidates considered to replace him the Governors decided to appoint Hubert Cunliffe-Jones,[23] the son of a former student (Walter Jones) who had emigrated to Australia in 1895 to become minister at Strathfield, Sydney. In order to distinguish himself from many other Congregationalists with the same surname, Walter Jones added his mother's maiden name to become Walter Cunliffe-Jones. Hubert Cunliffe-Jones's early theological training was at Melbourne University and Camden College, Sydney,[24] and was followed by a short pastorate and over a year as a travelling secretary with the Australian SCM. At this period he made many lifelong ecumenical friendships and developed the passionate belief in the need to heal the divisions of the Church which remained with him until his death.[25] He also acquired the nickname by which henceforth he was universally known, 'Jonah'.

In 1930 he came, as did many other young Australians, to Oxford for further study, in his case at Mansfield College. Here he encountered W. B. Selbie in the final years of his principalship, Nathaniel Micklem in the first year of his, and as other teachers, J. S. Whale, J. P. Naish, H. Wheeler Robinson and W. H. Cadman. It was Nathaniel Micklem more than anyone else who encouraged him to think for himself. He continued his theological studies and wrote a thesis under Clement C. J. Webb on 'The Problem of Evil with Special Reference to the *Theodicee* of Leibniz'. Equally formative was his experience on the executive of the World Student Christian Federation. 'This was a wonderful experience for a young man, to learn the newer movements in theology not through books but through people. Visser t'Hooft, Hans Lilje, Pierre Maury and others – the personal friendship of these people, this had a tremendous effect on my life. And Barth I learned through his disciples, not through books.'[26]

At the end of his course he was called to the pastorate at Witney, a dozen miles from Oxford, and remained for four years. In 1933 he married Maude Clifton, one of his Australian SCM circle of friends, in Mansfield College Chapel. She came from a Methodist background, and

[23] Hubert Cunliffe-Jones (1905–91). See *URCYB 1991/2* 226.

[24] His principal at Camden College was Griffiths Wheeler Thatcher, who had studied and taught at Mansfield College, Oxford, under A. M. Fairbairn.

[25] One of his daughters has recorded that within weeks of his death, while watching Songs of Praise on television, he heard the words, 'One Church, one Faith, one Lord' from the hymn 'Thy hand, O God, has guided' and exclaimed quite fiercely, 'NOT one church'.

[26] 'Talking to Jonah' – Cunliffe-Jones in conversation with John Sutcliffe and Roger Tomes in *Reform* September 1973.

loyally supported her husband in all his work; it was a happy and fruitful partnership which was to last for 56 years.

A fine biblical scholar and theologian, with a wide-ranging, exploratory mind, he was a worthy successor as principal when the time came for Price to retire. At first he was shy, and somewhat disorganised as a lecturer, though a ready wit and a sense of humour were never far under the surface. He loved 'to raise the issues' for his students; his task was to encourage them to think for themselves, and in this they later recognised that he had succeeded. He would challenge them at the beginning of their course to 'invent' a new heresy. A favourite phrase of his was, 'Inasmuch as you've got a mind, use it.' Even more, they valued his sensitive pastoral concern for them, which frequently continued long after college days. His interest in literature led him to take groups of students to the theatre in Bradford. Horton Davies remembers him in the late 1930s as 'the living embodiment of genuine Christianity, fair to all ecumenical viewpoints and thinkers, free of all faddishness, yet always open to new insights and ever encouraging'.[27] He was associated with the group of Congregational ministers, many of them connected with Mansfield College, who believed that the denomination was in danger of losing its theological roots and needed a revival of churchmanship. Their views were expressed in a series of 'Forward Books', edited by John Marsh; Cunliffe-Jones wrote the one on *The Holy Spirit* (London 1943), and also contributed to *The Presbyter*, 'A Journal of Confessional and Catholic Churchmanship', which ran from 1943 until 1950.

Another person who joined the staff in the mid-1930s was the part-time elocution tutor, Edward Broadhead, a former professional actor who loved giving performances of Dickens characters. He arrived in 1936 and remained until the College's closure in 1958. He was devoted to the College and students, many of whom acknowledged their debt to the very high standards of 'clear, correct and expressive speech' which he set.

In 1936 a Commission on the Colleges reported to the Congregational assembly. One of its recommendations encouraged the principal to suggest to the Governors something he had long wanted – a chapel appropriate to the size of the college community; the assembly hall, in which college worship took place, was of congregational rather than collegiate size. At first a new building was envisaged, but this idea had to be shelved when insufficient money was raised. Instead, one of the classrooms was adapted, and eventually opened in January 1940. The design of this beautiful little chapel was the work of William Illingworth of Saltaire, one of the oldest members of the Governing Board, and a skilled architect who generously gave his service to the College.

[27] Horton Davies, 10.

The prosperity which had characterised the leading Bradford Nonconformists at the end of the nineteenth century was now less secure. Both the 1920s and the 1930s witnessed a dramatic loss in trade, causing bankruptcies and unemployment, and despite some generous legacies and a number of loyal supporters the College's financial situation was a cause for anxiety for the rest of its history.

When war broke out in 1939, the general College attitude was very different from that in 1914. The Education Committee's response to the request from one of the students for leave of absence in order to continue ARP duties, was that 'there is no form of National Service which can possibly outweigh his obligation to continue his preparation for the work of the ministry.'[28] Those students who were already on the College list were exempt from military service, though they were required to do fire-watching within the College. Potential candidates, on the other hand, were all called up, and the numbers were diminished until the war ended. The war had very little direct impact on the city itself, which largely escaped the bombing raids.

In 1942 J. C. Ormerod moved to Mansfield College.[29] At this time Paton College had found itself unable to support its full complement of staff, and R. R. Turner was 'borrowed' for the rest of the war years. The staff at Rawdon College also offered to help with the teaching of biblical studies. At the end of the war Professor Turner returned to Nottingham, and in 1946 two new appointments were made: James Stewart,[30] who had been teaching Hebrew in the College since 1931, was appointed full-time Professor of Old Testament, and W. D. Davies[31] Professor of New Testament. James Stewart had come to Yorkshire from Scotland, after study at Edinburgh University, the Scottish Congregational College, and a final year at Mansfield College, Oxford, and two short ministries, to the Upper Chapel, Heckmondwike, where he was minister for 15 years (apart from war-time service as an RAF Chaplain). W. D. Davies, who was at the beginning of an outstanding academic career, was already at work on a major scholarly book on *Paul and Rabbinic Judaism: Some Rabbinic Elements in Pauline Theology*, which was published in 1948.

It cannot be claimed that the College was the most welcoming one to

[28] Education Subcommittee Minute Book 1934–58, entry for 26 September 1939, JRL.

[29] Almost immediately he suffered a serious breakdown of health and had to retire to the West Country.

[30] James Stewart (1898–1956). See *CYB 1957* 526 (this obituary is in error about his year of birth). He contributed regular articles to journals such as *The British Weekly* and the *Expository Times*, and after his death a book on which he had been working for many years, *The Message of Job*, was published in 1959.

[31] William David Davies (1911–). Educated at University College, Cardiff, Brecon Memorial College and Cheshunt College, Cambridge. He was minister at Fowlmere and Thriplow from 1941 until 1946.

women ministerial students, though this no doubt reflected the attitude prevailing in the churches of the area. Miss H. B. Walker of Dewsbury was the first woman to join the Board of Governors, in 1928. By 1937 Miss F. J. Dale of Bradford had joined her. In 1936, Dorothy Gill was appointed correspondence secretary in the College, and gradually acquired a unique position within the community; her annual letter to old students was one of the chief forms of continuing contact. She became very well known in the area, and as a lay preacher may have helped to prepare the way for the college's first female student. Daisy Beryl Russell entered the College in 1943, and at the end of her course married a fellow-student, Harold Bennett. Doreen Speck was accepted in 1946 but had to resign two years later when she married a fellow-student, Malcolm Rogers. When Cynthia Brook was accepted a year later, the Education Committee expressed concern about the 'unregulated situation' in regard to women candidates. In October 1947 they passed the following resolution:

> ... that this College welcomes every opportunity given for the theological education of women; that it is prepared, in principle, to admit women for the Christian ministry as well as men; but as there are at present few openings in the Home Churches, they feel that women should be admitted as ministerial candidates only for strong reasons and under proper safeguards.[32]

No more women students were admitted before the College closed.

It is appropriate to refer to the contribution made by the wives of the principals and professors to the atmosphere and happiness of the College community during these years. They were generous in entertaining, and in offering a home atmosphere to men whose 'digs' were often bleak and spartan; they were able quietly to offer encouragement to men who were going through a difficult period. In that era they were not expected to have careers of their own,[33] but they did make a great contribution to the life of neighbouring Congregational churches, as deacons and leaders within the women's organisations.

In 1947 the principal, E. J. Price, reached the age of 65, and his wife's breakdown in health made it necessary for him to retire. They moved to Broadway, Worcestershire, where he took charge of the small Congregational church until his death in 1952. Cunliffe-Jones seemed the natural successor, and was immediately appointed. He and his wife and four young children moved into the Principal's Lodgings.

In retrospect he recognised that the generation of students in the College at the beginning of his principalship was the most satisfying to

[32] Education Subcommittee Minute Book, entry for 2 October 1947.

[33] Ella Sophia Armitage, wife of Elkanah Armitage, was unusual in taking a public role and in gaining a scholarly reputation on her own account.

teach of his whole career: 'I taught them the words but they knew the realities; they'd hammered them out in six years of war.'[34] He introduced some innovations in sermon class, such as asking one student to read the sermon of another, and (before tape recorders were in general use) recording and re-playing student sermons. Liturgy was given more emphasis; all students had to study Gregory Dix's *The Shape of the Liturgy* in detail, and sermon class involved not only a sermon, but the form of a complete service (in which the New Testament lesson had to be read in Greek).

The College now recovered its intellectual vitality after the disrupted years of the war. Cunliffe-Jones had a particular concern for the development of theology in the mid-twentieth century, especially for an adequate theology of the Bible. In an article in the *Congregational Quarterly* in 1947 he wrote of the need not to break with nineteenth-century theology, but 'to integrate the disrupted elements of the Church and of the traditions of the Church in a new positive affirmation of Christian truth'.[35] In a book[36] published in the following year he wrote of being hampered in his work of theological reconstruction because of the lack of an appropriate theology of the Bible, and therefore of feeling compelled to write something himself 'in default of some strictly Biblical scholar answering the question'. He was at one with biblical critics in rejecting fundamentalism, but found that they had no adequate theological doctrine of the Bible within which to interpret their work. There was a need to integrate historical with theological study, and to understand and articulate the essential relation between the two Testaments. 'We are called to strenuous theological labour, to the positive exposition of the divine Revelation to which the Bible witnesses, in such a way as to do full justice to its historic actuality.'[37] It was with this purpose in mind that he wrote two small commentaries in the SCM Torch Commentary series, the first on Deuteronomy (1951, reprinted three times) and the second on Jeremiah (1960, reprinted twice).[38] His standing as a theologian in the denomination was recognised in his appointment as Chairman of the Commission (until 1962) which produced *A Declaration of Faith* for the Congregational Church in 1967.

One of his innovations was to invite Harry Guntrip (1901–75),[39] a Congregational minister who was doing pioneering work as a psycho-

[34] *Reform*, September 1973.

[35] 'Christian Theology for the Twentieth Century', *CQ 1947* 128.

[36] *The Authority of the Biblical Revelation* (London 1948).

[37] Ibid 11.

[38] These commentaries were based on his expositions of consecutive biblical passages used at the regular Tuesday morning services.

[39] See Jeremy Hazell, *H. J. S. Guntrip: A Psychoanalytical Biography* (London 1996).

therapist within the Leeds Medical School, to lecture at the College on pastoral psychology, and to require the students to study Guntrip's *Psychology for Ministers and Social Workers* (London 1949), subjecting it to critical theological analysis.

When C. J. Cadoux died in 1947 it was at Bradford that a memorial lecture in his memory was instituted. Many distinguished scholars, Nonconformist and Anglican, were invited: T. W. Manson, H. H. Rowley and John Huxtable among Nonconformists, A. M. Ramsey, A. R. Vidler and S. L. Greenslade among Anglicans. The Cadoux Memorial Lecture became an important academic occasion in the West Riding and drew a large ecumenical audience; 'those who come must be prepared to make an effort to understand on the technical theological plane.'[40] A less academic public lecture with the average church member in mind was given by a member of staff at the beginning of each academic session.

In 1950 W. D. Davies, who already had an international reputation, was appointed Professor of Biblical Theology at Duke University, North Carolina.[41] To cover immediate needs in church history and New Testament, Harold Leatherland of Leeds and John Baker of Batley gave tutorial help, until the appointment in 1951 of A. R. Vine,[42] the author of works on Nestorian Christianity,[43] and a keen advocate of church unity. His previous experience had been in pastoral ministry, notably at Broad Street, Reading.

Plans were already in hand for the coming bicentenary of the College in 1956. Kenneth Wadsworth, a former student then in ministry in Leyburn, was asked to write a history of the College. This was published[44] in 1954, in advance of the bicentenary in 1956, a worthy record of what had been achieved over 200 years, from its beginnings in Heckmondwike Academy in 1756. A further volume was prepared on *The Congregational Ministry in the Modern World: An Interpretation by Past Students and Present Staff of the Yorkshire United Independent College*, and published by the Independent Press in 1955, edited by Cunliffe-Jones. The fifteen authors[45] had all achieved distinction in

[40] *Annual Report* 1953.

[41] He subsequently continued his distinguished career at Princeton and published a number of notable books, such as *The Setting of the Sermon on the Mount* (1964), *The Gospel and the Land* (1974) and a three-volume commentary on Matthew's Gospel (1988–).

[42] Aubrey Russell Vine (1900–73). See *URCYB 1973–4* 282–3.

[43] *The Nestorian Churches* (1937) and *An Approach to Christology* (1948).

[44] *Yorkshire United Independent College: Two Hundred Years of Training for the Christian Ministry by the Congregational Churches of Yorkshire* (London 1954).

[45] W. J. Coggan, Horton Davies, J. Trevor Davies, J. A. Figures, Daniel Jenkins, R. O. Latham, H. F. Leatherland, Johnston McLellan, John Marsh, B. C. Plowright, C. T. Rae, Vernon Sproxton, James Stewart, and A. R. Vine, as well as Cunliffe-Jones.

pastoral or educational ministry. It was a significant contribution to Congregational theological education and theology of ministry. It was also fitting that in this bicentenary year, Cunliffe-Jones was not only chosen as Chairman-elect of the Congregational Union, but had the honorary degree of Doctor of Divinity conferred on him by the University of Edinburgh.

The actual celebrations of the bicentenary took place on 19 June 1956 when a service in Salem Church, at which H. S. Stanley, a former student who had just been appointed Secretary of the Congregational Union, was the preacher, was followed by a great rally in St George's Hall, attended by over 2,000 people. Sir Cuthbert Ackroyd, Lord Mayor of London, who was brought up in Heckmondwike in a Congregational family, and John Huxtable, principal of New College, London, were the main speakers. The BBC Home Service broadcast a documentary feature on the College's history.

It was a great festival of Bradford Congregationalism, but more retrospective than contemporary. Beneath the atmosphere of celebration was a realistic and depressing recognition that the College was able to balance its books only because of a few recent generous legacies, and that the number of students (ten in Bradford, with no student in the first year) hardly justified the provision of sufficient staff to cover the curriculum properly. The number of church members in Bradford Congregational churches had almost halved since 1914.[46] It was in 1954 that Cunliffe-Jones had first proposed to the Education Subcommittee that a letter should be sent to the General Secretary of the Congregational Union suggesting another Colleges Commission to consider whether the number of theological colleges should be reduced. He had then discussed the matter informally with Gordon Robinson, principal of the Lancashire College at the May Assembly of the Congregational Union. The proposed commission was appointed, with representatives of the seven colleges, and began work early in 1956.

It was not long before this Commission invited the two northern colleges to enter into discussion about the possibility of amalgamation. The first joint meeting of representatives of both Colleges was held on 15 February 1957, and from the first they reached general agreement that amalgamation should proceed (though there were many others who opposed such a move). From that time on, events moved fast. In June a circular letter was issued to supporters of the Bradford college, explaining why the Governors favoured the proposal, and inviting continuing support for a new joint college. It had already been decided that the new college should be based on the Manchester site, partly

[46] In 1914 there were 4,220 members; in 1957 there were 2,247. See *CYB 1915* 319–20, and *CYB 1958* 264–5.

because it could offer residential accommodation, and partly because of its proximity to Manchester University.

Meanwhile there were further changes in the Bradford staff. Because of James Stewart's illness in the session 1955–6 the help of two former students was sought, Leslie Green for Hebrew and Stanley Wilton for biblical studies. James Stewart died in March 1956, aged only 56, and was succeeded by Edgar Jones for the next session, during which Aubrey Vine accepted the invitation to become Secretary of the Free Church Federal Council and left the College in the summer of 1957. In view of the negotiations then proceeding with Lancashire College no new full-time appointment was made, but Roger Tomes (minister at Gomersal) and Kenneth Wadsworth were appointed part-time tutors in Hebrew and church history respectively.

During the academic year 1957–8 there was almost daily correspondence between the two principals, and much detailed legal and financial work had to be done in the background, involving innumerable long committee meetings and frequent drives over the Pennines. It was an exceptionally busy year for Cunliffe-Jones, who as Chairman of the Congregational Union for the year 1957–8 travelled over the country preaching and lecturing. It was agreed to call the new college 'The Northern Congregational College', indicating that it was now the college for ministerial education for the whole of the north of England. In 1954 Cunliffe-Jones had told Gordon Robinson that 'if we go forward, we want to unite not as an act of defeat but as an act of statesmanship contributing to the wider welfare of our churches.'[47] In order to maintain the interest and support of the Yorkshire constituency, it was decided to continue to hold the Cadoux Memorial Lecture in a Yorkshire church, and to include in the occasion a report by the Principal of the year's work of the new college.

The formal decision to move to Manchester was taken at a special Subscribers' Meeting on 19 February 1958, and the final meeting was held in Bradford on 18 June. After the end of term, many of the portraits, books and furnishings of the College were moved to Manchester. Cunliffe-Jones was appointed associate principal and Edgar Jones was to be a member of staff. An Inaugural Rally was arranged for 18 October, to which Yorkshire subscribers were invited.

It was a sad moment for West Riding Congregationalists, who for 200 years had felt pride in their colleges.

[47] H. Cunliffe-Jones to W. G. Robinson 6 April 1954, NCA.

14

Lancashire Independent College 1919–58

THE military authorities did not vacate the Lancashire College until the end of 1919, finally enabling the staff and 21 students on the roll to re-occupy the building in January 1920 after some necessary repair work. Plans could now at last be made to celebrate the centenary of the College, postponed since 1916. In May therefore there was a great gathering of 100 past and present students; J. D. Jones[1] preached at the commemoration service, and a number of speakers addressed a conference on 'Theological training in the light of the modern situation' (which the students and alumni found disappointing), and both the Bishop of Manchester (E. A. Knox) and the Vice-Chancellor of the University (the historian T. F. Tout) were guests at a special dinner. The Student Newsletter (June 1920) reported: 'The meetings were marked by that unique combination of deep seriousness and irresponsible gaiety that is to be found nowhere else save in Lancashire College.' Their seriousness led them to seek a meeting with the College Committee 'to lay before it the urgent need for a revisualisation of all that is involved in the phrase[2] that the builders carved over the main entrance to the College'.[3] They felt that the existing ministerial course did not prepare men to face adequately the problems of the post-war world.

One of their requests already made known was for a room in the College to be set apart as a chapel to be used for daily worship, and it was now agreed that a spare classroom should be designated and appropriately furnished for this purpose. The principal accepted this, little knowing that within months his own ashes would be buried beneath the floor of the new chapel.[4] It was in September of 1920 that Dr Bennett died quite suddenly, in the same month as his predecessor, Dr Adeney,

[1] A former student (1886–9), one of Congregationalism's greatest preachers, who was minister of Richmond Hill, Bournemouth. When he died in 1942 the *Annual Report* described him as 'the most lustrous jewel on our crown'. See Alan Argent, 'The Pilot on the Bridge: John Daniel Jones (1865–1942)' in *JURCHS* 5/10 June 1997.

[2] *Eis ergon diakonias*: 'for the work of ministry'.

[3] See Lancashire Independent College Old Students Association Newsletter, June 1920.

[4] In the course of the years the ashes of his widow and daughter were buried alongside his.

and G. Lyon Turner, former professor, at the age of 65. The upheaval of the war and requisition of the buildings meant that he had had restricted opportunities to develop the work of the College or make a distinctive contribution.

A few weeks after Dr Bennett's death the designated deputation from the past and present students met with the College Committee and put their suggestions for some new elements in the curriculum: elocution, sermon construction, pastoral theology and the pathology of spiritual experience. They suggested that a resident College tutor could help those who came to the College with limited educational background. They expressed the hope that preaching and pastoral skills would be an essential requirement for a new principal (Dr Bennett was not a notably popular preacher in the Manchester area). Within the next few years most of these suggestions were incorporated into the life and work of the College.

Before making any decision concerning a new principal, the Committee gave full consideration again to the possibility of amalgamating with the Yorkshire college. A suggestion that the arts course might be taken in Edinburgh and the theology course at Manchester was unacceptable to Bradford; another proposal that the arts course should be taken in Manchester and theology at Bradford was abandoned when the University Vice-Chancellor made it clear that Bradford could not be recognised as a divinity school of Manchester University. The idea was therefore abandoned and the search for a new principal began in earnest. J. D. Jones was approached first, but refused after several weeks' deliberation. The second person to be approached was A. J. Grieve, principal of the Edinburgh Theological Hall. He readily accepted.

Alexander James ('Sandy') Grieve[5] was now 48. He came to the College with considerable literary, pastoral and educational experience. His father was a Scottish businessman who after moving to Wales to sell tweed established a place for himself as deacon, local preacher, and local councillor and mayor in Pembroke, an area sometimes known as 'Little England beyond Wales'. His mother was Welsh; she also took a public role in the life of the town; she was the first woman member of the Board of Guardians for the Dock Ward, and a leader in the Women's Liberal Association and Sunday School Union. Both parents were active members of the local Congregational church, and they helped to inculcate the love and phenomenal knowledge of the Bible which their son revealed in later life. Grieve took an English degree at University College, Aberystwyth in 1894, and then proceeded to Mansfield College, Oxford, where he gained a first class theology degree after studying

[5] Alexander James Grieve (1874–1952). See C. E. Surman, *Alexander James Grieve: A Biographical Sketch* (Manchester 1953), and *CYB 1953* 508–9.

under A. M. Fairbairn. This was followed by a year in Berlin during the ascendancy of Adolf von Harnack. Before exercising pastoral ministry in Romsey, Hampshire, between 1905 and 1909, he undertook a variety of educational and literary tasks in London and in India: writing articles for the *Encyclopaedia Britannica*, editing and writing introductions for literary classics, acting as Registrar of Madras College, and teaching at the Government Central College in Bangalore.[6]

In 1909 he embarked on the task of theological education to which he was to devote his energies until retirement, when he was appointed as professor of New Testament and church history at the Yorkshire College in Bradford. Here he enjoyed the contacts with colleagues and students (Albert Peel was his outstanding student in church history) and took an active part in Yorkshire Congregational life. He contributed a regular column to the *Yorkshire Observer* under the pseudonym 'Gamma Minus'. When the College was closed because of the war he acted as minister of Salem Church in Bradford.

In 1917 he succeeded J. M. Hodgson as principal of the Theological Hall of the Scottish Congregational Churches in Edinburgh, then struggling with few students and unsuitable premises in George Square. He was energetic in raising money for new premises in Hope Terrace and oversaw the change of name to 'Scottish Congregational College'; his own contacts were widened through attending the Fourth International Congregational Council in Boston in 1920, at which he gave an address on 'The Relation between Church and College'.

He was installed as principal of the Lancashire College on 13 January 1922. As in Edinburgh, he was faced with several serious problems. The premises were in poor condition after war-time requisition, and the finances were not healthy. There were only 12 students, and some of these were mature students who had served in the war and did not take kindly to a discipline they felt to be more appropriate to school leavers. On the other hand, some members of the Committee felt discipline was too lax. This situation inevitably led to clashes, and a difficult few years before Grieve's authority was fully accepted and appreciated.[7] An indication of the high standards which he demanded of his students (which later they came to appreciate), as well of his wit, is given by his alleged response to the question, 'How many students have you?', – 'About one in ten.'

Supported by the Committee, he tackled the practical problems with vigour. After considerable negotiation the College had been registered as an official University Hall of Residence, and from 1922 until the building was sold in 1985, the 'hostel men', most of them from Congregational

[6] He was never actually a missionary of the London Missionary Society, though he did a little teaching at the LMS College in Bangalore.

[7] Surman 34.

backgrounds, were an integral part of College life; there were only two or three at first, but their numbers rose to more than 30 in the later years of the century. These students brought greater intellectual and social diversity to the College, as well as an essential financial contribution. An annual Lancashire Union Ministers Summer School of Theology was initiated in 1922; this not only brought much-needed income, but strengthened links between the College and churches. The premises were let in vacations for other appropriate conferences. Student numbers slowly began to increase; by 1925 there were 31, and by the end of the decade there were 35.

The improving finances allowed repair work and modernisation of the premises to be undertaken. Electric lighting replaced oil lamps first in the students' studies, then in bedrooms; hard tennis courts were laid out and the hot-water system was improved. Nevertheless the living conditions remained spartan.

The principal threw the Committee and the students into some confusion in November 1923 by suddenly deciding to stand as Liberal candidate in the impending General Election. He was allotted the constituency of Kelvingrove, Glasgow, and spent an exhausting fortnight canvassing. What would have happened to the College had he been elected had not been thought out. Despite not being elected, he thought it had been a good experience. 'One tends in a college life like ours to become rather detached from the every day issues and contentions of life, and in this experience I have touched mother earth again.'[8]

Grieve's own scholarly work and teaching was in the fields of biblical studies and church history; he was also, as principal, responsible for pastoral theology. His own ministerial education owed much to A. M. Fairbairn, and like Fairbairn he struggled constantly, though not always successfully, to raise the standards expected of new entrants. The Annual Report for 1926–7 stated: 'In view of the facilities for secondary education now existing, the Committee has decided that the normal educational standard of entrance to the College shall be Matriculation or one of the equivalent certificates recognised by the University.'

When called to the Chair of the Congregational Union in 1936 Grieve chose as the theme of his main address, 'Christian Learning and Christian Living'.[9] The year 1936 was the quatercentenary of the death of Erasmus and the publication of Calvin's *Institutes*, and to each of these great thinkers he paid respect.[10] He referred to 'our unceasing and increasing debt to sacred scholarship' and, reflecting on his experience as a

[8] Surman 66.
[9] Delivered on 12 May 1936. See *CYB 1937* 70–83. It is also reprinted in Surman, 79–96.
[10] In 1917 he had edited a quatercentennial edition of Erasmus' *The Complaint of Peace*.

theological educator, offered his conclusion that 'other things being equal, the better the intellect and its training, the more valuable will be the service rendered to the Kingdom of God by a consecrated and vigorous Christian personality.' Others sometimes accused the College of being too academic; 'my frequent fear is that we are not academic enough.' 'Our need, our endeavour, is to send men out with some desire and some aptitude for further study.' He expressed the hope that he might instil in his students the Nonconformist tradition of 'scrupulosity', for 'only by securing exactitude in that which is least can the determination and the toil involved in the quest for truth reach any permanent satisfaction'. He made a plea for more biblical scholars in the denomination, and for a greater appreciation of history: 'I suggest to you that we shall better understand the problems of the present and fit ourselves for the future, the more we know of the past, and of our own past.' His lecture ended: 'Christian learning and Christian living have been divinely joined together; may we never put them asunder.'

He wrote no 'magnum opus', though he edited the New Testament section of Peake's *Commentary on the Bible*, contributed to Hastings' *Dictionary of the Apostolic Church*, wrote reviews regularly for the *Congregational Quarterly* and contributed articles to the *Transactions of the Congregational Historical Society*. A colleague described him as 'one of the discoverers in this century of Congregationalism as Catholic Independency'. He once told the members of the Church at Carrs Lane, Birmingham that 'it is one of the divine paradoxes that separatism and catholicity meet in the Congregational way.'[11] He believed that history mattered, and for Congregationalists that meant studying and valuing the history of their own tradition. For 20 years, 1929–49, he was the President of the Congregational Historical Society. One of his indirect contributions to the study of Congregational history was the encouragement he gave to his former student and future son-in-law, Charles E. Surman, to compile a register of all the known former students of the two northern colleges, a register which was gradually extended to include all known Congregational ministers (the Surman Index now at Dr Williams's Library), which has been an invaluable aid to succeeding generations of researchers. Grieve's strong Congregational convictions led him to oppose the moves towards organic union with the Presbyterian Church of England which eventually led to the formation of the United Reformed Church. He valued the Congregational conception of ministry – 'I like to think of a minister as a member of the (local) Church,

[11] Quoted Surman 47. In 1939 Grieve's former pupil, Albert Peel, dedicated his edition of the Savoy Declaration of Faith and Order of 1658 to 'Alex J. Grieve MA DD, President of the Congregational Historical Society, who, in this year of grace 1939, is not ashamed to be "of the Congregational way" and to rank with "the Dissenting brethren"'.

which has discerned in him certain gifts of God qualifying him for the discharge of certain pastoral duties' – too much to yield to what he discerned as Presbyterian distinctions between clergy and laity.[12]

His colleague until 1930 was Robert Mackintosh, who continued to teach ethics, Christian sociology, apologetics and historical theology. Following the students' suggestions in 1920, four part-time tutors, all former students, were appointed successively: George Phillips (1925–9), W. Gordon Robinson (1929–32), Gordon Hawes (1933–5) and R. K. Orchard (1935–7); the first two were to return later as full-time members of staff. At the University the students attended the lectures on biblical exegesis given by A. S. Peake, and a variety of other lectures too. Reciprocally, Grieve was appointed Lecturer in Ecclesiastical History at the University in 1923; Mackintosh was already Lecturer in the Philosophy of Religion. Thus the students in all theological colleges attached to the University Faculty had the benefit of being taught by staff of different ecclesiastical and theological outlooks.

Robert Mackintosh retired, aged 72, in 1930. He was succeeded by John Murphy,[13] whom Charles Surman remembered as 'a man of tremendous erudition, supreme modesty and grace, though often quite unintelligible to his students'. A Scotsman educated at Glasgow University, the Edinburgh Theological Hall and Berlin and Heidelberg, he came to Manchester in 1930 after 29 years in pastoral ministry in Scotland. His great interest was in anthropology and comparative religion, and his time was to be shared between teaching the history of doctrine in the College and acting as Professor of Comparative Religion in the University. He had already published *Primitive Man: His Essential Quest* (London 1927) and while in Manchester worked on two further works in the same field which were published after his retirement.[14]

A. S. Peake, Rylands Professor of Biblical Criticism and Exegesis in the University, died suddenly in 1929, before reaching the age of 65. His two successors in the Rylands Chair, covering the next 28 years, were both scholars from the Reformed tradition. C. H. Dodd[15] came from Mansfield College, Oxford, in 1920; he lived in the College until his family was able to join him in their new home, and continued to attend College prayers sometimes. He immediately caused a stir by failing almost all the New Testament class in terminal examinations, 'on the ground that they did not begin to approach the standard of scholarship

[12] A. J. Grieve, 'Presbyterian-Congregational Union? II – I am Against', *CQ* 1947 302.

[13] John Murphy (1876–1949). See *CYB 1950* 520–1.

[14] *Lamps of Anthropology* (Manchester 1941) and *The Origins and History of Religion* (Manchester 1949).

[15] Charles Harold Dodd (1884–1973). See F. W. Dillistone, *C. H. Dodd: Interpreter of the New Testament* (London 1977) and *DNB 1971–80*.

for biblical exegesis'.[16] The impact he made was such that two of his former students could write this vivid account of his teaching more than 40 years later:

> At the appointed hour this small, dynamic figure would walk briskly into the lecture room, take his place on the rostrum, open his notes and for forty minutes or so, at a rapid pace, would proceed first to expound the linguistic data of a passage – with a wholly unjustified assumption that his hearers would follow his quotations in Greek, Hebrew, Latin, Syriac, German and French (he condescended to his audience sufficiently to write the Syriac on the blackboard); next, the relevant passages from the Bible would be brought to illumine the text under notice; then would follow a precis of different lines of exegesis, where he regarded these as well-founded and important, with his assessment of them. Five or ten minutes before the end, the spectacles would be removed, the note book closed; we, gasping a little from this rapid immersion in the deeper waters of scholarship, would be given a brief, lucid and penetrating exposition of the theological import of the passage, related to contemporary philosophical ideas, or social change, or ethical issues. In those last few minutes of each lecture we saw the relevance of all the preceding linguistic and exegetical study to the understanding of what God was saying to men to-day through the witness of the Bible.[17]

After only five years he moved to Cambridge, but he was succeeded in the University by another outstanding biblical scholar, T. W. Manson,[18] who was a member of the Presbyterian Church of England, and who over the succeeding years not only provided outstanding scholarly teaching to the Lancashire students but was also a great strength on the College Committee as University representative. Another Nonconformist biblical scholar, the Baptist H. H. Rowley,[19] who was trained at Mansfield, was appointed Professor of Semitic Languages in 1945.

At the end of the first war, the Lancashire College, in common with some other Congregational theological colleges, had had to consider its attitude to potential women applicants, in the light of the ordination of Constance Coltman in London in 1917. The College Committee had taken a positive initiative in 1918, and agreed to a resolution proposed by Dr F. J. Powicke: 'That in the opinion of this meeting it is desirable that the College should make provision for the training of women, with a

[16] Ronald and Eileen Orchard, students at LIC in the early 1930s, in an unpublished typescript written in 1975, deposited in NCA.

[17] Ibid.

[18] Thomas Walter Manson (1893–1958). In 1953 he was Moderator of the General Assembly of the Presbyterian Church of England. Among his books were *The Teaching of Jesus* (Cambridge 1931) and *The Servant-Messiah* (Cambridge 1953). See *DNB 1951–60*.

[19] Harold Henry Rowley (1890–1969). See *DNB*.

view to their entrance into the Congregational ministry on the same terms as men' (25 November 1918). The policy was put to the test when an application was received from Margaret Hardy, and considered by the College Education Committee on 19 June 1924. Margaret Hardy[20] was 33; she had studied at Westhill College, spent some years as a teacher, had already taken charge of Milton Congregational Church, Hanley for 18 months, and was currently full-time assistant to the minister of Hanley Tabernacle. She 'impressed all members of the Committee as an able and consecrated woman'.[21] 'At the close of a long and very interesting interview it was unanimously agreed to receive Miss Hardy as a student of the College.'[22] The condition was that she should reside outside the College.

Almost exactly one year later, three more women candidates presented themselves; all were interviewed, and two were accepted. Constance Clark[23] and Kathleen Hall[24] were both more than a decade younger than Margaret Hardy. Like Margaret Hardy, they had to live out of college. All three women concerned achieved considerable academic distinction during their course, and all three were called to pastorates immediately after their course of education and training. The first woman Committee member, Constance Pilkington, was appointed in the same year. The women were welcomed by the members of the Common Room, and though they were not allowed to become formal members, they were able to attend meetings of the Literary and Debating Society on Friday evenings. The Assembly Hall was adapted as a badminton court: 'And now the flutter of the shuttlecock mingles sweetly with the flutter of the petticoat, and all is joyance within,' wrote one wag in the Old Students Newsletter (April 1925).

The reports of the discussions in the 1920s concerning women candidates convey a much more sympathetic and positive attitude than that in other similar colleges. But a few members of the Committee began to harbour doubts about the willingness of churches to call women ministers (possibly reflecting their own uncertainties), and although three more women were accepted in the next six years, their admission was suspended in 1931 on three grounds: the small number of churches willing to call a woman minister, the alleged need for 'specialised

[20] Later Margaret Fullerton (1890–1980). She exercised a notable ministry in Leeds. See *URCYB 1981* 249.

[21] Entry for 19 June 1924, LIC Education Committee Minutes 1907–31, NCA, JRL.

[22] Entry for 19 June, LIC Committee Minutes 1924–34, NCA, JRL.

[23] Ada Constance Clark (1902–69). She too had a notable ministry in Leeds, at first in partnership with Margaret Hardy, and continued there almost until retirement. See *CYB 1969–70* 429.

[24] Kathleen Mallalieu Hall, later Hendry (1906–). She has written an account of her experiences in *Don't Ask Me Why: Sixty Years a Woman Minister* (London 1991).

training' for which there was as yet no provision, and the perceived unsuitability of the College's traditions and accommodation for co-education.[25] No further women were accepted until 1951.

Despite the restriction on women, the student numbers throughout the 1930s were healthy. In 1938 there were 35 ministerial students and eight hostel men. When war came in 1939 the work continued, though numbers inevitably fell; but even in the session for 1943–4 there were 15 ministerial students and 15 hostel men. Valuable manuscripts, books and portraits were stored in the Muniment Room and cellars. This proved a wise precaution, for on 22 December 1940 the College was damaged in an air raid. Fortunately the students were not in residence, and the caretaker's house and the principal's house at each end of the building escaped serious harm. It took time to repair all the damaged windows and doors, and those students who could not temporarily travel daily from home lived in cramped conditions in the west wing for a time. All resident students were required to take a turn in fire-watching, and many were also ARP Wardens or first aid workers.

The year 1943 was marked by both the celebration of the centenary of the Whalley Range building and by the resignation of the principal (who had reached the age of 69) after 21 years at the College.[26] A special service of commemoration was held at the College on 28 April at which the preacher was John Whale, president of Cheshunt College, Cambridge.[27] As a church historian and one of the leaders of the Neo-orthodox movement in Congregationalism, Whale was well equipped to expound the true nature of the Puritan heritage of the College. While he and his Neo-orthodox colleagues were seeking to recover the tradition of church order in the Reformed tradition, and commemorating the tercentenary of the convening of the Westminster Assembly, publishing their findings in the pages of *The Presbyter* and the series of 'Forward Books', three alumni of the Lancashire College collaborated in the publication of a short book on Christian freedom, *The Fourth Freedom* (taking their title from F. D. Roosevelt's enumeration of 'freedom from want, freedom from fear, freedom of speech and freedom of worship'). The contributors were Leslie Cooke, then minister of Warwick Road Congregational Church, Coventry (later Secretary of the Congregational Union), George Phillips, recently appointed to the staff of the College, and John M. Phillips (later Editor of the *Congregational Quarterly*). In

[25] Entry for 26 September 1930, LIC Education Committee Minutes 1907–31, NCA.

[26] Grieve accepted an invitation to become pastor of Cavendish Congregational Church in Suffolk, where he ministered happily for seven years. He finally retired to the home of his daughter in Erdington, Birmingham, and died in 1952.

[27] John Seldon Whale (1896–1997) was minister at Bowdon Downs from 1925 until 1929 and taught at Mansfield College, Oxford, for four years until 1933.

the foreword, Principal Grieve referred to the fact that the year 1943 was not only the College's centenary year, but also the 350th anniversary of the death of Henry Barrow, John Greenwood and John Penry, martyrs to the cause of Christian freedom and representatives of the tradition to which Congregationalists were heirs. 'A people that exhibits the fullest possible association of the freest possible units has yet something to say to the Church and the world.' Leslie Cooke's chapter was entitled, 'The witness of historic Independency re-examined and re-affirmed'. George Phillips examined the claim 'that there are now no theological differences between the Church of England and Congregationalism sufficiently grave to warrant our remaining a separate Christian body', and expressed the view that the historic witness of Congregationalism would be submerged in any scheme for organic union so far proposed. Differences over church government, the doctrine of ministry and the doctrines of the sacraments, were sufficient to justify maintaining the 'historic Congregational witness'. J. M. Phillips used the contemporary situation in Germany in particular, and totalitarian states in general, to point to the need for an abiding witness to Christian freedom.

There was reason to be proud of what the College had achieved. Charles Surman, who had completed his register of the College alumni, produced a booklet to commemorate the centenary, which included a complete list of the 547 students who had completed the full course of training in Manchester (including those who were transferred from Blackburn). Of these, 215 were still surviving. In an earlier list of 'Facts and Figures', produced in 1935, the compiler had noted that 57 former students had worked overseas with the London Missionary Society or a kindred missionary society, 10 had been appointed college principals, and 16 taught on the staffs of theological colleges. Ten alumni and eight members of staff had been elected to the Chair of the Congregational Union. Fifty had left the Congregational denomination for another – mostly the Church of England – after a period of ministry within the Congregational Union.

John Murphy had already retired, in 1940. His successor in the chair of historical theology and philosophy of religion, on a part-time basis until the end of the war, was George Phillips.[28] Phillips was a native of Kingham, Oxfordshire, where his father was a farmer, and educated at Oxford High School and Jesus College, Oxford. His family was Strict Baptist, but through the influence of W. B. Selbie, principal of Mansfield College (whose father had been a student at Lancashire Independent College), he became a Congregationalist. He taught in Rugby for six years before experiencing a call to the ordained ministry and entering Lancashire College in 1922. After leaving the College in 1925 he

[28] George Phillips (1893–1967). See *CYB 1968* 440.

continued his connection with the College first as part-time tutor and then as Secretary, alongside ministry in Salford and Marple. He was a modest and generous man of great pastoral gifts – much loved by students for his eccentricities, real or assumed – whose interests extended beyond theology to literature, music (he played piano and organ and produced and conducted Gilbert and Sullivan operas) and astronomy. Despite 'an almost pathological horror of the limelight' he served on many denominational committees, and was for many years a member of the Manchester Education Committee.

The man chosen to succeed A. J. Grieve was another former student, Gordon Robinson,[29] then a comparatively young man of 40. Born and educated in Liverpool, where his father was a journalist and his mother a teacher, he was a graduate in philosophy of Liverpool University. Both his parents were Congregationalists. He had begun his ministerial training at the Lancashire College under A. J. Grieve, but completed it at Mansfield College, Oxford under C. H. Dodd and W. B. Selbie. He returned to the north of England and for four years acted as part-time tutor at the Lancashire College during his first ministry in Gatley, before moving to Oldham, where he was minister for 11 years. As principal he was responsible for biblical studies and church history, homiletics and pastoral theology. Before he was principal he had already become fascinated by the character and work of William Roby, the effective founder of the College, and it was to the life and times of Roby that he now devoted much of his research time, eventually presenting a thesis on 'The Revival of Independency in Lancashire and the North in the Late Eighteenth and Early Nineteenth Centuries' for the degree of PhD at Manchester University in 1951. The fruits of this research were distilled in a book published by the Independent Press in 1954, *William Roby (1766–1850) and the Revival of Independency*. The manuscripts which Robinson unearthed during his research are now preserved in the John Rylands University Library, Manchester.

He had a great love for the local churches of Lancashire, and saw his ministry as a dual one to both College and to the churches, which looked to the College not only for student preachers but also for leadership and teaching. Most Sundays were spent preaching somewhere out of Manchester. The lack of a car seemed no deterrent to his continual travelling round the county. His memory for people and names was remarkable, and his close knowledge of the churches stood him in good stead when he was asked to write the history of the Lancashire Congregational Union in 1955, a volume which pulsed with pride in what had been achieved through the sacrificial work of his predecessors

[29] William Gordon Robinson (1903–77). See *URCYB 1979* 265.

in Lancashire Congregationalism.[30] He had no time for the pretentious, and was very approachable.

His contributions to the *Congregational Historical Society Transactions* revealed his pride in the Congregational tradition, and his election as President of the Society in 1955 confirmed the respect in which he was held by the members. At the same time he had a vision of greater unity within the Church, and believed that union between Congregationalists and Presbyterians might be the first step. In his presidential address to the Congregational Historical Society in 1958 on 'The Savoy Declaration of 1658 and To-day' he emphasised the insight of his forebears of 1658 that differences of conscience were not 'schism'; 'our heritage in Congregationalism has to be preserved and deepened, but charitably and tolerantly, if we are to bring our treasures into the great Church which shall yet come into being.'[31]

As well as historical works, he produced a number of more general books on the New Testament, and one on the Old Testament. In these he revealed his gifts as a skilled communicator of biblical scholarship to church members without any theological background. *The Gospel and the Church in a Pagan World* (London 1958), a study of I Corinthians, was the Congregational Union's Lent Book for 1958, a skilful 'contemporisation' of Paul's letter to the Corinthian church. The same was true of his articles in *The Christian World*, 52 of which were published in *New Testament Treasure* (London 1954).

He was a skilled administrator as well as a teacher, dealing with business efficiently without the help of a secretary. He was Secretary and tutor to the University Theology Faculty for 20 years from 1948; he was appointed as a University Lecturer in Ecclesiastical History in 1951. He was proud that the Theology Faculty chose to hold its Jubilee Thanksgiving Service in 1954 in Lancashire College as the constituent college which had the longest connection with it.

His leading of morning prayers made a great impression on the students, who regarded him as a master of the art of free prayer. When the Congregational Union decided to produce a booklet on 'our heritage of free prayer', it was to Gordon Robinson that they turned to write it.[32]

Gordon Robinson and George Phillips were the two full-time members of staff. They were assisted by two part-time tutors, Vincent Knowles,[33] who was responsible for Greek, and G. L. Brook[34] a lively University

[30] W. G. Robinson, *A History of the Lancashire Congregational Union* (Manchester 1955).

[31] *CHST* XVIII (1958) 88.

[32] Published without attribution by the Independent Press in 1950.

[33] He was later University Registrar.

[34] George Leslie Brook (1910–1987) was Professor of English Language 1945–77 and of Mediaeval English Literature 1951–77. See *Who Was Who 1981–1990*.

lecturer who lived in bachelor quarters in the College until his marriage in 1949, and in return gave tuition to the students in elocution. From 1945 the University offered the option of taking a BA in Theology within the Faculty of Arts, though the College was reluctant to abandon the practice of taking an arts degree followed by the postgraduate BD. Those whose course had to be curtailed could work for the Certificate in Theology.

The numbers of students and hostel men began to build up again after the war. By 1948 there were 40 ministerial students and 19 hostel men. Life was still quite spartan. Each student had a study and a bedroom, but the weekly allowance of one bucket of coal (often riddled from slack using a garden sieve) for rooms which had no other form of heating meant that in the winter the students either shared with each other the comparative warmth of a room with a coal fire, or went out from the College to work in the John Rylands Library. The students were not allowed to marry during their training without special permission, and those who were already married sometimes had to live separate lives during the term if their finances would not run to a rented house or flat.

In 1955 the principal was elected to the chair of the Congregational Union for the year 1956–7. The students gave him a great reception on his return from delivering his Chairman's address, with the College jazz band playing 'Home on the Range'. It was during his year in that office that the negotiations with the Yorkshire College began; a joint committee began work in February 1957 under the chairmanship of Dr John Prentice, chairman of the Yorkshire Governors. In September 1957 a letter was sent to all the subscribers informing them what was afoot. By the beginning of 1958 an application was being made to the Ministry of Education for a scheme of amalgamation. An extraordinary meeting of subscribers was held on 24 February 1958, and despite a snowstorm, 58 attended and voted to approve the scheme. The joint committee wished to emphasise that they saw the move as the creation of a new college (to be named the Northern Congregational College), inheriting the traditions of both Yorkshire and Lancashire. Because the Whalley Range site was to be used, the Lancashire subscribers did not experience the sense of loss felt by those in Yorkshire.

15

Establishing a New Identity 1958–86

THE combined students and staff of the Lancashire and Yorkshire Colleges began work in Whalley Range in October 1958 under the name of the Northern Congregational College. Nearly 800 visitors from both the two counties attended a service of inauguration and At Home on 18 October. Twenty-four students who had begun their course in the Lancashire College, eight students from Bradford, nine new students and twenty-five hostel students were on the College list. A few of the students were not in residence, for various reasons, leaving thirty-six ordinands and the twenty-five hostel students actually in residence. Inevitably the Lancashire students predominated and it took time for the Yorkshire students to feel at home.

Gordon Robinson continued as principal and Hubert Cunliffe-Jones was designated associate principal. This was not an easy situation, but one which both men accepted with grace; Cunliffe-Jones was also appointed University Lecturer in the History of Doctrine. George Phillips was already 65, but it was agreed that he should continue for another three years before retirement; his successor was to be Eric Hull, who was to continue as a part-time tutor and minister at Chorlton-cum-Hardy until 1961. Edgar Jones moved his sphere of work to Manchester as Professor of Hebrew and Old Testament, though he continued to live in Bradford for another two or three years. He never actually held a University post, but his lectures to students preparing for the Manchester BD degree were recognised by the University for that purpose. With four staff instead of two, each with something distinctive to contribute, the atmosphere changed. Edgar Jones lived in College during the week until he and his family finally moved to Manchester.

The legal process of amalgamation was complicated and was not finally completed until May 1961. It was delayed by long negotiations with the Ministry of Education concerning which sums of money could be treated as reinvested income (and therefore available for the general purposes of the College) and which as capital. Before the formal amalgamation a Board of Governors had already begun to function as one committee, with half appointed by the Lancashire subscribers and half by the Yorkshire subscribers. Their chairman until 1962 was Dr

John Prentice from Yorkshire. The new constitution allowed for the appointment of up to thirty Governors from each body of subscribers, a very large committee which was later reduced. Subcommittees were formed to deal with education and finance.

Great efforts were made to maintain the Yorkshire connection, and the contribution of Governors who travelled regularly from Yorkshire helped in this respect. The whole company of staff and students travelled each year to different churches in West Yorkshire for the Cadoux Lecture,[1] and, despite its frequently taking place during the examination period and therefore being the subject of student complaint, for the Heckmondwike Lecture (which was now reduced to one sermon and accompanied by a cricket match).[2]

The students came to know the churches of Yorkshire as well as Lancashire through their regular preaching engagements and they often formed lifelong friendships in this way. The allocation of these preaching engagements was the responsibility of the student 'List Manager', and was the subject of frequent debate at the Theological Students Meeting, as was the fair distribution of preaching fees. Churches had to be reminded of their responsibility to pay adequate fees to student preachers.

The basic scheme of training continued to be a course of six years, the academic part of which included an arts degree taken at the University followed by the postgraduate BD course in theology. Older students took a course of four or five years, taking either the BA (Theology) degree or the University's Certificates in Biblical Knowledge and Theology alongside some general arts education. As time went on, the number of those taking the BD declined.[3] The Governors announced that they were prepared for some students to take the arts course in Edinburgh (following the Bradford tradition), but this seems not to have come about. One unusual feature of the Lancashire College, originally introduced by A. J. Grieve, continued: on one Saturday a term, the students had to take an examination on a book of the Bible, set by the staff in turn. Any who failed had to re-take the examination until they passed. The scheme was designed to ensure that each student would have been examined on every book of the Bible at the end of six years. This

[1] Cunliffe-Jones encouraged the Governors to regard this as an important part of the teaching ministry of the College.

[2] The last Heckmondwike Lecture took place in 1977, when Leslie Green was the preacher.

[3] In 1959 five students took the BD examinations. In 1968 no students took the BD, and the majority took the Certificates rather than a degree course. The numbers taking the BD increased again later. Of those who entered the College between 1968 and 1985, 18 per cent gained the BD.

scheme lasted until 1975, when 'Bible Essays' were substituted for examinations.

A new class in sermon preparation was introduced by Cunliffe-Jones, to supplement the traditional sermon class conducted by Gordon Robinson. Cunliffe-Jones gave each student a different biblical text. In the first term the student had to produce an order of service based on the given text, which the associate principal would then criticise in detail and discuss with the whole class. In the second term the student would have to develop the outline into a fully scripted service, which (following a practice he had introduced in Bradford) another student would have to deliver.

Despite the fact that the buildings were in a poor state, and that student accommodation was badly in need of renovation, the general atmosphere was positive and forward-looking. The Governors decided that this was the moment to launch an appeal; at the Annual Meeting on 20 June 1963 they announced an appeal for £40,000, to be raised, if possible, over the next three or four years. The sum was almost reached by 1967, and by 1969 the total raised had reached £45,147, well exceeding the original target. The money came from churches and individuals all over the north of England. As it was received, the College embarked on improvements: a new central heating system and new bathrooms were installed, the kitchens were completely renovated, the whole building was redecorated, and in 1969 six rooms were prepared for women students, who for the first time could now come into residence. In addition, better changing facilities were provided for sports, which had always been a strong feature of college life.

The Appeal helped to maintain the strong links between local churches and the College. In October 1964 the College held its first Open Week, when 700 people from 60 churches in the area came to see something of its work, and over 1,000 attended the four performances of the students' concert. Quite apart from the special appeal, a large number of churches and individuals continued to give regular subscriptions to the College, and a further sum of £47,805 was received through special gifts and legacies between the years 1968 and 1976.

The coincidence of Northern's appeal with appeals from other Congregational theological colleges, especially that being launched by Mansfield College on a nation-wide scale, led many to question the lack of co-operation between the Colleges, and to consider whether there were not still too many colleges. The Governors, confident that there would always be a need for a college in the north of England, told the subscribers in 1964 that they were 'pioneering in pressing the Council and the Assembly of the Congregational Union of England and Wales to consider the present situation of our Colleges and to make recommendations to the denomination'. Two years later they were able to report that more than 25 per cent of the students in the eight Congregational theological colleges of England and Wales[4] were in the Northern Congregational College.

The Commission on theological colleges which met in 1964 and 1965 recommended certain amalgamations – Cheshunt and Westminster, Mansfield and Western, and Paton and New, and indicated that continuing help from the denomination was contingent on further amalgamations. The failure of the negotiations recommended by the Commission which involved Western and Paton led those two colleges (as described earlier) to make an approach to the Northern Congregational College. Paton was the first, in 1966, and by June 1967 a draft scheme for the amalgamation of Paton and the Northern College was agreed, to take effect the following year.

Meanwhile changes in staffing in Manchester were imminent. Cunliffe-Jones resigned his position in the College in 1966 on his appointment as University Professor of the History of Doctrine,[5] though Northern students continued to attend his lectures in the University. He had a very happy final seven years teaching in the University and writing before retirement. He published *Christian Theology since 1600* (London 1970) during these years, as well as being at work editing a new edition of G. P. Fisher's *History of Christian Doctrine*, which was published after his retirement, in 1978. His post at the College was not filled immediately, as other changes were impending. A year later Gordon Robinson told the Governors of his wish to retire in the summer of 1968, and the search for a new principal began. On 16 February 1968 the Education Committee, having considered eight candidates, put forward the name of Basil Sims, currently principal of Western College, a nomination which was accepted by a majority of Governors, though not unanimously. Basil Sims' acceptance of the post a month later persuaded the Council of Western College that amalgamation with the Northern College would now be the best course, and between March and June of 1968 negotiations with both Northern and Paton were speedily conducted. On 9 July Basil Sims addressed the Northern College Governors as principal-elect, pointing out that Western College had a higher proportion of graduating students than Northern College, and expressing the hope that under his principalship the academic standards would rise. It was a shock to all concerned when he withdrew his acceptance on 13 August, in the middle of the summer vacation.

[4] The others were Mansfield, Paton, Western, New and Cheshunt Colleges in England, and Memorial College, Swansea and Bala–Bangor Independent College in Wales.

[5] The title of the Chair was changed in 1968 to 'Professor of Theology', indicating a change of emphasis in the teaching of the theology department from the strictly historical to the more systematic.

In October 1968 therefore the College re-assembled with extra students from Nottingham and Bristol, but no principal; Edgar Jones was appointed acting principal. Four students had moved from Bristol and three came from Nottingham. They joined the twenty Congregational students and three Moravian students who were already part of the College,[6] and thirty-three hostel students. The fact that some of the Paton students were married led to a gradual relaxation of the rule that College students could not marry during their course. The Governors agreed at their meeting on 25 March 1969 that in future applications to marry would be considered individually. It was some time, however, before accommodation was provided for married students.

In recognition of the amalgamation with Western College the word 'Northern' was now (temporarily) abandoned, and the College was known for the next 14 years as 'The Congregational College Manchester'.[7] Members of the Paton College General Committee and of the Western College Council attended Governors' meetings until the Scheme of Foundation for the new amalgamated College was sealed by the Secretary of State for Education and Science (Margaret Thatcher) on 24 September 1970, when many of them became elected members of the enlarged Governing Body. The legal process of amalgamation was an easier task than that of 1958 because much of the groundwork had already been done, though it nevertheless put a heavy burden of work on the College Secretary, Arthur Chadwick.

Edgar Jones,[8] who some felt had been overlooked in the original search for a new principal, was now approached with an invitation to assume the role, which he accepted willingly, though he was now 56. A Welshman, he was brought up in the Rhondda Valley during the years of depression, and had worked in the mines for a time before becoming conscious of a call to ordained ministry. He took an arts degree in Cardiff and ministerial training in Brecon. He had three pastorates, in Flint, Oldham and Swansea (Walter Road Church, where he was a successor to Maurice Charles) before becoming a theological teacher in Bradford and Manchester. It was during his ministry in Oldham that he studied for a PhD through Manchester University on an Akkadian text.[9] His enthusiasm for Hebrew and the Old Testament was equalled by his enthusiasm for cricket. 'When Edgar said "OT" you never quite knew whether he meant Old Testament or Old Trafford.'[10] As a scholar he was a

[6] From 1962 onwards the Moravian Church in Great Britain used the College for training ministerial students, after the closure of their own college.

[7] This title was unsatisfactory after 1972 because most of the ordinands were then preparing for ministry in the United Reformed Church, though a few students were sponsored by the Congregational Federation.

[8] Edgar Jones (1912–91). See *URCYB 1991–2* 229.

[9] His supervisor was Professor T. Fish, Professor of Mesopotamian Studies.

[10] Anthony Burnham, Funeral Sermon for Edgar Jones 1991.

popular iser and exponent of the scholarship of others rather than an original thinker, one who could bring the Old Testament to life vividly.[11] The students enjoyed his strong sense of humour. He suffered a heart attack early in his principalship, but this did not diminish his capacity to lead the College.

Eric Hull[12] had been full-time New Testament tutor since 1961 and was now designated Senior Lecturer. His *The Holy Spirit in the Acts of the Apostles* (London 1967) revealed him to be a careful and thorough New Testament scholar. He was a former student of Gordon Robinson's, a Lancastrian who was proud of the College's tradition, and whose whole life was spent in the north west, as minister (at Oakvale, Timperley and Chorlton-cum-Hardy) and tutor. Edgar Jones and Eric Hull formed a very effective team, sharing the same priorities, ministry, teaching and social concern. Both were active in local churches and in lay training through the local WEA.

During the last years of the 1960s pressure from students all over Europe and the United States against the values of the existing social institutions did not leave theological colleges entirely unscathed. It was deemed wise at Northern College not only to agree to the request of the students that two of their number should be appointed to the Board of Governors (they first attended in June 1970) but also to recruit one or two new members of staff who were nearer to the age of the students. A recent former student, David Jenkins (1959–65),[13] joined the staff as a part-time lecturer in 1968, combining his teaching one day a week with pastoral ministry at Morley across the Pennines. He was joined a year later by another former student, Anthony (Tony) Burnham (1955–61), as full-time lecturer in psychology, sociology and ethics, and librarian.[14] The students continued to have the advantage of attending lectures in the University's theology faculty.[15]

The tradition of Paton in taking older students, sometimes without formal academic qualifications, and in giving special attention to

[11] He wrote several comparatively short books introducing the interested reader to the fundamental ideas of the Old Testament. Perhaps the best was *The Triumph of Job* (London 1966).

[12] John Howarth Eric Hull (1923–77). See *URCYB 1979* 260.

[13] After studying in Manchester he spent a year at Berkeley, California on a World Council of Churches Scholarship. He continued to do a variety of teaching in the College until 1981. He was later Moderator of the Northern Province and was elected Moderator of the General Assembly for the year 1997–8.

[14] Anthony Burnham was a former Lancashire student who returned to teach at Northern College after ministries in Blackburn and Poulton-le-Fylde and Hambleton. He was later Moderator of the North Western Province and is now General Secretary of the United Reformed Church.

[15] Among those who lectured to the Congregational students for many years were F. F. Bruce (New Testament), S. G. F. Brandon (Comparative Religion) and R. H. Preston (Christian Ethics).

sociology and education, combined with the more academic traditions of the Northern and Western Colleges, was reflected in the variety of courses now offered. The curriculum was also adapted to the fact that the transformation of the Congregational Union into the Congregational Church in 1966 brought with it a move towards a more centralised policy for ministerial recruitment and education. In 1968 a new form of interviewing all candidates on a national basis came into operation, and colleges began to have less control over their acceptance. There were five different academic courses adapted to the range of qualifications of students now entering the College. Those who already held a degree could take a three-year course leading to the University BD examination. Those who entered with a General Certificate of Education adequate for admission to a degree course could take the traditional Lancashire course, that is, a choice of BA degrees[16] followed by the BD, taking six years in all. Older students who were appropriately qualified could take the BA (Theol) in three years, followed by a further year of training. Others who were not qualified to take a degree course were offered the opportunity, given the ability and the motivation, to work for the necessary A Levels alongside a general arts course, enabling them to take the BA (Theol). The final option was to take a general arts course and University Certificates in biblical knowledge and theology. As the average age of students rose, very few took a course lasting more than four years.

In addition to the academic courses, there was now a stronger emphasis on practical experience, and guided reflection on it. A new University course leading to a Diploma in Pastoral Studies included a considerable amount of field work and could be taken in the final year of a course. Didsbury College of Education offered an ecumenical course in education, including a good deal of practical work. There was a growing emphasis throughout the training on psychological, sociological and educational theory and practice, and on the church's role in community relations. Visiting speakers helped to enrich this dimension of training. This was in part a reflection of the College's social and geographical context. It was now surrounded by a number of decaying inner-city churches, hardly an encouraging background to ministerial education. From the College emerged the idea of forming a group of churches in South West Manchester in which students might learn of the problems and challenges of such an area, and share in developing such churches' mission. Tony Burnham took on the leadership of the ministerial team (reducing his hours at the College to part-time) in 1973 and was joined by David Jenkins, who now moved from Morley to Manchester. Both

[16] For example, the BA in biblical studies, in religious studies, in theology, or a general arts course.

continued to serve the College part-time, Tony Burnham being given overall responsibility for practical training. A year later, in 1974, the principal reported to the Annual Meeting that the churches of South West Manchester had 'opened their churches and their hearts to our students'. Whereas student preaching and student pastorates had always been a significant part of ministerial training, they had hitherto been unsupervised. From this point onwards, the emphasis was on student 'placements' and work in the community as an educational process in which local ministers as well as tutors could play a part.

Another new dimension of the College's work was in education and training for the whole Church. The College's proximity to such a large conurbation provided an excellent opportunity for offering evening lecture courses and weekend conferences to local church members, often through the WEA. For example, in the autumn and winter of 1970 and 1971, four well-attended courses, each of six lectures, were held on contemporary worship, the Psalms, the book of Revelation, and on 'a future for the Church'. Many lectures were provided in the College, but in other cases members of staff travelled to places like Bolton and Sheffield to deliver regular series of lectures. In 1972 staff and students visited both Leeds and Liverpool to lead conferences on 'Training for Tomorrow's Ministry' – leading to a series of similar visits to other northern cities and to Bristol.

In 1972 the majority of Congregational churches and almost every one of the churches of the Presbyterian Church of England united, forming the United Reformed Church (URC); most of the Congregationalists who remained outside the new Church chose to join either the Congregational Federation or An Evangelical Fellowship of Congregational Churches. The College now trained ministers for both the URC and the Federation, and included representatives of both bodies on its Board of Governors. One result of the acceptance of the new Basis of Union of the URC was that students were no longer authorised to preside at communion services, and this caused considerable discussion and protest at the theological students' house meetings.

The work of theological education was now becoming increasingly ecumenical throughout the country, reflecting the development of the ecumenical movement as a whole.[17] In 1970 the Queen's College, Birmingham, became the first college to attempt ecumenical theological training and education. The theological colleges in Manchester had long worked together through the University's Faculty of Theology, and it was a natural development of this collaboration to initiate ecumenical courses, of a more practical nature, through the colleges. During the

[17] In 1964 the Faith and Order Conference of the British Council of Churches in Nottingham had called for its member churches to seek union by 1980.

academic year 1969–70 Tony Burnham, together with R. G. Jones of Hartley Victoria Methodist College and Michael Taylor of Northern Baptist College, had organised an ecumenical course for first-year students. The following year this was continued, and the final year students of the three colleges shared in an ecumenical course on the practical work of ministry, focusing particularly on mission, worship, pastoral work and communication. In 1973 the Congregational College and the Baptist College shared in the appointment of David Goodbourn as lecturer in sociology and adult education, based at the Baptist College, an arrangement which lasted until 1985. The Unitarian College was soon involved in these courses as well. This process of ecumenical training gathered momentum during the 1970s and early 1980s and prepared the way for the establishment of the Northern Federation for Training in Ministry in 1984.

The College building was being fully used. Although the number of ordinands was not increasing significantly, the number of hostel students, now including women, was growing rapidly. By the academic year 1976–7 there were 116 students on the College roll, 104 of them in residence in newly-furnished study-bedrooms (no longer did the students have a study and a bedroom each). These included 33 preparing for the ministry of the United Reformed Church, two for the ministry of the Churches of Christ, two for the Moravian ministry, and six taking a special non-residential ministerial course for which the College now took responsibility.

Edgar Jones retired in 1977, and Tony Burnham resigned in the same year. Their work was now entrusted to two full-time lecturers. Stanley Russell, who had succeeded John Salsbury[18] in 1976, was the first to be appointed specifically to teach systematic theology. A graduate of the University of Birmingham, he trained for the ministry at New College, London, and later at Mansfield, where he wrote a DPhil thesis on Augustine and Calvin under the supervision of John Marsh. He had been a tutor at Adams Theological College in South Africa for five years between pastorates in England. Edgar Jones's work in teaching Hebrew and Old Testament was continued by Roger Tomes, a former student of Mansfield College, where he had been a research scholar. He had been associated in both a teaching and a governing capacity with the Yorkshire College during his first pastorate in Gomersal. Subsequently he spent four years as a part-time member of staff at New College during his time as minister at the King's Weigh House and at Whitefield Memorial Church in London.

Edgar Jones's successor as principal was Eric Hull, the senior lecturer.

[18] John Salsbury lectured to the first year students in theology and philosophy on a part-time basis from 1972 until 1976, while minister in Wallasey.

Sadly, Eric Hull died during his first term of office, in November 1977, at the age of 54. His widow, Dr Winifred Hull, herself a classical scholar, took over the teaching of Greek and temporarily fulfilled the role of acting warden. Stanley Russell was appointed Lecturer-in-Charge until a new appointment could be made.

The search for a new principal led the College to approach Robert John (Jack) McKelvey. Originally from Northern Ireland, he had studied at Paton College in the 1950s, and spent a year on a World Council of Churches scholarship at Western Theological Seminary, Pittsburgh, where he gained his Master's degree. In 1956 he proceeded to Mansfield College, where he did New Testament research for a doctorate under Austin Farrer.[19] McKelvey went to South Africa under the auspices of the London Missionary Society in 1959. He served as tutor and subsequently as principal of Adams United Theological College and President of the Federal Theological Seminary of Southern Africa in Alice, Cape Province. He spent some time in the United States in the mid-70s, studying internship training and clinical pastoral education, and from 1976 was personally involved in setting up internship training for ordinands of the United Congregational Church of Southern Africa. He also assisted in setting up the Theological Education by Extension College in Southern Africa. He began his work as principal in Manchester in January 1979, bringing particularly strong international interests and contacts, which bore fruit in the growing number of overseas students who came to the College.

One thing required of the new principal (which had attracted him to the post), as set out in the job description, was 'to engage in a radical review of ministerial training, its nature, where it should take place, and its ecumenical dimension, and taking into account contemporary developments in patterns of theological education'. The denominational background to this was the Report of the Commission on the Ministry, presented to the General Assembly of the United Reformed Church (URC) in 1975.[20] The Commission had been appointed by the Assembly of 1973, a year after the formation of the URC, a union of the Presbyterian Church of England and the majority of churches which had hitherto belonged to the Congregational Church of England and Wales. Much hard work had been done in defining the role of the ordained ministry. The Commission, chaired by Professor Roy Niblett, a leading Congregational layman who had recently retired from the Chair of Higher Education in the University of London, had wide-ranging terms of reference to explore the forms of ministry needed in the URC in the

[19] His thesis was published as *The New Temple: The Church in the New Testament* (London 1969).

[20] The Report forms Appendix III of the Minutes of the General Assembly of the URC in 1975.

foreseeable future, and the scope, content and provision of the training needed. Each existing college was represented on the Commission (Northern College was represented by Edgar Jones; Roger Tomes was also a member in his capacity as a member of the Supplementary Ministries Committee). Economic factors (including unpredictable rates of inflation), declining church membership, and enormous social changes had all to be taken into account. Ecumenical developments formed a wider context – 'the Commission has taken very seriously the declaration made by the URC from its inception that it is in deliberate search for the fuller unity of the Church of God.' Though the Commission recognised that still further closures or amalgamations were needed, they recommended 'that Westminster and Manchester should for the present be retained'.[21]

The College's own Review Group consisted of the principal and nine others, four of them Governors, and was convened by John Young (Chairman of Governors). It met first in November 1979 and immediately set up a number of sub-groups. Staff and students were consulted. The Group's conclusions, in the *Report of the College Review Group*, were presented to the Governors in January 1981, after a year's work. Their review of the academic content of the course led them to recommend that the University Faculty of Theology should be asked to make provision for courses in pastoral studies, in Judaism, and in the interpretation of scripture, philosophy and doctrine for today. Within the College, they recommended that theology should be taught systematically as well as historically. The spiritual development of the ordinands should be given a higher and more sustained priority. Practical training, properly supervised and rigorously assessed, should be a more significant part of every ordinand's training, using the summer vacations in a more organised way. The Review also set out a number of options for the development of the ecumenical context of training. The lines of development suggested by the Report guided the College throughout its work in the 1980s.

McKelvey reorganised the final year of training at the College by introducing internship. Instead of college-based courses, students learnt 'on the job' through sharing in ministry in a local congregation and community. Under David Goodbourn and later John Francis, students of Northern College and Northern Baptist College spent several days of each week in major church placements and one day mid-week at the College for reflection and input. Local ministers and lay persons played an important part in the College's teaching programme and students gained a great deal from one another through peer group methods of

[21] The Governors of New College decided during the course of the Commission's deliberations that it would not continue as a theological college beyond 1977.

learning. Clinical pastoral education courses in local hospitals under resident chaplains enriched pastoral training. Internship training was commended by the URC and eventually adopted by both Mansfield and Westminster Colleges. At Northern the experience gained led the staff to revise the practical training of earlier years and to make greater use of industrial mission and youth leadership programmes of training.

Arising out of discussion in a class on worship and preaching, a series of annual College missions was organised in co-operation with local churches within reach of Manchester. Staff and students shared together in a week's activity, including street theatre and school visits, and found the experience of working together with local churches in identifying needs and goals to be valuable preparation for ministry. Students who differed from each other theologically were sometimes surprised to find how much they could gain from working together.

One of the great changes in theological colleges in the last years of the twentieth century has been the increase in the number of women ordinands, reflecting the changing position of women in society in general. Over the period 1968–85 the proportion of women among those admitted to the full course at Northern College was 12 per cent, but the proportion for the years 1981–5 was 18 per cent. Whereas in 1970 the Governors discussed the difficulty that women students faced of finding churches worthy of their abilities, a decade later the situation had changed to the extent that in four of the five years 1977–82 it was a woman who was the first final-year student to receive a call from a church (a reflection of the growing acceptance and appreciation of the ministry of women by the churches in general). It was not however until 1986 that a woman (Jean Forster, who helped part-time with student placements and education) was appointed to the staff. The first woman to be elected Chairman of the Board of Governors was Mrs Beti Onions in 1987.

The ecumenical context became increasingly significant. The College had already been training Moravian students and latterly students preparing for the ministry of the Churches of Christ, for whom John Francis, former principal of Overdale College, Selly Oak, acted as supervisory tutor.[22] In 1981 he became an official part-time lecturer of the College. More ambitious ecumenical schemes were now discussed. The Review Group had invited the principals and chairmen of the Governing Bodies of the Baptist, Methodist[23] and Unitarian Colleges, together with representa-

[22] When Overdale College closed in 1975, its principal, John Francis, was appointed as Churches of Christ Ministerial Training Advisor and part-time member of staff of the Congregational College. By this time the Churches of Christ were already involved in the negotiations which led to the union of many congregations with the URC in 1981.

[23] Hartley Victoria College, which had been sharing the same site with the Baptist College since 1973.

tives of the Northern Ordination Course, to discuss the possibility of operating ecumenically from one site. Of the four possible options proposed, it was that of a federation of separate colleges working under a shared agreement that the Review Group proposed. This view was supported by the Northern College Governors at their meeting on 6 January 1982, and by the other colleges, and an ecumenical committee was appointed to draw up proposals. It was agreed from the beginning that it would be best to work from one site, and there was general agreement that the site would be that of the Baptist and Methodist Colleges in Rusholme. On 12 January 1984 the Northern College Governors agreed to join the Federation, and the following day an estate agent was instructed to seek a buyer for the Whalley Range building.

Great efforts had been made to keep the Whalley Range site financially viable, especially through increasing the number of hostel students. But the level of fees which the University set out for student residence was insufficient to cover costs, and in practice every hostel student was being heavily subsidised. The Review Group had warned that the costs of maintaining the building would increase, and that the URC could not hope to keep up with the continuously increasing costs of tuition and residential training.

The Northern Federation for Training in Ministry was inaugurated on 6 October 1984, at a service at which the preacher was Bishop Lesslie Newbigin, a former Moderator of the URC with long ecumenical experience in the Church of South India. Jack McKelvey was elected the first President of the Federation. Each of the participating colleges was to retain its own identity and governing body, but a joint council would be responsible for all ecumenical training and future planning. There was some debate over whether or not the Unitarian College could be a full member of the Federation; this was resolved by giving it the status of an associate member.

Since the formation of the URC it had been felt that the title of the College was anomalous, and suggestions for a new name had been solicited. This provoked a great deal of discussion; in the end the only name on which general agreement could be reached was 'Northern College (United Reformed and Congregational)'. This was agreed in 1982, and came into effect on 24 October 1983 as part of a new constitutional scheme sealed by the Charity Commissioners. The size of the unduly large Board of Governors was reduced from 60 to 30.

A purchaser for the Northern College building was found early in 1985: the General Municipal Boilermakers and Allied Trades Union (GMBATU), who paid £500,000.[24] Contracts were exchanged on

[24] The money realised from the sale created the Whalley Range Fund, the interest of which was to be used for the work of the College.

3 April, and the agreed completion date was 1 July 1985, which meant that the move to Rusholme had to be carried out in the few days between the end of term on 22 June and completion date. Some furniture was sold to students, the rest at an auction on 26 June. A Service of Thanksgiving and Commitment was held on the last day of term, at which the preacher was the historian and College Governor Dr Clyde Binfield.[25] Many found it hard to take their leave of a building which had been a great symbol of Congregationalism in the North-West for almost a century and a half, but the College community was reminded by the preacher that the College had moved twice before, and that its identity and traditions were not inextricably linked with a building. It is however sad to recount that most of the portraits inherited from each of the colleges which now formed Northern College had already been somewhat thoughtlessly disposed of in the 1970s. On the other hand it is a matter of much satisfaction to former students and staff of the College that the GMBATU have preserved an interest in the history of the building and have invested a great deal of money in its restoration and maintenance.

The Rusholme site was already the home of Northern Baptist College, Hartley Victoria Methodist College, the Northern Ordination Course and the Manchester Christian Institute (which provided a non-residential Christian leadership course, open to lay people as well as to Baptists, Moravians and members of the URC training for non-stipendiary ministry). Northern College and the Unitarians moved onto the site in September 1985 when their own buildings were sold. At the same time the building was re-named Luther King House. In the year that followed, 157 students were in training in the five constituent bodies, either full-time or part-time, training for both stipendiary and non-stipendiary ministry; 46 were also in training with the Manchester Christian Institute for various forms of Christian leadership. As many of these students were non-resident, there was still room for a few hostel students, who helped to create a wider intellectual and social context at the House. In the vacations, the House provided residential training weekends for students of the Northern Ordination Course and the Christian Leadership Course of the Manchester Christian Institute.

For some time it had been felt desirable to appoint a College Chaplain, someone whose role would be entirely pastoral and not involved in any assessment or disciplinary structures. At the beginning of 1985 a former student, Fred Noden, began work in this capacity alongside his ministry in Wilmslow, and fulfilled a perceived need.

Two new initiatives in the year 1985–6 were indicative of the continuing intention to keep abreast of new needs. The first was the

[25] The sermon was published as 'Habakkuk in Pykecrete: A Sermon in Celebration and Anticipation', *Free Church Chronicle* 40/3 (1985).

establishment of the Mona Powell Fellowship, funded largely through a generous legacy from a church member at Worsley Road, Swinton. The purpose of this was to enable a younger minister-scholar to undertake postgraduate research over a period of three years. The first holder of the Fellowship, from October 1985, was David Stec, who was preparing an edition of the Targum of Job. The other innovation was the inauguration of a new course, known as the FourC course: Church, Community, College Course. Essentially a pilot project, it sought to develop lessons gained from internship by widening the context of training. Greater effort was made to expose the students to the community and its needs. This course eventually led to a further review at the College and the introduction of a fully integrated form of training.

16

Northern College 1986–97

As the end of the twentieth century approached, the College continued to question and refine its goals and means of achieving them in the light of a changing context. Manchester as a city continued to flourish in its economic and cultural life, but had within its borders areas of great deprivation, particularly Hulme and Moss Side, which were not far from Luther King House. Society was changing rapidly, in ethnic composition, the distribution of wealth and patterns of employment. In facing these changing patterns and problems, the Federation proved to be a source of strength. Further support was derived from the contribution of theological educators from other parts of the world, whose critical observations brought a global dimension to the College's life and work.

The movement towards a more fully integrated training programme, already foreshadowed by the introduction of the internship year, continued. Two developments provided a further impetus. One was the University's introduction of a new part-time BA degree in theology at the end of the 1980s, enabling the College to develop a more flexible programme. The other was the appointment of David Peel to the new post of tutor in community-based training in 1988, with a particular responsibility to develop ministerial training through placements in the local community. David Peel was a former student of Northern College (1971–4), a native of Keighley, Yorkshire; he had taken a degree in chemistry at London University before beginning his ordination training in Manchester. As well as his own College education in the 1970s, he brought a variety of experience to his new task: attendance at the World Council of Churches (WCC) conference in Uppsala in 1968 while working at a WCC work camp in Sweden, and at the WCC conference in Nairobi in 1975 as a steward, a year's study at Perkins School of Theology, Dallas on a WCC Scholarship, pastoral ministry in Kettering and Stockton-on-Tees, and a PhD in systematic theology.[1]

The first fully-integrated, community-based course had begun in the Northern Baptist College in 1988, under the leadership of Heather Walton, a Methodist lay theologian on the staff of the Baptist College in succession to David Goodbourn. A year later, two Northern College

[1] His thesis was entitled 'The Theology of Schubert M. Ogden: A Dialogue with his Critics', prepared under the supervision of David Pailin.

students were accepted for this course with David Peel as URC tutor. Their work was based principally at Moss Side, involving churches and community groups. Thus the local community as well as the College became the context of training, and ministers and church members now played an important role in the students' learning process.

The College had to decide how far it should go down the road of integrated training; should it be an option for a minority of students, or should it become the normal course of training? That issue, and the impending retirements of three of the four members of staff, contributed to the decision of the Governors to appoint another Review Group in February 1990, with a remit 'to identify the requirements for education in Northern College in the light of the changing requirements of church bodies and the experience of being involved with the Federation and the University of Manchester' and to advise on the resources needed. The Group of ten members, including representatives of the Congregational Federation and of the University's theology faculty, was convened by former Yorkshire student Leslie Green,[2] and consulted widely among former students, local churches and others. In April and May 1991 David Peel, as part of a sabbatical term, visited several seminaries in the United States to study developments in ministerial education, and offered a report of his findings to the Group. Their recommendations, in a report entitled 'Enhancing Effective Ministry', were presented to the Governors one year later. The report was a contribution to the general debate within the URC on the nature of the ordained ministry and the needs of the Church in the future. Assuming a missionary rather than a maintenance model of the Church, the Review Group emphasised particularly the need for ordained ministers to be able to reflect and to help others to reflect theologically on experience, both individually and in community. Their recommendations, which were adopted by the Governors with only minor modifications, affirmed the value of the integrated course and implied its adoption as the principal mode of training.

Following this report, therefore, the College moved swiftly towards adopting an integrated course as the basic programme for most students. Together with some of their partners in the Federation, the College negotiated with the University the status of 'Affiliated Institution'. This meant that the Federation was able to devise its own integrated four-year course, 'Faith in Living', designed to lead either to a degree or a diploma in theology which the University agreed to validate. The first students, from Northern College, Northern Baptist College and the Manchester Christian Institute, began the first year of the course in the autumn of 1994. It was to be a flexible, modular course which could be undertaken

[2] He had long experience of chaplaincy in higher education as well of pastoral ministry. The College owes him a very great debt for his contribution to the thinking about ordination education and training, as well as to its implementation.

on a part-time or full-time basis, open to lay students as well as ordinands.

One of the recommendations of 'Enhancing Effective Ministry' was that students should be more closely involved in formulating goals and assessing their own achievement. These recommendations were built into the new course, which was to be assessed by regular assignments rather than by traditional examination. The students were designated 'participants' in the course.

Despite the difficulties of having to meet the needs of a variety of student life-patterns (part-time, full-time, residential and non-residential), regular worship continued to be at the heart of the community's life. In 1991 the Federation was officially recognised as a Local Ecumenical Partnership (LEP), which not only helped the constituent members to grow together through joint worship, but provided relevant experience for those ordinands who would move to other LEPs after leaving college.

Jack McKelvey retired in 1993 after almost fifteen years as principal. After public advertisement of his post, and enquiries concerning suggested candidates, the Governors came to the conclusion that the right candidate as successor was a member of the existing staff, David Peel. He began work as principal in September 1993, and continued to take a leading role in the planning for the integrated degree course. As far as teaching was concerned, he now concentrated upon systematic theology. Roger Tomes retired after 16 years at the College in the same year. The staff now assumed a more ecumenical character. Two part-time biblical scholars were appointed, Helen Bond (an Anglican) from the Universities of St Andrews, Durham and Tübingen, to teach New Testament,[3] and Walter Houston, from the staff of Westminster College, Cambridge, to teach Old Testament.[4] Frances Ward, an Anglican deacon from St Andrews University, the Royal London Hospital and Westcott House, Cambridge was appointed tutor in practical theology.[5] When Stanley Russell retired a year later, his work in systematic theology was undertaken by David Peel, and John Parry was appointed to teach mission studies and world faiths when he had completed his work as Mona Powell Fellow in 1995. A former student of the College (1966–73), he had served with the Council for World Mission in Bangladesh, and later had a pioneering ministry in Southall, Middlesex, an area with a high Asian population, where he had developed an excellent short programme for ordination students. His research thesis,

[3] Her doctoral thesis was on Pontius Pilate.

[4] His *Purity and Monotheism: Clean and Unclean Animals in Biblical Law* was published in 1993 (Sheffield).

[5] Her experience of and preparation for ministry is recounted in Mary Loudon, *Revelations* (London 1994).

Figure 11: Luther King House (quadrangle), home of Northern College today
Photo: David Yeo Poulton

for which the University of Birmingham awarded him a PhD, was on Christian–Sikh dialogue. His experience of multi-faith dialogue was a valuable addition to the College's resources, building on the openness to people of other faiths which Roger Tomes had tried to encourage. In addition, a steady flow of international students enriched the College's life.

Collaboration between staff, students, local churches and governors was now enhanced. In 1996 the College Governors appointed another Review Group, with wide representation, to make recommendations for the future shape of the College's programmes. After sharing its interim findings with a wide constituency, the Group presented its final report to the Governors in November 1997. This report built on the developments of the previous few years, and recommended that the College should widen its existing pattern of education and training to include preparation for non-stipendiary ministry, for church-related community work, the ministry of elders and deacons, and lay ministries in secular spheres.

The Group also recommended strong support for the most recent developments of the Federation, of which David Peel was made president in 1996. The Federation was now poised to move forward with new vitality and hope by widening the partnership and recognising the importance of part-time training, by making more intensive use of Luther King House for different forms of theological education and training (and thereby reducing the hostel accommodation for lay students to weekdays only), and by entering into discussions concerning the possible future common ownership of the building and site.

Former students continued to make distinguished contributions to the life of the denomination and to scholarship. For example, Tony Burnham was elected General Secretary of the URC in 1992, and in 1997 Alan Sell was the first former student of the College, and only the seventh person, to be awarded the DD degree of Manchester University.

The late 1990s have been a time of change and opportunity. The college has tried to keep abreast of developments in contemporary theology, but without abandoning a critical stance. There has been the opportunity to re-vision the role of a theological college, and, in David Peel's words to the subscribers in 1995, to rediscover the role of such colleges as 'the theological conscience and voice of the churches.' It was ever more necessary to respond to the Church's need for educated and educating theologians.[6] While hope grounded in faith, rather than optimism, was the outlook of the College, there were many excitements and challenges opening up for the future, which those responsible will surely face with as much courage and imagination as their predecessors.

[6] See David Peel's article, 'A View from the Tower: The Need for a Teachable Spirit in the United Reformed Church', in *Reformed Quarterly*, 1993.

Appendix

College Staff who taught arts and theological subjects

The Western Academy/College		Higher Education and Ministerial Training
Senior Tutors/Presidents/Principals		
Lavington, John Jnr	1752–64	Private study
Rooker, James	1765–79	Bedworth Academy
Reader, Thomas	1780–94	Bedworth Academy and Northampton Academy
Small, James	1796–1828	Taunton Academy
Payne, George	1829–48	Hoxton Academy and Glasgow University
Alliott, Richard	1849–57	Homerton College and Glasgow University
Charlton, John	1857–75	Highbury College
Chapman, Charles	1876–1910	Western College, Plymouth
Franks, Robert Sleightholme	1910–39	St John's College, Cambridge and Mansfield College
Parry, Kenneth Lloyd (Acting)	1939–41	University of Liverpool and Mansfield College
Cocks, Harry Francis Lovell	1941–60	Hackney College
Sims, Basil	1960–68	Corpus Christi College, Oxford and Mansfield College
Tutors/Professors		
Anthony, Frederick Evans W.	1857–1901	Western College, Plymouth
Currie, Daniel	1829–31	Axminster Academy
Dobbin, Orlando Thomas	1840–45	Trinity College, Dublin and Hoxton Academy
Downes, William John	1947–62	University of London and New College
Glyde, Jonathan	1831–35	Highbury College
Griffiths, William Henry	1854–57	Coward College
Macey, Thomas Stenner	1886–1924	Western College, Plymouth
Newth, Samuel	1845–54	University College, London and Coward College

Pope, John White	1836–39	Western Academy, Exeter
Sims, Arnold Walter	1927–47	Western College, Bristol

Bristol Theological Institute

Allan, John Petherick	1879–91	Western College, Plymouth
Hartland, Edward Joseph	1863–79	Cheshunt College
Knight, Thomas Broughton	1867–91	Western College, Plymouth

The Yorkshire Colleges

Heckmondwike and Northowram: *Tutors*

Scott, James	1756–83	University of Edinburgh
Walker, Samuel	1783–94	Heckmondwike Academy

Rotherham Independent Academy/College

Theological Tutors/Principals

Williams, Edward	1795–1813	Abergavenny Academy
Bennett, James	1813–28	Gosport Academy
Perrot, Clement	1829–33	(not known)
Stowell, William Hendry	1834–50	Blackburn Independent Academy
Falding, Frederick John	1852–88	Rotherham Independent College and University of Glasgow (see also under Yorkshire United Independent College)

Tutors

Armitage, Elkanah	1884–88	Owens College and Trinity College, Cambridge (see also under Yorkshire United Independent College)
Barker, Philip	1872–84	Spring Hill and University of Glasgow
Bennett, William Henry	1884–88	Lancashire Independent College and St John's College, Cambridge (see also under Lancashire Independent College)
Clark, Thomas	1852–54	Highbury College
Gilbert, Joseph	1810–17	Rotherham Independent Academy
Phillips, Maurice	1796–1810	Oswestry Academy
Smith, James	1872–76	University of Glasgow and Rotherham Independent College
Smith, Thomas	1817–50	University of Edinburgh
Tyte, Cornelius Curtis	1854–73	Rotherham Independent College

Idle Academy/Airedale Independent College

Theological Tutors/Principals

Vint, William	1800–33	Northowram Academy
Scott, Walter	1834–56	Hoxton Academy
Fraser, Daniel	1858–76	University of Glasgow and Glasgow Theological Academy (see also below)
Fairbairn, Andrew Martin	1877–86	University of Edinburgh and Evangelical Union Academy, Glasgow and study in Germany

Tutors

Clulow, William Benton	1835–43	Hoxton Academy
Creak, Henry Brown	1848–64	Spring Hill College
Duff, Archibald	1878–88	McGill University, Andover Theological Seminary, Halle and Göttingen (see also under Yorkshire United Independent College)
Fraser, Daniel	1843–58	University of Glasgow and Glasgow Theological Academy (see also above)
Harley, Robert	1864–68	Airedale College
Hartley, Richard Griffiths	1858–62	Lancashire Independent College and Owens College
Shearer, William Campbell	1863–88	University of Edinburgh and Cheshunt College (see also under Yorkshire United Indpendent College)
Taylor, Thomas Rawson	1833–34	Idle Independent College

Yorkshire United Independent College

Principals

Falding, Frederick John	1888–92	Rotherham Independent College and University of Glasgow (see also under Rotherham)
Simon, David Worthington	1893–1907	Spring Hill College and study in Germany
Griffith-Jones, Ebenezer	1907–32	Presbyterian College, Carmarthen and New College
Price, Ernest Jones	1932–47	University of Manchester and Lancashire Independent College
Cunliffe-Jones, Hubert	1947–58	Melbourne University and Camden College, Sydney, Australia (see also below and under Northern College)

Tutors/Professors

Allan, James Baxter	1925–32	University of St Andrews and Scottish Theological Hall
Armitage, Elkanah	1888–1914	Owens College and Trinity College, Cambridge (see under Rotherham)
Cadoux, Cecil John	1919–33	University of London and Mansfield College, Oxford
Davies, William David	1945–50	Cardiff University College, Brecon College and Cheshunt College
Duff, Archibald	1888–1925	McGill University, Andover Theological Seminary, Halle and Göttingen (see also under Airedale)
Escott, Harry	1935–38	University of Edinburgh and Yorkshire United Independent College
Green, Leslie Craven	1955–58	University of Edinburgh and Yorkshire United Independent College
Jones, Edgar	1956–58	Cardiff University College and Brecon College
Martin, George Currie	1903–09	University of Edinburgh, Marburg and New College
Mee, Arnold Francis	1933–35	University of Leeds and Yorkshire United Independent College
Ormerod, Joseph Charles	1933–43	Trinity College, Oxford and Mansfield College
Pope, Ambrose	1908–28	Jesus College, Oxford and Mansfield College
Russell, Hunter	1928–29	(not known)
Shearer, William Campbell	1888–1902	University of Edinburgh and Cheshunt College (see also under Airedale)
Stewart, James	1946–56	University of Edinburgh, Scottish Congregational College and Mansfield College
Turner, Robert Reynolds	1942–45	University of Edinburgh and Cheshunt College (see also under Paton)
Vine, Aubrey Russell	1951–57	University of London and New College
Wilton, Stanley	1955–58	University of Edinburgh and Yorkshire United Independent College

Lancashire Colleges

Roby's Academy

Roby, William	1803–08	Trevecca College (for six weeks)

Leaf Square Academy

Phillips, George	1811	Wymondley Academy and University of Glasgow
Lewis, Jenkin	1811–13	Abergavenny and Oswestry Academy

Blackburn Independent Academy

Theological Tutors/Presidents

Fletcher, Joseph	1816–22	Hoxton Academy and University of Glasgow
Payne, George	1823–29	Hoxton Academy and University of Glasgow
Wardlaw, Gilbert	1830–43	Glasgow Theological Academy (see also below)

Tutors

Alexander, William Lindsay	1827–31	University of St Andrews
Hayward, Daniel Burgess	1833–43	Blackburn Independent Academy
Hope, William Johnstone	1817–22	University of Edinburgh and Selkirk Theological Academy
Howle, William	1819–21	(not known)
Miller, Ebenezer	1824–28	Glasgow Theological Academy
Wardlaw, Gilbert	1821–23	Glasgow Theological Academy (see also above)

Lancashire Independent College

Presidents

Vaughan, Robert	1843–57	Private education
Rogers, Henry	1858–69	Highbury College
Scott, Caleb	1869–1902	Airedale College
Adeney, Walter Frederick	1903–13	New College
Bennett, William Henry	1913–20	Lancashire Independent College and St John's College, Cambridge (see also below and under Rotherham)
Grieve, Alexander James	1922–43	Aberystwyth University College and Mansfield College
Robinson, William Gordon	1943–58	University of Liverpool, Lancashire Independent College and Mansfield College

Tutors/Professors

Davidson, Samuel	1843–57	Royal Belfast Academical Institution
Corbold, R. E.	1905–15	(not known)
Ferguson, Joseph	1898–1904	Universities of St Andrews and London and Lancashire Independent College
Grime, J. E.	1910–18	(not known)
Hall, Theophilus Dwight	1856–66	University College, London
Halley, Robert	1850–56	University College, London and Coward College
Hawes, Gordon K.	1933–35	University of Manchester and Lancashire Independent College
Herbert, Thomas Martin	1876–77	Spring Hill and Lancashire Independent College
Higgins, A. J. B.	1940–46	Universities of Wales and Manchester and Lancashire Independent College
Hodgson, James Muscutt	1875–94	University of Glasgow and Lancashire Independent College
Knowles, Vincent	1938–48	(not known)
Lewis, Thomas	1895–98	Universities of St Andrews and London and Lancashire Independent College
Martin, George Currie	1904–09	University of Edinburgh, Marburg and New College (see also under Yorkshire United Independent College)
Mackintosh, Robert	1894–1930	University of Glasgow, New College, Edinburgh, Jena and Marburg
Mason, Charles Peter	1943–49	University of London
Murphy, John	1930–41	University of Glasgow, Scottish Theological Hall, Berlin and Heidelberg
Newth, Alfred	1856–75	Homerton College
Orchard, Ronald Kenneth	1935–37	University of Manchester and Lancashire Independent College
Peake, Arthur Samuel	1895–1912	St John's College, Oxford
Phillips, George	1925–29 and 1941–61	Jesus College, Oxford and Lancashire Independent College
Robinson, William Gordon	1929–32	University of Liverpool, Lancashire Independent College and Mansfield College (see also above)
Russell, William C.	1870–75	(not known)
Scott, Caleb	1865–69	Airedale College (see also above)

Thomson, Alexander	1875–95	University of Aberdeen and Spring Hill College
Titchmarsh, Edward Harper	1920–21	University of London and New College
Turner, George Lyon	1880–89	University College, London and Cheshunt College

Cavendish Theological College, Nottingham Theological Institute and Paton College

Principals

Parker, Joseph	1860–62	Private study
Paton, John Brown	1863–98	Spring Hill College
Mitchell, James Alexander	1898–1903	New College (see also below)
Ritchie, David Lakie	1903–19	University of Edinburgh and Scottish Theological Hall
Henderson, Alexander Roy	1921–37	University of Edinburgh and Scottish Theological Hall
Taylor, Thomas Samuel	1937–48	St John's College, Oxford and Mansfield College
Charles, Maurice	1948–64	New College and Mansfield College
Turner, Robert Reynolds	1966–68	University of Edinburgh and Cheshunt College

Tutors

Bumby, Frederick	1886–97	(not known)
Hodgkins, Harold	1951–68	Cheshunt College
McKenzie, John Grant	1921–51	University of Aberdeen and Yorkshire United Independent College
Sanders, Harold Freer	1898–1938	Victoria University and Lancashire Independent College
Thomas, David Arafnah	1951–60	Cardiff University College, Brecon College and Merton College, Oxford
Turner, Robert Reynolds	1939–42 and 1946–66	University of Edinburgh and Cheshunt College (see also above)
Williams, Frederick Smeeton	1863–86	University College, London and New College

Congregational/Northern College

Principals

Robinson, William Gordon	1958–68	University of Liverpool, Lancashire Independent College and Mansfield College (see also under Lancashire Independent College)

Cunliffe-Jones, Hubert	1958–66	(see also under Yorkshire United Independent College)
Jones, Edgar	1968–77	Cardiff University College and Brecon College (see also under Yorkshire United Independent College)
Hull, John Eric Howarth	1977	University of Manchester and Lancashire Independent College
McKelvey, Robert John	1979–93	Paton College, Pittsburgh Theological Seminary and Mansfield College
Peel, David	1993–	University of London, University of Manchester, Northern College and Perkins School of Theology, Dallas

Tutors

Berry, Janet Nesta	1997–	University of Bristol, Bristol Baptist College and Regent's Park College, Oxford
Bond, Helen	1993–96	Universities of St Andrews, Durham and Tübingen
Burnham, Anthony Gerald	1969–77	University of Manchester and Northern College
Francis, John Ewart	1981–91	University of London and Overdale College
Houston, Walter John	1993–	St John's College, Cambridge and Mansfield College
Hull, John Eric Howarth	1961–77	University of Manchester and Lancashire Independent College (see also above)
Jenkins, David	1968–80	University of Manchester, Northern College and University of Berkeley, California
Oakes, Peter	1996–	Jesus College, Cambridge, University of Liverpool, London Bible College and Worcester College, Oxford
Parry, John Maldwyn	1995–	University of Manchester, Northern College and University of Birmingham
Peel, David	1988–93	University of London, University of Manchester, Northern College and Perkins School of Theology, Dallas (see also above)
Ponnusamy, John Samuel	1996–	Tamil Nadu Theological Seminary and Madurai Kamaraj University

Russell, Stanley Herbert	1976–94	University of Birmingham, New College and Mansfield College
Salsbury, John Derek	1972–76	University of Manchester and Northern College
Tomes, Francis Roger	1977–93	Jesus College, Oxford and Mansfield College
Ward, Frances	1993–97	University of St Andrews and Westcott House, Cambridge

Bibliography

1. Manuscript Sources and College Reports

(All records are in the Congregational/Northern College Archive at the John Rylands University Library, Manchester, unless otherwise stated.)

Western College

Letter, Joseph Chadwick to Joshua Wilson 1820 (DWL)
Annual Reports 1837–55 (Plymouth Local Studies Library)
Annual Reports 1855–61, 1874–6
Annual Reports 1899–1910 (Bristol Local Studies Library)
Annual Reports 1911–67
Rules and Regulations of Western College, Plymouth
S. Newth, MS Autobiography (DWL)
College Council Minute Book 1891–1936
Education Committee Books 1935–68
Bristol Congregational Council Minute Books 1893–1904, 1947–56 (Bristol Record Office)
Bristol and District of Gloucester and Hereford Congregational Union Minute Book 1930–56 (Bristol Record Office)

Yorkshire Colleges

Heckmondwike and Northowram Academies

An Account of the Rise, Nature and Progress of a Society for Educating Young Men for the Work of the Ministry, in the West Riding of the County of York (c.1765)

Idle Academy, Airedale Independent College and Rotherham Independent Academy/College

Idle Academy Minute Book 1804–31
Idle Academy Reports 1800–31

Letter, J. P. Clapham to John Blackburn 1831 (DWL)
Airedale College Building Committee Minute Book 1830–33
Airedale College Committee Minute Books 1831–87
Airedale College Annual Reports 1830–87
Papers relating to the Hanson Trust
Papers relating to negotiations between Airedale and Rotherham Colleges
Report on the site of Airedale College in a Sanitary Point of View (W. Burnie) 1864
Rotherham Independent Academy Minute Books 1796–1876
Rotherham Independent Academy Annual Reports 1812–89
Records of Rotherham students 1796–1888
Edward Williams, Lecture Notes (DWL)

Yorkshire United Independent College

Minute Books: College Committee 1924–34, Finance Committee 1934–58, Education Committee 1934–58, Library Committee 1934–58
Annual Reports 1887–97, 1943–58
Papers relating to A. Duff (Bradford Record Office)
Cadoux papers (Bodleian Library, Oxford)
Minutes of Leeds and Bradford Theological Circle 1935–49 (Leeds Archive Office)

Lancashire Colleges

Leaf Square, Blackburn Independent Academy and Lancashire Independent College

Leaf Square Academy Minute Books
Blackburn Independent Academy Minute Books and Annual Reports
Memorandum from Blackburn students to the Committee April 1827
Correspondence and Scrapbook of George Hadfield
William Roby papers
Lancashire Independent College Minute Books: College Committee, Education Committee, House and Finance Committee, Debating Society, Samuel Davidson Subcommittee, Liverpool Bazaar
MSS relating to Robert Mackintosh
Old Students Association Newsletters
Annual Reports
Centenary Booklets 1920, 1943
Correspondence relating to College Centenary 1943
R. K. and E. K. Orchard, ‘C. H. Dodd at the University of Manchester’
Lancashire Independent College Register of Students

Cavendish Theological College, Nottingham Congregational College and Paton College

R. R. Turner, unpublished History of Nottingham Congregational Institute
Annual Reports
College Committee Minutes 1867–1902
College Committee Minutes 1947–68, Executive Committee Minutes 1902–33, Executive and Finance Committee Minutes 1933–68 (Congregational Centre, Nottingham)

Congregational College/Northern College Manchester

(The most recent records are kept at the College.)
Annual Reports
Governors Minute Books
Education Committee Minute Books
Theological Students Minute Books
Report of the College Review Group (1981)
'Enhancing Effective Ministry: Report of the College Review Group' (1992)
'Enhancing Effective Ministry: The Next Steps' (1997)

Other Records

Surman Card Index of Congregational and URC Ministers (DWL)
Senatus Academicus Minute Book (DWL)
Congregational Union of England and Wales, Ministerial Training Committee Minute Book 1930–47 (URC Archive, Westminster College, Cambridge)
D. W. Bebbington, 'The Dissenting Idea of a University: Oxford and Cambridge in Nonconformist thought in the Nineteenth Century', Hulsean Prize Essay, University of Cambridge, 1973
R. E. Chadwick, 'Church and People in Bradford and District 1880–1914', Oxford DPhil Thesis (1986)

2. Periodical Publications

British Quarterly Review
Congregational Magazine
Congregational Quarterly
Congregational Year Books
Congregational Federation Year Books
Evangelical Magazine
Journal of the United Reformed Church History Society
Manchester Times

Record
Reform
United Reformed Church Year Books
Transactions of the Congregational Historical Society

3. Printed Books, Pamphlets and Articles

Abram, W. A. — *The History of Independency in Blackburn* (Blackburn 1878)

Adamson, W. — *The Life of the Rev Joseph Parker 1830–1902* (London 1902)

Anderson. K. C. — *The New Theology* (1907)

Argent, Alan — 'The Pilot on the Bridge: John Daniel Jones (1805–1942)', *JURCHS* 5/10 (1997)

Axon, W. — *The Annals of Manchester* (Manchester 1886)

Ayres, W. F. — *The Highbury Story* (London 1963)

Baker, Frank — *William Grimshaw 1708–63* (London 1963)

Balgarnie, R. — *Sir Titus Salt* (London 1977, reprinted Settle 1970)

Bebbington, David — *Evangelicalism in Modern Britain: A History from the 1730s to the 1980s* (London 1989)

Bellot, H. Hale — *University College London 1826–1926* (London 1929)

Bennett, James — *Memorials of the Rev James Bennett* (London 1863)

Binfield, Clyde — *So Down to Prayers: Studies in English Nonconformity 1780–1920* (London 1977)

Pastors and People: The Biography of a Baptist Church: Queen's Road Coventry (Gloucester 1984)

'Samuel Morley' and 'Titus Salt' in J. O. Baylen and N. J. Grossman (eds), *Biographical Dictionary of Modern British Radicals* vol 2 1830–70 (Brighton 1984)

'Three Personalities and a Theological College', *Transactions of the Hunter Archaeological Society* 14 (1987)

'The Wills Family of Bristol', *Congregational History Circle Magazine* 2/6 (1990)

'True to Stereotype? Vivian and Dorothy Pomeroy and the Rebels in Lumb Lane' in S. Mews (ed), *Modern Religious Rebels* (London 1993)

'Hebrews Hellenized: English Evangelical Nonconformity and Culture 1840–1940' in S. Gilley and W. J. Sheils, *A History of Religion in Britain: Practice and Belief from Pre-Roman Times to the Present* (Oxford 1994)

'The Story of Button Hill: An Essay in Leeds Nonconformity' in A. Mason (ed), *Religion in Leeds* (Stroud 1994)

Bogue, D. and Bennett, J. — *A History of the Dissenters from 1688 to 1808* vol IV (London 1812)

Bolam, C. G., Goring, Jeremy, Short, H. L. and Thomas, Roger — *The English Presbyterians: From Elizabethan Puritanism to Modern Unitarianism* (London 1968)

Briggs, Asa — *Victorian Cities* (London 1963)

Brockett, Allan — *Nonconformity in Exeter 1650–1875* (Manchester 1962)

Brown, K. D. — 'College Principals – A Cause of Nonconformist Decay?', *Journal of Ecclesiastical History* 38 (1987)

A Social History of the Nonconformist Ministry in England and Wales 1800–1930 (Oxford 1988)

Burnley, E. G. and Walker, J. W. — *History of Upper Independent Church, Heckmondwike 1674–1924* (Heckmondwike 1924)

Campbell, R. J. — *A Spiritual Pilgrimage* (London 1916)

Chislett, C. J. (ed) — *Masbro' Independent Chapel* (Rotherham 1960)

Church, R. A. — *Victorian Nottingham* (London 1966)

Clark, J. C. D. — *English Society 1688–1832: Social Structure and Political Practice During the Ancien Regime* (Cambridge 1985)

Cockin, John (ed) — *Memoirs of the Rev Joseph Cockin* (London 1841)

Cocks, H. F. Lovell — *The Nonconformist Conscience* (London 1943)

The Religious Life of Oliver Cromwell (London 1960)

Coleman, B. — 'Nineteenth Century Nonconformity' in N. Orme (ed), *Unity and Variety: A History of the Church in Devon and Cornwall* (Exeter 1991)

Conder, G. W. (ed) — *Memoir and Remains of Jonathan Glyde* (London 1858)

Congregational Union of England and Wales — *Congregational Union Assembly: Official Handbook October 1911*

Congregational Union Assembly: Official Handbook October 1938

Commission on the Colleges (London 1958)

Coote, T. and Falding, F. J. *Notes of a Journey Round the World Made in 1875* (Sheffield 1876)
Cottle, B, and Sherman, J. W. *The Life of a University* (Bristol 1959)
Crowther, Freda and Greene, Dorothy *Rotherham* (Rotherham 1971)
Cudworth, William *Round About Bradford* (Bradford 1876)
Cunliffe-Jones, H. 'Christian theology for the Twentieth Century', *CQ* 25 (1947)
The Authority of the Biblical Revelation (London 1948)
Cunliffe-Jones, H. (ed) *The Congregational Ministry in the Modern World: An Interpretation by Past Students and Present Staff of the Yorkshire United Independent College* (London 1955)
Cunningham, C. and Waterhouse, P. *Alfred Waterhouse 1830–1905: The Biography of a Practice* (Oxford 1992)
Cunningham, Valentine *Everywhere Spoken Against: Dissent in the Victorian Novel* (1975)
Currie, R., Gilbert, A. and Horsley, L. *Churches and Churchgoers: Patterns of Church Growth in the British Isles since 1700* (Oxford 1977)
Dale, R. W. 'The History of Spring Hill College' in *Mansfield College Oxford: Its Origin and Opening (London 1890)*
'Memoir of Henry Rogers' in Henry Rogers, *The Superhuman Origin of the Bible* (Eighth edition, London 1893)
Davidson, A. J. *The Autobiography and Diary of Samuel Davidson* (Edinburgh 1899)
Davidson, Samuel *Facts, Statements and Explanations Connected with the Publication of the Second Volume of the Tenth Edition of Horne's Introduction to the Scriptures* (London 1857)
Davies, D. R. *In Search of Myself* (London 1961)
Davies, Horton *A Church Historian's Odyssey: A Memoir* (Allison Park and Grand Rapids 1993)
Davis, V.D. *A History of Manchester College: From its Foundation in Manchester to its Establishment in Oxford* (London 1931)
Dictionary of Welsh Biography Down to 1940 (London 1959)

Dillistone, F. W. — *C. H. Dodd: Interpreter of the New Testament* (London 1977)

Drummond, J. S. — *Charles A. Berry DD* (London 1899)

Duff, A. — 'A Theological College Professor's Training in the Nineteenth Century', *CQ* 14 (1936)

Fairbairn, A. M. — *The Philosophy of the Christian Religion* (London 1902)

Studies in Religion and Theology (London 1910)

'Experience in Theology: A Chapter of Autobiography', *Contemporary Review* 91 (1907)

Fiddes, E. — *Chapters in the History of Owens College and of Manchester University 1851–1914* (Manchester 1937)

Fletcher, Joseph — *Memoirs of the Life and Correspondence of the Late Rev Joseph Fletcher DD* (London 1846)

Flew, N. and Davies, R. E. (eds) — *The Catholicity of Protestantism* (1950)

Franks, R. S. — *The Atonement* (Oxford 1934)

Fraser, Lucy A. (ed) — *Memoirs of Daniel Fraser* (London 1905)

Gilbert, J. — *Memoir of the Life and Writings of Edward Williams* (London 1825)

Gill, Crispin — *Plymouth: A New History* vol II (Newton Abbot 1979)

Gladstone, W. E. — *The Gladstone Diaries* vol IX (ed H. C. G. Matthew) (Oxford 1986)

Glover, Willis B. — *Evangelical Nonconformists and Higher Criticism in the Nineteenth Century* (London 1954)

Gomme, A., Jenner, M. and Little, B. — *Bristol: An Architectural History* (London 1979)

Grant, J. W. — *Free Churchmanship in England* (London n. d. [1955])

Greenfield Congregational Church, Bradford — *Jubilee Volume* (Bradford 1902)

Grieve, A. J. — 'A Hundred Years of Ministerial Training', *TCHS* 11 (1930–2)

'Presbyterian-Congregational Union? II I am Against', *CQ* 25 (1947)

Griffin, James — *Memories of the Past* (Manchester 1883)

Griffin, S. — *The Sherwell Story* (Plymouth 1964)

Griffith-Jones, E. *The Ascent through Christ* (1899)
The Challenge of Christianity to a World at War (London 1915)
Providence – Divine and Human (1925)

Hadfield, George *An Address Intended to have been Delivered on the Occasion of the Laying of the Foundation Stone of Lancashire Independent College* (Manchester 1842)

Halley, R. *Lancashire: Its Puritanism and Nonconformity* 2 vols (Manchester 1869)

Helmstadter, R. J. 'Orthodox Nonconformity' in D. G. Paz (ed), *Nineteenth Century English Religious Traditions* (Westport USA 1995)

Hendry, Kathleen *Don't Ask Me Why: Sixty Years a Woman Minister* (London 1991)

Heywood, Oliver *His Autobiography, Diaries, Anecdotes and Event Books* 4 vols (ed J. H. Turner) (Bingley 1881–5)

Hora, Mary 'The Age of Great Cities' (forthcoming in *JURCHS*)

Hunter, L. S. *John Hunter DD: A Life* (London 1922)

Huxtable, John *As It Seemed to Me* (London 1991)

James, David and Beesley, Ian *Undercliffe – Bradford's Historic Victorian Cemetery* (Bradford 1991)

James, John *History of Bradford* (London 1841)

Jay, William *Autobiography* (Second edition, ed G. Radford and J. A. James, London 1855)

Johnson, Dale A. 'The End of the Evidences: A Study in Nonconformist Theological Transition', *JURCHS* 2/3 (1979)

Johnson, Mark D. *The Dissolution of Dissent 1850–1918* (New York and London 1987)

Johnstone, J. C. 'The Story of Western College', *TCHS* 7 (1916–18)

Jones, Ignatius *Bristol Congregationalism* (Bristol 1947)

Jones, R. Tudur *Congregationalism in England 1662–1962* (London 1962)

Kaye, Elaine *C. J. Cadoux: Theologian, Scholar and Pacifist* (Edinburgh 1988)
'Constance Coltman – a Forgotten Pioneer', *JURCHS* 4/2 (1988)
Mansfield College: Its Origin, History and Significance (Oxford 1996)

Kelly, John — *An Examination of the Facts, Statements and Explanations of the Rev Dr Samuel Davidson* (London 1857)

Kingsland, J. P. — 'Lancashire College Sixty Five Years Ago', *TCHS* 14/3 (1943)

Koditschek, T. — *Class Formation and Urban Industrial Scoiety: Bradford 1750–1850* (Cambridge 1990)

Lancashire Independent College Jubilee 1893 (Manchester 1893)

Lees, Andrew — *Cities Perceived: Urban Society in European and American Thought 1820–1940* (Manchester 1985)

Loudon, Mary — *Revelations* (London 1994)

Lovegrove, D. — *Established Church, Sectarian People: Itinerancy and the Transformation of English Dissent* (Cambridge 1988)

Macfadyen, D. — 'The Apostolic Labours of Captain Jonathan Scott', *TCHS* 3 (1907–8)

Mackennal, A. — *The Life of John Allison Macfadyen* (London 1891)

Mackintosh, R. — 'My Experiments in Authorship', *CQ* 9 (1931)

Macqueen, J. G. and Taylor, S. W. (eds) — *University and Community: Essays to Mark the Centenary of the Founding of University College Bristol* (Bristol 1976)

Marchant, James — *J. B. Paton: Educational and Social Pioneer* (London 1909)

Matthews, W. S. — *Memoirs and Select Remains of T. R. Taylor* (London 1836)

McLachlan, H. — *English Education under the Test Acts* (Manchester 1931)

Warrington Academy: Its History and Influence (Manchester 1843)

Medway, John — *Memoirs of the Life and Writings of John Pye Smith* (London 1854)

Memorial of the Opening of the New and Enlarged Buildings of Lancashire Independent College (Manchester 1878)

Messinger, G. — *Manchester in the Victorian Age* (Manchester 1985)

Miall, A. — *Life of Edward Miall* (London 1884)

Miall, J. G. — *Congregationalism in Yorkshire* (London 1868)

Micklem, Nathaniel — 'Memoir of Arnold Thomas' in *Arnold Thomas of Bristol: Collected Papers and Addresses* (London 1925)

The Box and the Puppets (London 1957)

Milner, D. — 'J. P. Chown 1821–86', *Baptist Quarterly* 25 (1973)

Minutes of the Proceedings of a Conference of Committees of the Various Theological Colleges Connected with the Independent Churches of England and Wales held in the Congregational Library 7–8 January 1854 (London 1845)

Minutes of the Proceedings of a Conference of Delegates from the committees of the Theological Colleges and Institutes Connected with the congregational Churches of England 1865 (London 1865)

Moon, N. S. *Education for Ministry: Bristol Baptist College 1679–1979* (Bristol 1979)

Munford, Tony *Victorian Rotherham* (Huddersfield 1989)

Newell, J. P. 'A Nestor of Nonconformist Heretics: A. J. Scott (1805–66)', *JURCHS* 3/1 (1983)

Nicholas, Thomas *Dr Davidson's Removal from the Professorship of Biblical Literature in the Lancashire Independent College, on account of Alleged Error in Doctrine. A Statement of Facts, with Documents, Together with Remarks and Criticisms* (London and Edinburgh 1860)

Nicholson, F. and Axon, E. *The Older Nonconformity in Kendal: A History of the Unitarian Chapel in the Market Place with Transcripts of the Registers and Notices of the Nonconformist Academies of Richard Frankland MA and Caleb Rotheram DD* (Kendal 1915)

Nightingale, B. *A History of the Old Independent Chapel, Tockholes, near Blackburn, Lancashire* (London and Manchester 1886)

Lancashire Nonconformity vol II (London and Manchester 1891)

The Story of the Lancashire Congregational Union 1806–1906 (London and Manchester 1906)

Nuttall, G. F. *Howel Harris 1714–73: The Last Enthusiast* (Cardiff 1965)

The Significance of Trevecca College 1768–91 (London 1969)

'Assembly and Association in Dissent 1689–1931' in G. Cuming and D. Baker (eds), *Councils and Assemblies*, Studies in Church History 7 (Oxford 1971)

'Training for Hoxton and Highbury: Walter Scott of Rothwell and his Pupils', *JURCHS* 5/8 (1996)

O'Brien, P. *Warrington Academy 1757–86: Its Predecessors and Successors* (Wigan 1989)

Odgers, W. J. *A Report on the Sanitary Condition of Plymouth* (1847)

Owen, W. T. *Edward Williams DD 1750–1813: His Life, Thought and Influence* (Cardiff 1963)

Parker, I. *Dissenting Academies in England* (Cambridge 1914)

Parker, Joseph *The Operative College* (Manchester n. d. [c.1861])

Parrish, H. G. *From the World to the Pulpit* (London 1863)

Paton, J. L. *John Brown Paton: A Biography* (London 1914)

Payne, George *Lectures in Christian Theology* 2 vols (London 1850)

Peake, A. S. (ed) *Inaugural Lectures Delivered by Members of the Faculty of Theology* (Manchester 1905)

Peake, L. S. *Arthur Samuel Peake: A Memoir* (London 1930)

Pearson, Mark *Northowram: Its History and Antiquities* (Halifax 1898)

Peel, Albert 'The Autobiography of David Everard Ford', *TCHS* 11 (1930–2)

These Hundred Years: A History of the Congregational Union of England and Wales 1831–1931 (London 1931)

Peel, David 'A View from the Tower: The Need for a Teachable Spirit in the United Reformed Church', *Reformed Quarterly* (1993)

Peel, Frank *Nonconformity in the Spen Valley* (Heckmondwike 1891)

Spen Valley: Past and Present (Heckmondwike 1893)

Phillips, George 'Freedom in Religious Thought' in L. Cooke (ed), *The Fourth Freedom* (London 1943)

Picton, James Allanson 'The College Crisis' in A. J. Davidson, *The Autobiography and Diary of Samuel Davidson* (Edinburgh 1899)

Porritt, Arthur *John Henry Jowett CH MA DD* (London 1924)

Powicke, F. J. *David Worthington Simon* (London 1912)

Price, E. J. 'The Place of Systematic Theology', *CQ* 23 (1945)

Our Churches and the Ecumenical Mind (Chairman's Address to the Congregational Union of England and Wales 1937) (London 1937)

The Churches, the Ministry and the Colleges (London 1937)

'The Yorkshire Academies and the United College', *TCHS* 10 (1927–9)

Priestley, Joseph *Memoirs* (Centenary edition, London 1904)

Raffles, T. S. *Memoirs of the Life and Ministry of the Rev Thomas Raffles* (London 1864)

Religious Census of Bristol 1881 (Bristol 1881)

Reynolds, J. *The Great Paternalist: Titus Salt and the Growth of Nineteenth-Century Bradford* (London 1983)

Robinson, W. G. 'William Roby's Missionary Candidates', *TCHS* 16 (1949–51)

William Roby and the Revival of Independency in the North (London 1954)

A History of the Lancashire Congregational Union (Manchester 1955)

'The Savoy Declaration of 1658 and Today', *TCHS* 18 (1958)

Rogers, Henry *Essays on Some Theological Controversies of the Time* (London 1874)

Rogers, J. Guinness *Autobiography* (London 1903)

Rogerson, J. *Old Testament Criticism in the Nineteenth Century* (London 1984)

Ross, J. *W. Lindsay Alexander* (London 1887)

The Savoy Declaration of Faith and Order (ed A. G. Matthews, London 1959)

Scoresby-Jackson, R. E. *The Life of William Scoresby* (London 1861)

Scott, Caleb *In Memoriam: Alexander Thomson MA DD* (Manchester 1895)

Seed, John 'Gentlemen Dissenters: The Social and Political Meanings of Rational Dissent in the 1770s and 1780s', *Historical Journal* 28 (1985)

Selbie, W. B. *The Life of Andrew Martin Fairbairn* (London 1914)

Sell, Alan P. F. 'The Life and Work of Robert Mackintosh 1858–1933', *JURCHS* 1/3 (1973)

Robert Mackintosh: Theologian of Integrity (Bern 1977)

Dissenting Thought in the Life of the Churches (San Francisco 1990)

Commemorations: Studies in Christian Thought and History (Cardiff 1993)

'A Renewed Plea for "Impractical" Divinity', *Studies in Christian Ethics* 7/2 (1995)

Seymour, A. C. H. *The Life and Times of Selina, Countess of Huntingdon* 2 vols (London 1844)

Shaw, W. A. — *Manchester Old and New* 3 vols (Manchester 1894–6)

Simon D. W. — *The Bible an Outgrowth of Theocratic Life* (Edinburgh 1886)

Sims, Arnold — *The Western College, Bristol: An Outline History* (Bristol 1952)

Slate, R. — *A Brief History of the Lancashire Congregational Union and Blackburn Academy* (London 1840)

Slugg, J. T. — *Reminiscences of Manchester Fifty Years Ago* (Manchester 1881)

Smith, Bertram — *In Memoriam: F. J. Falding MA DD* (Bradford 1893)

Smith, J. W. Ashley — *The Birth of Modern Education* (London 1954)

Stowell, William (ed) — *Memoir of the Life and Labours of William Henry Stowell* (London 1859)

Surman, C. E. — 'Roby's Academy, Manchester 1803–8', *TCHS* 13 (1937–9)

'Leaf Square Academy, Pendleton 1811–13', *TCHS* 13 (1937–9)

Alexander James Grieve: A Biographical Sketch (Manchester 1953)

Thomas, Peggy — *The Story of Redland Park United Reformed Church* (Bristol 1995)

Thompson, David — 'The Liberation Society 1844–68' in P. Hollis (ed) *Pressure from Without in Early Victorian England* (London 1974)

Thompson, Joseph — *The Owens College* (Manchester 1886)

Lancashire Independent College 1843–93 (Manchester 1893)

Tomes, F. Roger — ' "We are Hardly Prepared for this Style of Teaching Yet": Samuel Davidson and Lancashire Independent College', *JURCHS* 5/7 (1995)

Toothill, Jonathan — *Funeral Sermon for the Rev James Scott* (Huddersfield 1783)

Turner, J. H. — *Nonconformity in Idle, with a History of Airedale College* (Bradford 1876)

Turner, R. R. — 'Cavendish Theological College (1860–63)', *TCHS* 21 (1972)

Turner, R. R. and Wallace, I. — *Serve Through Love: A History of Paton Congregational College, Nottingham* (privately published)

Turquand, P. — *A Brief Historical Sketch of the Educational*

	Institutions Connected with the Congregational Fund Board (London 1896)
United Reformed Church	*The Commission on the Ministry in the United Reformed Church in England and Wales* (London 1975)
Vaughan, R. A.	*Essays and Remains, with a Memoir by R. Vaughan* (London 1858)
Vaughan, Robert	*On the Study of History* (London 1834)
	Congregationalism: Or, the Polity of Independent Churches, Viewed in Relation to the State and Tendencies of Modern Society (London 1842)
	The Age of Great Cities: Or, Modern Society Viewed in its Relation to Intelligence, Morals and Religion (London 1843)
Venn, Henry	*The Life and a Selection from the Letters of Henry Venn* (London 1834)
Waddington, J.	*Congregational History 1800–50* (London 1878)
Wadsworth, K. W.	*Yorkshire United Independent College* (London 1954)
Ward, W. R.	*Religion and Society in England 1740–1850* (London 1972)
Watson, S. J.	*Furnished with Ability: The Lives and Times of the Wills Families* (Salisbury 1991)
Watts, Michael	*The Dissenters: From the Reformation to the French Revolution* (Oxford 1978)
Welch, Edwin	*Spiritual Pilgrim: A Reassessment of the Life of the Countess of Huntingdon* (Cardiff 1995)
Whittingham, Sarah	'Dandy Design', *Nonesuch* (University of Bristol Magazine 1996)
Wilkinson, J. T.	*Arthur Samuel Peake: A Biography* (London 1971)
Williams, Edward	*An Account of the Rotherham Independent Academy* (Sheffield 1797)
Williams, F. S.	*Nottingham Past and Present* (Nottingham 1878)
Williams, Rhondda	*How I Found my Faith* (London 1938)
Wright, D. G. and Jowitt, J. A. (eds)	*Victorian Bradford: Essays in Honour of Jack Reynolds* (Bradford 1982)
Wrigley, F.	'George Hadfield, Joseph Parker and Other Correspondents', *CQ* 17 (1939)
Wykes, David	'The Dissenting Academy and Rational Dissent' in K. Haakonssen, *Enlightenment and Religion: Rational Dissent in Eighteenth Century Britain* (Cambridge 1996)

Wylie, W. H. and Briscoe, J. P. *A Popular History of Nottingham* (Nottingham 1893)

The Yorkshire Colleges: The Amalgamation Question (Sheffield c.1872, reprinted from *The English Independent*)

Yorkshire United Independent College: Two Hundred Years of Training for the Christian Ministry by the Congregational Churches of Yorkshire (London 1954)

Index